"That's Not What We Meant to Do"

Also by Steven M. Gillon

America during the Cold War
(editor, with Diane B. Kunz)

The Democrats' Dilemma:
Walter F. Mondale and the Liberal Legacy

Politics and Vision:
The ADA and American Liberalism,
1947–1985

"That's Not What We Meant to Do"

Reform and

Its Unintended

Consequences in

Twentieth-Century

America

W · W · Norton & Company

New York

London

Steven M. Gillon

For information about permission to reproduce selections from this book, write to
Permissions, W. W. Norton & Company, Inc., 500 Fifth Avenue, New York NY 10110

The text of this book is composed in 12/13.5 Perpetua
with the display set in Bodega Serif Medium and Perpetua Italic
Composition by Allentown Digital Services Division of R.R. Donnelley & Sons Company
Manufacturing by the Hadden Craftsmen
Book design by Margaret M. Wagner

Library of Congress Cataloging-in-Publication Data
Gillon, Steven M.
    "That's not what we meant to do": reform and its unintended consequences in
twentieth century America / Steven M. Gillon.
        p.   cm.
    Includes bibliographical references and index.
    ISBN 0-393-04884-5
    1. United States—Social policy.   2. United States—Politics and government—
20th century.   3. Social legislation—United States.   4. Campaign funds—United
States.   I. Title: Reform and its unintended consequences in twentieth century America.
II. Title.
    HV57.G56 2000
    361.6'1'0973—dc21
                                                                        99-059626

W. W. Norton & Company, Inc., 500 Fifth Avenue, New York N.Y. 10110
www.wwnorton.com

W. W. Norton & Company Ltd., 10 Coptic Street, London WC1A 1PU

1 2 3 4 5 6 7 8 9 0

For James T. Patterson
and the memory of
John Kennedy

Contents

●

. .

Acknowledgments

*T*HE idea for this book was born in the spring of 1996 during a lunch conversation in New York City with two old friends from Brown University, Gary Ginsberg and John Kennedy. When he launched *George* magazine in 1995, John asked Gary to serve as a senior editor, and he invited me to be a contributing editor. On this particular day we were sitting around discussing ideas for future stories. Since I had spent the previous weeks digesting a steady diet of books examining how results often strayed from intent, I suggested that the magazine consider an article that looked at the unintended consequences of significant pieces of legislation. Both liked the idea, and John invited me to write the article, which he then skillfully edited and published in the July 1997 issue.

I had so much fun writing the piece, and *George*'s readers responded so warmly to it, that I decided to expand it into a book. Over the next few years I incurred numerous debts while working on this project. During that time I had the privilege of teaching at two wonderful universities that provided me with an intellectually stimulating environment that rewarded both teaching and research. At Oxford University I could always count on John Rowett of Brasenose College and Byron Shafer of Nuffield College for insightful commentary and friendly conversation. My thanks to David Boren, the dynamic president of the University of Oklahoma, for inviting me to join his team as the first dean of the Honors College. My staff at the Honors College, especially Carolyn Morgan, have shielded me from burdensome administrative duties, while research assistants Paul Kelton, Lorien Foote, Heather Clemmer, and Holly Furr worked tirelessly to track down sources. A special thanks to Ron Green, a diligent researcher and a demanding editor. At the History Channel, I am indebted to Libby O'Connell for introducing me to the network, to Abbe Raven for having the confidence to put me on the air, and to Steven Jack for his patience and skill.

A number of people have read the manuscript and offered useful suggestions. At the University of Oklahoma, Larry B. Hill, Ron Schleifer, and Ron Peters read early drafts of the introduction and Nick Hathaway read every chapter. My wise and generous colleague David Levy (aka the Great Levy) provided a number of helpful substantive and stylistic suggestions. Gary Ginsberg, who has since left *George* for more lucrative pastures, read an early version of the manuscript and showed that he has not lost his editorial touch. Hugh Graham shared with me his considerable knowledge of civil rights and affirmative action. Alan Brinkley offered an especially helpful critique. Julian Zelizer, Jim Ryan, and David Courier volunteered sound advice. Joao Souza provided valuable support and advice. My agent, Gerry McCauley, guided the project to completion. At Norton, Ed Barber's well-deserved reputation as an accomplished editor is matched only by his patience and good cheer.

Finally, this book is dedicated to two very special people. As he has done so often in the past with other projects, James T. Patterson read this manuscript with great care, making perceptive comments along the way. Since I took his graduate seminar at Brown in the spring of 1981, Jim has been an unfailing source of encouragement, good advice, and warm friendship. His example has inspired me to become a better historian. It was while working as a teaching assistant in Jim's class on modern American political history in 1981 that I met John Kennedy. Over the next two decades John would have a profound impact on my life. He was a wonderful friend. I shall miss him.

"That's Not What We Meant to Do"

Introduction

American Exceptionalism and the Promise
of Unintended Consequences

- Congress imposes a nationwide 55 mph speed limit to lower gas consumption and reduce highway fatalities, but the legislation saves little gas and may actually result in a greater highway death rate.

- Rent control legislation designed to protect poor tenants at the expense of landlords evolves into a set of rules that benefit middle-class tenants while providing little help for the poorest residents.

- President Reagan promises that a 25 percent across-the-board tax cut will revive the economy and balance the budget, but eight years later the nation is drowning in a sea of debt.

WHAT do these reforms have in common? They all fell victim to one of the most immutable rules of nature, the law of unintended consequences, which states that you cannot always predict the results of purposeful action. Life is frequently too complicated and unpredictable, the universe too random, to bend to the will of any individual or group of individuals.

It is not a new idea. The contradiction between intention and result has influenced some of the greatest works of literature and shaped our understanding of religion, science, economics, and politics. The great Greek classical writers—Aeschylus, Sophocles, and Euripides—blamed the "gods" and human passion for the tragic fate of the protagonists in their plays, what classical scholar

Richard Lattimore called "love and hate working simultaneously to force distorted action." In Goethe's masterpiece *Faust,* Mephistopheles described himself as a "part of the force that always tries to do evil and always does good." Martin Luther, the father of the Protestant Reformation, suggested that unintended consequences were part of God's master plan. "God uses lust to impel man to marriage, ambition to office, avarice to earning, and fear to faith," he observed. In the seventeenth century Sir Isaac Newton raised the idea of unnoticed consequences to the level of scientific certainty with his third law of motion, which asserted that "to every Action there is always opposed an equal Reaction." According to Adam Smith, unintended consequences drove the engine of capitalist societies. His *Wealth of Nations,* published in 1776, created the image of the "Invisible Hand" to show how an individual, acting entirely in his own interest, "promote[d] an end which was no part of his intention." In his study of the French Revolution, Alexis de Tocqueville showed how revolutions were frequently the unintended consequence of reform. "[E]xperience teaches us," he wrote, "that generally speaking the most perilous moment for a bad government is one when it seeks to mend its ways."[1]

As Newton's law suggests, scientists have been grappling with the tension between action and result for centuries. Some of the most significant scientific discoveries are the products of unintended consequences and have in turn produced unforeseen results of their own. Take penicillin, for example. In 1928, as British scientist Sir Alexander Fleming grew staphylococcus bacteria in a culture plate near an open window, some mold spores blew in. He noticed that the uninvited mold possessed a unique power: It killed off all the bacteria that had been growing on the plate. Fleming's surprise discovery of penicillin became one of the most important medical breakthroughs in history. The chain of unintended consequences in this story had only begun. Experts predicted that penicillin would eradicate such sexually transmitted diseases as syphilis and gonorrhea. But effective treatment allowed people to engage in risky behavior that spread the diseases more than ever. Governments virtually halted education programs, and the sexual revolution, spurred at least in part by a belief that venereal diseases were now easily curable, created new opportunities for both microbes to spread. By the early 1980s, 2.5 million Americans contracted gonorrhea every year, and syphilis ranked as the third most common infectious disease in the nation. Then the casual use of antibiotics—in another striking demonstration of the law of unintended consequences—produced drug-resistant strains of gonorrhea that ate penicillin and rendered other antibiotics useless. Antibiotics are miracle drugs that have saved millions of lives, but in the end they have also helped spread and strengthen the diseases they were intended to conquer.[2]

Unintended consequences have also produced some of the most spectacular scientific follies in this century, confirming the observation of the social critic Gerald Sykes that "Man rushes first to be saved by technology, and then to be saved from it." Efforts at biological control—fighting nature with nature—have been especially prone to failure. Scientists have learned a great deal about the ecosystem, buty they still cannot predict what will happen when they introduce a new species. Witness the case of the cane toad. Imported into Australia during the 1930s, the poisonous cane toad was meant to get rid of a beetle that devastated sugarcane crops. However, because the beetles flew at night and were inaccessible to the toads, the voracious toads ate everything else. Soon 102 toads turned into a trillion. Between 1883 and 1885, Hawaii imported the Indian mongoose to eat rats that were destroying the island's cane fields. The mongoose, however, discovered that local birds tasted better than rats and proceeded to wipe out ground-nesting birds on the island. During the 1930s, southern farmers in the United States planted kudzu, a fast growing Japanese vine that promised to stem soil erosion. Within a few decades the vine had strangled native plants and blanketed whole landscapes.[3]

Today technology has accelerated the pace of change, making life more complicated and increasing the possibilities of unintended consequences. According to Edward Tenner, things "bite back" because we have tried to subdue nature rather than live with it. The inspiration for his popular book *Why Things Bite Back: Technology and the Revenge of Unintended Consequences* came from his observation that the personal computer, heralded as the cornerstone of a tidy, eco-correct "paperless office" of the future, actually created more paper, not less. "The real revenge," Tenner wrote, ". . . is the tendency of the world around us to get even, to twist our cleverness against us." In other words, the knowledge of scientific consequences lags behind the knowledge of science. "Scientists leave their discoveries like foundlings on the doorstep of society," observed the British science analyst Lord Ritchie-Calder. "The step-parents do not know how to bring them up."[4]

With so many examples of unintended consequences, it is not surprising that a number of thinkers have tried to incorporate unanticipated events into their theories of how the world works. Some scientists now propose that chaos, not order and certainty, rules the universe. Chaos theory holds that certain phenomena involve so many factors that they are inherently unpredictable. James Gleick, in his 1987 best seller *Chaos,* presented an unforgettable image of the so-called butterfly effect. In Gleick's words, "a butterfly stirring the air today in Peking can transform storm systems next month in New York." The tiny air currents that a butterfly creates travel across thousands of miles, mixing with other breezes and eventually changing the weather. In other words, trivial-seeming changes in initial conditions can produce huge differences in final outcomes.[5]

Many scientists have hailed the articulation of chaos theory as the third great scientific revolution of the twentieth century, along with relativity and quantum mechanics. Though barely a quarter of a century old, it has influenced fields from medicine to management. The conventional wisdom of medicine dictated that healthy bodies seek to reach a steady state, or homeostasis, in which everything is predictable and regular. But doctors using sophisticated new technology have suggested abandoning that idea. "The wisdom of the body is not homeostasis, but chaos," declared one physician. Management experts meanwhile have used chaos theory to redefine the laws governing modern corporations. The old paradigm of organization management, which viewed bureaucracies as rigid and mechanistic, has given way to a "new institutionalism" that emphasizes flexibility, unpredictability, and paradox. Charles Handy, a professor at the London Business School and a popular management guru, called his book *The Age of Paradox* "because so many things, just now, seem to contain their own contradictions, so many good intentions to have unintended consequences, and so many formulas for success to carry a sting in their tail." His American counterpart, Tom Peters, author of the best-selling *Thriving on Chaos,* concurred. "Unintended consequences outnumber intended consequences," he wrote. "Certainty is a delusion." Since nothing is predictable, Peters urged managers to evaluate everyone in the company "on his or her love for change."[6]

The unintended consequence theme has even invaded the hallowed halls of the academy. In a pioneering study the political scientists Jeffrey Pressman and Aaron Wildavsky demonstrated how ambitious federal programs were frequently warped by reality on the local level. Their book, *Implementation: How Great Expectations in Washington Are Dashed in Oakland,* provides a classic case study of chaos theory in action, as the good intentions of policy makers become distorted by poor implementation. "Promises can create hope, but unfulfilled promises can lead to disillusionment and frustration," they argued. "By concentrating on the implementation of programs, as well as their initiation, we should be able to increase the probability that policy promises will be realized." That insight has produced a growing body of literature that looks at how bureaucracy redirects legislative will. According to James Q. Wilson, American bureaucracy is "unlike that found in almost any other advanced nation" because it is both "laden with rules" and "suffused with participation." That divided spirit, he suggests, makes it difficult for large bureaucracies effectively to translate legislative intent into practice.[7]

The gap between human intention and actual outcome has also shaped the way historians look at the past. Brown University historian Gordon S. Wood has argued that unlike the other social sciences, "which try to breed confidence in managing the future," history "tends to inculcate skepticism about people's ability to order their own destinies." History "that shows that the best-laid plans of people in the past often went awry and that most people struggled against forces which they never clearly understood and over which they had little control tends to dampen that naive conquer-the-future spirit that Americans above all other peoples possess." Wood practices what he preaches. In his Pulitzer Prize-winning book *The Radicalism of the American Revolution,* he argued that one of the founding principles of the Republic, democracy, was itself an unintended consequence of the American Revolution. The founders, he suggested, were actually trying to create a society based on benevolence, selflessness, and social responsibility but instead unleashed the forces of social competitiveness and individualism. American revolutionaries, looking back at the movement for independence from old age, did not recognize their own child and despaired of their revolution's success.[8]

Perhaps no discipline has struggled more with the distance between action and consequences than sociology. Some of the most important works in the field are based on the unpredictability of human actions. The French sociologist Émile Durkheim postulated that material progress frequently had the unfortunate side effect of producing social isolation. Robert Michels's study of social organizations led him to postulate an "Iron Law of Oligarchy," which held that despite the best of intentions, democratic movements and political parties inevitably become controlled by an elite. Robert K. Merton wrote what is still widely regarded as the best, most dramatic examination of factors that contribute to unintended results. In a 1936 article, "The Unanticipated Consequences of Social Action," he examined the efficacy of purposeful action and uncovered a world informed by irony, where good produces evil, and evil produces good. Yet Merton remained optimistic about the possibilities of purposeful social action, arguing that "widespread, even typical, failures in planning . . . cannot be cited as evidence for pessimism." It was, he maintained, "the successful experiment which is decisive and not the thousand and-one failures which preceded it. More is learned from the single success than from the multiple failures. . . ."[9]

THE shadow of the 1960s hangs over any discussion of unintended public policy consequences. Many of the ambitious social experiments launched during the decade have evolved in directions far different from those anyone had predicted. Conservatives, who have dominated the airwaves for more than twenty years, have insisted that Lyndon Johnson's war on poverty, a series of programs designed to lift the poor out of poverty, instead acted as an incentive to those working or potentially working at low wages or salaries to flock to the welfare rolls and to stay there, to become forever "trapped" in sloth and poverty. "We tried to provide more for the poor and produced more poor instead," declared Charles Murray in his influential book *Losing Ground.* "We tried to remove the barriers to escape from poverty and inadvertently built a trap." Murray based part of his argument on the Law of Unintended Rewards, which specifies that "any social transfer through welfare programs increases the net value of being in the condition that prompted transfer." Since he said all welfare programs fail, Murray called for "scrapping the entire federal welfare and income-support structure for working-aged persons." Though critics have attacked Murray for oversimplifying a complex issue, his interpretation has become a staple in modern debate over the welfare state. "The Great Society," Republican House leader Newt Gingrich declared in 1994, "has had the unintended consequences of snaring millions of Americans into the welfare trap."[10]

Nowhere are the laws of unintended consequences more evident than in race relations. Lyndon Johnson made implementation of the Supreme Court decision in *Brown v. Board of Education* (1954), which called for an end to racial segregation in the public schools, the centerpiece of his Great Society agenda. He persuaded Congress to pass two monumental legislative landmarks in American history: the Civil Rights Act of 1964 and the Voting Rights Act of 1965. Johnson, and most liberals who supported the legislation, hoped that it would lead toward a color-blind society. But both laws have spawned race-conscious policies: affirmative action and racially gerrymandered legislative districts. When voluntary desegregation failed, the courts stepped in. In 1974 U.S. District Judge W. Arthur Garrity, Jr., ordered a massive system of busing to promote desegregation in the Boston public school system. But a well-intentioned program designed to improve educational opportunity for African-American children eroded financial and political support for public schools and did little to promote interracial classrooms. Indeed it helped in many places to accelerate an already large-scale movement of white middle-class parents to the suburbs, thereby heightening racial divisions in America. Boston, a system that had ninety-six thousand students and was 61 percent white in 1972, twenty years later had sixty-three thousand pupils and was 80 percent minority. South Boston and Charlestown, neighborhoods that the 1990 census counted as 95 percent white, have public high schools with white enrollments of 27 percent and 16 percent respectively. As more middle-class whites move to the suburbs or send their children to private schools, they are less willing to support tax increases to improve services in public schools. The pattern has been repeated in many, though not all, metropolitan areas across the country.[11]

President Johnson's attempt to extend his vision of the Great Society abroad also produced unintended results. In Vietnam the United States used the military to attempt to fashion a Western-style democracy in the middle of Southeast Asia. Instead it killed millions, devastated the Vietnamese economy, and cost taxpayers billions. "Each escalation of the conflict was undertaken as a compromise, and each step was taken with the conviction that just a little more firepower would win the day," commented the historians James Olson and Randy Roberts. "But the sum total of dozens of small escalations was the dreaded land war in Asia." In the end a crusade to preserve America's standing in the world further eroded U.S. stature and power. A cause designed to unite the nation around preventing the spread of communism instead drove a wedge through the nation and eroded public support for government and its leaders. "All during Vietnam, the government lied to me," declared the journalist Richard Cohen. As a result, "I'm cynical. I'm the credibility version of the depression baby. I've been shaped, formed by lies."[12]

The unintended consequences of liberal social legislation in the 1960s have contributed to a souring of the public mood and to growing public cynicism about the possibility of achieving change through politics. The public saw a direct connection between government ambition and the events that accompanied it: racial violence, the war in Vietnam, student protest, Watergate, and economic stagnation. Not only was government unable to solve these problems, but many people believed Washington had accidentally created them in the first place. "Reflecting on all these matters," Philip Yancey wrote in *Christianity Today,* "I have become stubbornly resistant to grand schemes for changing society or the world, since most of them produce the opposite result." Those feelings have contributed to low levels of confidence in public institutions and government leaders. In 1964 three-quarters of the American public said that they trusted the federal government to do the right thing most of the time. In recent years, depending on the particular poll, only one-quarter to one-third do. Between 1966 and 1994 those expressing "a great deal" of confidence in the president declined from 41 percent to 12 percent. Public confidence in Congress fell even further, from 42 percent to only 8 percent.[13]

Not surprisingly, conservatives have made the unintended consequences theme a key weapon in their arsenal against liberalism. On issues from welfare to civil rights they have pointed out—often correctly—that the current practice is very different from the original intent. They have used these unintended consequences as a springboard for a more sweeping indictment of government activism: If politicians cannot accurately predict the outcome of legislation, the argument goes, then why act at all? Nathan Glazer, in an influential 1971 article titled "The Limits of Social Policy," stated: "Our efforts to deal with distress themselves increase distress." As the conservative thinker Irving Kristol has put it, "the unanticipated consequences of social action are always more important, and usually less agreeable, than the intended consequences." Since ambitious social policies are frequently tripped up by what Milton Friedman calls the "invisible foot," the only way to control unanticipated events is to have Washington do as little as possible.[14]

There are, however, a number of problems with the sweeping neoconservative indictment of government activism. First, it is not always easy to discern the "intent" of legislation. Some legislation passes in the heat of public passion with little opportunity for careful thought or reflection. The process of negotiation and compromise between competing interest groups often leaves legislation laden with vague and confusing language. As a result, Congress frequently passes bills that it does not fully understand, that cannot be enforced with any precision, and that are full of loopholes begging for court challenges and conflicting interpretations. In recent years a number of legal scholars have questioned the importance of legislative intent in trying to understand an ambiguous statute. Proponents of "legal textualism," they maintain that since it is impossible to discern the intent of a body as large and unruly as Congress, judges should limit themselves to interpreting only the intent captured in the actual language of the law. "It is the *law* that governs, not the intent of the lawgiver," noted Supreme Court Justice Antonin Scalia. "Men may intend what they will; but it is only the laws that they enact which bind us." While Scalia and other advocates of legal textualism push their case too far, often failing to appreciate the distinction between what Congress intended to say and what it hoped to accomplish, they underscore an important point: Seeking to discern intent can expose an ideological minefield that must be navigated with caution.[15]

Second, unintended consequences are not always bad. With the aid of hindsight, virtually everyone now hails the original GI Bill, which subsidized the schooling and mortgages of millions of World War II veterans. The journalist David Osborne and Ted Gaebler, authors of the best-selling book *Reinventing Government,* praised the GI Bill as "perhaps the most successful social program in American history," which "turned millions of battle-scarred young men into the educated backbone of a 30-year economic boom. . . . Future historians may consider it the most important event of the 20th century." The novelist James A. Michener claimed that the GI Bill "represented the soul of democracy" and was one of the two or three finest laws Congress has ever passed. In 1994 President Clinton confidently called it "the greatest investment in our people in American history."[16]

In 1944 neither President Roosevelt nor Congress intended to pass such an important piece of legislation. Congress enacted the measure to avoid a rerun of the chaos that had ensued after World War I, when the return of millions of veterans expanded the jobless rolls and prompted widespread labor strikes and race riots.

It took hardball lobbying from the American Legion to get the measure out of congressional committee. Most members of Congress considered the provision guaranteeing veterans twenty dollars a week in unemployment benefits to be the key feature of the bill and devoted little attention to the clauses offering free college education and low-interest housing loans. Roosevelt, who predicted that the number of vets taking advantage of the educational benefits would be "in the hundreds of thousands," signed the measure in June 1944 with little press fanfare. The GI Bill's authors did not foresee how the legislation would boost the earnings of millions of veterans or change American higher education forever. How could they have known that it would inspire the developer William Levitt to create low-cost housing, allowing millions of veterans to move to the suburbs?[17]

As the journalist David Whitman has pointed out, there are many other examples of unintended consequences producing a positive outcome. The administrators of the women, infants, and children (WIC) program, a government nutrition plan, provided parents with coupons to purchase iron-fortified foods in the hope of reducing anemia among children living in low-income families. They had not anticipated that manufacturers wanting to sell their breakfast cereals through WIC would raise the iron fortification levels for all American. Twenty years ago the Pentagon designed an obscure computer network to withstand bomb attacks. That system now has mushroomed into the Internet and has revolutionalized the daily lives of millions of Americans. The billions spent on federal cancer research have failed to find a cure, but they have produced a series of unanticipated spin-offs, from nicotine patches to the test used to detect the AIDS virus.[18]

Third, not only does the neoconservative critique fail to recognize that government can play a positive role in American life, but it ignores the fact that laws, for better or worse, sometimes perform precisely as intended. The Social Security Act, expanded and amended over time, provided economic security to millions of senior citizens; the Civil Rights Act of 1964 largely abolished legal segregation in America; the Voting Rights Act of 1965 ended white political monopoly in the South; and numerous pieces of environmental legislation have produced cleaner water and air. "I think the greatest argument for progressive government in my generation," noted the journalist Gregg Easterbrook, "is the success of pollution controls."[19]

When they do occur, unintended consequences often exist on the margins and do not undermine the principal goal of the legislation. The Voting Rights Act is a good example. The most effective civil rights legislation in history, it produced a dramatic increase in black voting, a rise in the number of black elected officials, and a cleansing of the poisoned atmosphere of southern politics, ridding it for the most part of hardened racists and allowing for the emergence of a generation of racial moderates. Critics, however, focus on a small spin-off of the bill, the creation of so-called safe minority districts.[20]

Finally, conservatives conveniently forget that unintended consequences can plague *any* attempt to challenge the status quo, whether by liberals trying to create a new government program or by conservatives fighting to slash government spending. Modern conservatives—the proactive Newt Gingrich types that now dominate the Republican party—are just as likely to fall prey to the laws of unintended consequences as were the Great Society liberals whom they often ridicule. Like the liberals who devised the Great Society, New Right conservatives may be seeding disappointment by promising more changes than they can deliver. "The mistake of the Democratic majority was believing it could create the good society by merely building government up," argued Don E. Eberly, the president of the Commonwealth Foundation, a conservative think tank. "The danger for the Republican majority may be believing it can recreate the good society by merely tearing government down."[21]

The experience with deregulation underscores the dangers of

conservative devolution. During the 1980s deregulation became an article of faith, "espoused more or less automatically, even unthinkingly, by a wide range of officeholders and their critics," wrote two social scientists. Concerned that Washington bureaucracies were stifling competition, increasing costs to the consumer and promoting inefficiency, an odd coalition of conservative intellectuals, consumer advocates, and liberals banded together to cut government control over a number of major industries, including airlines, telephones, trucking, and banking. In some cases the changes resulted in reduced costs and better services; in most, however, it has produced new monopolies, less competition, higher prices, and inferior service. "Twenty years later," observed the journalist Robert Worth, "liberals have plenty of reason to regret the notion that the way to fix regulations is by scrapping them."[22]

Few public policy mistakes have been more costly than deregulation of the banking industry. In the early 1980s conservatives erased the line that separated savings and loans, called thrifts, from commercial banks. Utah's Jake Garn, the principal sponsor in the Senate, argued that the change was necessary to save the thrifts and revive the banking industry. "In essence, what this legislation represents is a shifting of gears to facilitate the stability and growth of our financial system," he declared. Ronald Reagan, who never met a deregulation measure he did not like, called the law "the most important legislation for financial institutions in the last 50 years. . . . All in all, I think we hit the jackpot," he added. Instead of saving the S&Ls the law was a major step down the road to banking ruin that resulted in a $165 billion taxpayer-financed bailout. After all the court judgments are settled, the price could rise above $200 billion, making the S&L bailout the most expensive public policy disaster in American history. Texas Democrat Jim Wright, who supported the bill as House majority leader, later called it a "grotesque error."[23]

What happened? The "laws" of unintended consequences suggest that it is hard, if not impossible, to liberate an industry as big and diverse as S&Ls—nine hundred billion dollars of assets and thirty-four hundred institutions—and predict what will happen. Since S&L owners could choose to operate under either state or federal regulations, the bill produced a bidding war between Washington and the states to retain the favor, and the generous political contributions, of large S&Ls. The move set the stage for anarchy and fraud. Garn assumed that thrift owners would stick to conservative ventures, such as automobile or commercial loans. But the prophets of deregulation gave crafty thrift owners all the tools needed to make a quick killing. Charles Keating and company turned their thrifts into giant casinos, using federally insured deposits to bet on high-risk corporate take-overs and junk bonds. It was a game of blackjack that only consumers could lose. "We didn't see the buccaneers coming," admitted an official at the U.S. League of Savings Institutions, which supported the reforms. "We thought we were dealing with the traditional people we had always dealt with."[24]

WHY do unintended consequences plague modern politics? The obvious answer—the one offered by conservatives—is that the growth in the size and scope of government power has increased the opportunities for mischief. It is probably fair to say that historically unintended consequences are often a product of ambitious state power. The historian James Scott has argued that tragic public policy failures in modern times have a number of common elements. First, they all were led by people who possessed a "high-modernist ideology," an optimistic faith in man's ability to rationalize society. Second, the reformers inevitably turned to "an authoritarian state that is willing and able to use the full weight of its coercive power to bring these high-modernist designs into being." Third, the civil society was so weak that it lacked the capacity to resist the reforms. The massive social engineering schemes in this century, from agricultural collectivism in Russia to apartheid in South Africa, all have developed from the lethal combination of "utopian plans" and "an authoritarian disregard" for democracy.[25]

I contend, however, that the formula is different in the United States, where a deeply embedded democratic culture and a pronounced ambivalence toward state power change the calculus. At the heart of the problem of unintended consequences in the United States is a paradox: Americans look to Washington for solutions to complex problems, but they are reluctant to give government the power it needs to address most issues. "At the heart of American politics lies a dread and a yearning," wrote the political scientist James Morone. "Americans fear public power as a threat to liberty." The paradox has its roots in the nation's revolutionary past. The founders rebelled against the imperial designs of a distant and impersonal British government. Believing that "power" was antithetical to "liberty," they created a system of government that made it difficult for power to concentrate in any one branch of government. "The constant aim," Madison explained in *The Federalist Papers,* "is to divide and arrange the several offices in such a manner that they may be a check on the other—that the private interest of every individual may be a sentinel over the public rights." The founders also specified the limited powers of the federal government and added the Tenth Amendment, which stipulated that any powers not delegated to Washington were "reserved to the states respectively, or to the people." "Ours is a many-splendored, as well as many-splintered, system," observed the political scientist Thomas E. Cronin. "Tensions are inevitable and designed that way. The Constitution disperses power and invites struggle."[26]

For most of its history the United States resisted developing an expansive state presence. As the founding fathers had hoped, American political culture restricted the evolution of a powerful federal government. "The state plays a more limited role in America than elsewhere because Americans, more than any other people, want it to play a limited role," observed a political scientist. The United States also never developed a powerful labor movement, which was responsible for expanded government services in other Western democracies. At its peak in the 1950s labor had organized only a quarter of the labor force, including only a third of nonagricultural workers. The lack of class identity meant that social and cultural issues often dominated politics, frustrating efforts of reformers to build class-based coalitions for greater government services. Americans voted, noted the historian Richard Oestreicher, "on the basis of cultural and emotional loyalties that reflected the fundamental concerns of family, church, tradition, and daily life."[27]

Despite these inhibitions, Americans have witnessed a dramatic increase in the size and scope of government power. In the nineteenth century the federal government did little more than deliver the mail, collect customs duties, and conquer the Indians. Beginning with the Progressive Era, Washington assumed new responsibilities, regulating monopolies, inspecting food and drugs, and collecting income tax. Franklin Roosevelt built on the progressive foundation of regulatory agencies and added new programs, such as the Social Security and the National Labor Relations acts, which offered some government help to senior citizens and labor. The trend has been especially pronounced in the years after World War II, when Americans, their expectations whetted by prosperity and rising expectations of the "good life," have placed enormous pressure on government to increase services and benefits. The Great Society tackled issues that the New Deal had ignored: civil rights, health care, and the environment. Between 1950 and 1980 federal domestic expenditures exploded from 6 percent to 15 percent of the gross domestic product (GDP). State and local expenditures increased from 7 percent to 13 percent during the same time period.[28]

By the early 1990s government was touching nearly every aspect of American life. Washington provided pensions to senior citizens and loans to college students, subsidized farmers and research scientists, and provided food stamps to one of ten Americans. It insured bank deposits, regulated pollution emissions, and set safety standards for consumer products. By 1994 nearly half—48 percent—of all American households, including many with high incomes, received some form of federal entitlement check: unemployment compensation, Medicare, Social Security, food stamps, veterans' benefits, or welfare. Government spending at all levels accounted for about 38 percent of the nation's economic output—up from about 11 percent before the Great Depression. The *Federal Register* of national laws grew from 5,307 pages of rules and regulations in 1940 to 68,101 in 1995.[29]

The paradox is that the growth in the size of government has not been accompanied by a corresponding change in public attitudes. Americans have come to accept the benefits of a modern welfare state without abandoning doubts about the wisdom of federal power. Polls, for example, show overwhelming support for the large entitlement programs that make up a significant portion of domestic spending. Yet the same surveys show a clamoring for cuts in government spending, a reduction in Washington's power, and a demand for local control. A bellwether poll conducted by Princeton Survey Associates in 1995 found that by a margin of 61 to 24 percent, Americans trusted state government to "do a better job running things" than the federal government. The poll results confirm Arthur Schlesinger, Jr's. earlier assertion that America is "operationally liberal and philosophically conservative." Americans are against "big government," for example, yet also want Washington to provide for Social Security, Medicare, Medicaid, clean air and water, and safe streets. The federal budget deficit, which ballooned during the 1980s and early 1990s, was the most visible manifestation of this tension: Americans wanted a balanced budget but also lower taxes and more benefits.[30]

. .

Americans have responded to these "push and pull" pressures by constructing a haphazard administrative state that struggles to satisfy the demands for new services without offending conservative sensibilities. In most European nations, where the fear of state power is less palpable, governments have been able to consolidate authority. By contrast, in the United States, despite a considerable movement of power over the past half century from the states to Washington, the national government remains decentralized and pluralistic. No other nation, reported the political scientists Peter Marris and Martin Rein, "organizes its government as incoherently as the United States." The vacuum of power has led to the proliferation of "iron triangles" of power, in which subgovernments made up of interest groups, congressional committees, and corresponding executive agencies can shape and frequently distort the intentions of legislators. As early as 1964 the journalist Douglass Cater coined the word "subgovernment" to describe a common characteristic of these triangular arrangements: They are not under the control of the "general" government and are able to make laws and policies without the assent of superior authority. "There isn't any government down there to manage," said Lloyd Cutler, who worked in the Carter White House. "There is a series of subgovernments pursuing single interests of one kind or another."[31]

In modern America the possibilities of unintended consequences are compounded not only by the increased size of government, as most conservatives contend, but by the fragmentation of power and authority in Washington. The case studies discussed here—welfare, deinstitutionalization, affirmative action, immigration, and campaign finance—are by-products of government's growing prominence since the 1930s. Human error, ignorance, miscalculation, and misfortune—all the elements of the human condition—play a role in shaping their unintended consequences. But they are also products of a political culture that has difficulty reconciling public fear of a strong national government with increased demands for social services and of a weak government burdened by competitive institutions and overlapping and unco-ordinated authority. Of course no study of a subject as complex and multifaceted as unintended consequences can claim to be au-thoritative. This study looks at only a handful of cases, so the lessons drawn are by definition limited and tentative. My goal is fairly modest: to tell a few stories of how unintended conse-quences occur, to speculate about their significance, and to inspire more research and discussion about this often mentioned but in-frequently explored theme.

There is one final element in the complex brew that produces unintended consequences: a mystic faith in the ability of "the peo-ple" to solve all social problems. "A great part of both the strength and weakness of our national experience lies in the fact that Americans do not abide very quietly the evils of life," observed the historian Richard Hofstadter. "We are forever restlessly pitting ourselves against them, demanding changes, improvements, remedies, but not often with sufficient sense of the limits that the human condition will in the end insistently impose upon us." From Andrew Jackson's celebration of the "common man" to Bill Clinton's pledge to "put people first," American politics has been shaped by the image of a united and noble public capable, as John Adams noted, to "think, feel, reason and act." Politicians have tapped into this strong populist undercurrent by portraying pol-itics as a Manichaean struggle between the noble intentions of "the people" and the greedy interests of elites. Populism, noted the historian Michael Kazin, is a "grand form of rhetorical opti-mism," which establishes that "once [they are] mobilized, there is nothing ordinary Americans cannot accomplish." The populist impulse has shaped most major reform movements in America, from the agrarian populist in the late nineteenth century to the so-cial protests of the 1960s. Samuel Huntington coined the label "creedal passion period" to describe those recurrent periods in U.S. history characterized by "widespread and intense moral in-

· ·

dignation" about the gap between American ideals and practice and by a "rush to moral judgment on the rights and wrongs of politics."[32]

Moral outrage is hardly a substitute for enlightened public policy, however, and the gap between expectation and reality provides a fertile breeding ground for unintended consequences. The glorification of "the people" as a unified whole conceals deep social and ideological divisions, oversimplifies problems, and obscures potential solutions. By failing to educate the public to the role that competing interests play in the struggle for political power, the populist persuasion leaves people unprepared to engage politics, which, in the words of the nineteenth-century journalist Ambrose Bierce, is "a strife of interests masquerading as a contest of principles." An optimistic faith in the perfectibility of American society, and a growing habit of depending on Washington to realize that vision of an ideal society, contribute to the pressure on legislators to develop quick and easy answers to complicated questions and to pass legislation without taking the time to examine its potential impact. Ironically, the desire to enhance democracy often expands the administrative capacity, but not the authority, of the state. "A great irony propels American political development," James Morone noted. "The search for more direct democracy builds up the bureaucracy."[33]

The bundle of reforms that Congress passed following Watergate serves as a good example of America's penchant for using the legislative process as an outlet for moral outrage. "Watergate was the greatest political scandal of our time," said Fred Wertheimer, the president of Common Cause. "Out of it grew many reforms designed to control corruption, abuse of power, secrecy and government for personal gain." Most of the reforms, such as the War Powers Act to limit the president's power to send troops abroad, were simply ineffective. Many others, however, have backfired. "If we can draw any lesson from our study of the post-Watergate reforms," observed Benjamin Civiletti, attorney general during the

Carter administration, "it is the lesson of the unintended consequence."[34]

Take the example of the Ethics in Government Law (1978), which imposed new financial disclosure requirements and limited the lobbying activities of former government officials. Spurred by the "Saturday Night Massacre" in 1973, when Richard Nixon fired the special prosecutor Archibald Cox, Congress included a small provision giving the attorney general the power to appoint a special prosecutor to investigate criminal allegations against high-level White House officials. While many members of Congress complained about the tough new financial disclosure rules, few objected to the special prosecutor clause. The strongest objections came from a handful of Republicans who believed the legislation was unnecessary and from a few Democrats who wanted the law expanded to cover Congress. The Carter administration, which proposed the legislation, was clear about the intention. "The purpose was to remove all sense of politics and thereby restore confidence in government," said a Justice Department official.[35] Congressional Republicans, who were always skeptical about the legislation, turned hostile following Lawrence Walsh's six-year $48.5 million investigation of the Reagan administration's Iran-contra affair. With the support of the Bush White House, Congress refused to reauthorize the act in 1992, allowing it to die a quiet death. Ironically, Bill Clinton reinstated the clause in 1994. The statute, he declared, "has been in the past and is today a force for government integrity and public confidence."[36]

During its lifetime the legislation spawned twenty independent counsels, who collectively spent $148.5 million to produce dozens of indictments. The most notable of those investigations was Kenneth Starr's dogged four-and-one-half-year probe into nearly every aspect of Bill Clinton's public and private life. Starr, a conservative Republican with political ambitions, was appointed by a special court in August 1994 to investigate questions about Whitewater, a defunct land deal in Arkansas. Over the next few years he gradually expanded his probe to include the firing of the White House travel office, the suicide of the Clinton adviser Vincent Foster, and the improper collection of FBI files on Republicans. Unable to find incriminating evidence against Clinton on any of these matters, Starr enlarged his probe again in January 1998 and began investigating the president's sexual relationship with a young White House intern, Monica Lewinsky. After spending $40 million, the independent counsel produced an X-rated report of steamy sex (described in leaden lawyerly prose) between a reckless man and a desperate woman. Claiming that the president had lied about his affair with Lewinsky and then misused his office to cover it up, Starr called for Clinton to be impeached and removed from office. The charges moved a partisan House of Representatives to impeach a president for only the second time in history. Starr's overzealous investigation of Clinton's private life shocked many of the original authors of the legislation, who had Nixonian abuses of power and not presidential sexual peccadilloes in mind when they crafted the law. "We wanted to put a mechanism in place that would ensure a thorough and fair investigation in the event a President ever committed such acts in the future," recalled former Democratic Congresswoman Elizabeth Holtzman, one of the authors of the act. "I never dreamed that a special prosecutor would be using his enormous powers to investigate accusations about a President's private (and legal) sexual conduct."[37]

Following the Senate's acquittal of the president in early 1999, both Democrats and Republicans were willing to admit their mistake and let the legislation die. "In 1978, with the noblest of intentions, both Republicans and Democrats embarked on a path of mutually ensured destruction by passing what could be called the ultimate law of unintended consequence," observed Kentucky's Republican Senator Mitch McConnell. Liberal Christopher Dodd of Connecticut agreed. Renouncing his original support for the law, he confessed that the statute had unintentionally "criminalized the political process." Perhaps the most persuasive critic of the law was Kenneth Starr, who pleaded with the Senate to abolish the act. "The statute should not be reauthorized," he told the Senate Committee on Government Affairs. Referring to his own experience, he complained that his investigation "came to be characterized as yet another political game. Law became politics by other means." As a result, he declared, "the statutory mechanism intended to enhance confidence in law enforcement thus had the effect of weakening it."[38]

Since the 1960s Americans have experienced a dizzying array of social experiments. During the 1960s the pendulum swing of policy moved dramatically to the left, but a potent conservative backlash pushed it to the right during the 1970s and 1980s. Both movements achieved notable victories, but neither lived up to the unrealistic expectations of their leaders. For better or worse, Americans enter the twenty-first century more suspicious of politicians, more skeptical about government, and more cautious about the possibilities of reform. Bill Clinton, the first Democrat in sixty years to win reelection to a second term, captured the cautious mood when he declared in his second inaugural that government should be "humble enough not to try to solve all our problems for us but strong enough to give us the tools to solve our problems for ourselves."[39]

"Humility" is the key lesson to learn from the unintended consequences of the past. On this issue the Protestant theologian Reinhold Niebuhr is as relevant today as he was a half century ago, when he convinced a generation of liberals to abandon their Wilsonian idealism and embrace a tough-minded realism. Unlike modern liberals and conservatives, Niebuhr possessed a passionate sense of the tragedy of life, the fallibility of humans, and the irony of the past. But, as Arthur Schlesinger, Jr., has observed, he also possessed a "deep conviction of the duty, even in the face of these intractable realities, to be firm in the right as God gives us to see the right." Unlike conservatives, who can sometimes ra-

· ·

tionalize unintended consequences as an excuse to do nothing, Niebuhr never allowed his tragic sense to sever the nerve of action. Unlike some liberals, who often underestimated the resistance to change and overemphasized the malleability of social institutions, he recognized the role of power in society and appreciated the resilience of conservative values. Niebuhr talked about idealism without illusion and about realism without resignation. "Our realists are too cynical; our idealists are too sentimental," he wrote. "We need prophets who are not afraid to know the worst about man, and who will yet maintain their faith in him." We would do well to heed his advice again.[40]

Chapter 1

The Irony of Reform:
The Origins of Federal Welfare Policy,
1935

●

JANUARY 30, 1935: Even the hardened members of the House Ways and Means Committee were moved by the description of fatherless children being forced from their homes. Grace Abbott, a champion for social justice, told the committee of a young widow trying to raise her three children. "At the time of her husband's death they owned a home," she said, "but about a year later the mortgage was foreclosed. With the $500 that she received at the time of the foreclosure, she rented a basement flat in which they now live and turned the front room into a store, stocking it with candies and cigars." Despite working every day until ten or eleven in the night, "she does not make enough to pay the rent and take care of the family." Unless Congress approved a national program to aid mothers with dependent children, Abbott told the committee, this family, and thousands like it, would continue to suffer. Most would be evicted from their homes, the children forced into orphanages. "The whole idea of mothers' pensions is that it should be enough to care for the children adequately, to keep the mother at home and thus give some security in the home." The program of aid for dependent children, she said, "is not only the best but the cheapest method of taking care of children—much cheaper than taking care of them in an institution or in somebody else's home." Also, she added, it preserves "the relationship of the mother and the child."[1]

Advocating on behalf of women and children was nothing new to Grace Abbott. Growing up in Nebraska in the 1880s, both she and her older sister, Edith, absorbed their mother's concern for the oppressed, her passion for progressive causes, and, most of all, her commitment to equal rights for women. Because the Abbott sisters found few outlets for their reformist zeal in rural Nebraska, they moved to Chicago, a city burdened with all the new social problems associated with massive immigration and industrialization. "I always was happy in Nebraska," Grace reflected, "but there isn't much opportunity for a girl in a small city, and it seemed inevitable that I leave." In 1908, after completing her graduate studies and teaching briefly at the School of Social Work at the University of Chicago, Grace decided to take up residence in Jane Addams's Hull House settlement. During those years she became part of an extraordinary network of reform-minded women, including Florence Kelley and Julia Lathrop, who were determined to ameliorate the harsh conditions of urban life.[2]

During her years at Hull House, living in one of Chicago's toughest neighborhoods, Abbott witnessed how the harsh new industrial order imposed enormous hardship on young families. Private charity and emergency public relief could not sustain poor single mothers and their children. In many cases state authorities split up families, sending children to orphanages and poorhouses. In 1909 Abbott had joined other progressive women and convinced the White House to organize a Conference on the Care of Dependent Children. "Home life is the highest and finest product of civilization," the conference concluded. "It is the great molding force of mind and character. Children should not be deprived of it except for urgent and compelling reasons. . . . No child should be deprived of his family by reason of poverty alone." The conference successfully lobbied Congress to establish in 1912 a Children's Bureau within the Department of Labor to "investigate and report upon all matters pertaining to the welfare of children and child life among all classes of people." In 1921 Abbott left

Chicago to assume leadership of the bureau and help transform it into the most influential and effective lobby for children's issues.[3]

In addition to raising public awareness about the issue, women reformers lobbied state legislatures for passage of mothers' aid laws. In 1911 Abbott helped convince Illinois to enact the first statewide measure. By 1919 thirty-nine states had enacted mothers' pensions. By 1935 every state except Georgia and South Carolina had mothers' pension programs. "Their enactment constituted public recognition by the states that the contribution of the unskilled or semiskilled mothers in their own homes exceeded their earnings outside of the home and that it was in the public interest to conserve their child-caring functions," Abbott wrote. Every state established different guidelines, but all provided payments to the children of poor mothers who had been widowed, divorced, or abandoned. By 1931 the only families eligible in all states were those whose fathers were dead, imprisoned, or insane. Thirty-six states covered families whose fathers had deserted, twenty-one provided for mothers who had divorced, but only eleven extended benefits to mothers whose children had been fathered out of wedlock. "In effect," observed Christopher Howard, "states held that the families of felons were more worthy than those of deserters, deserters more than divorces, and divorces more than unmarried fathers." The Children's Bureau estimated that as of 1934 approximately 109,000 families, including 280,500 children, were receiving aid. The vast majority of recipients were widows, by most estimates more than 80 percent.[4]

The allowances were often small and hedged with moralizing restrictions. A survey in 1919 noted that in most states the grants were "woefully inadequate," ranging as low as $4.33 a month in Arkansas to $69.31 in Massachusetts. Many states established that the mother must be "physically, mentally, and morally fit" to have custody of the children—requirements that even women reformers accepted. "For successful administration of mothers' aid laws it is necessary to establish by investigation the need of the mother and her moral and physical fitness to maintain the home," Abbott wrote, "as well as the legal requirements as to citizenship and residence to determine eligibility for this form of assistance." Local administrators had wide discretion in determining eligibility. In many communities social workers visited recipients in their homes to make sure they were morally fit to receive benefits. A typical mothers' pension law directed social workers to investigate "the condition of the home and family and all other data which might assist in determining the wisdom of the measures taken and the advisability of their continuance." Studies showed that the restrictions often discriminated against ethnic and racial minorities. A 1931 survey covering one-half of all recipients nationwide found that 96 percent of the beneficiaries were white, 3 percent were black, and 1 percent "other." Mothers' aid programs were especially rare in southern states, where 80 percent of blacks lived. In 1931 North Carolina had only four black families on the rolls. Louisiana and Mississippi had none.[5]

The Great Depression, which gripped the country in the 1930s, shook the foundation of the nascent mothers' pension programs. As tax revenues dried up, many states were forced to give smaller pensions or discontinue the programs. Between 1929 and 1931 Los Angeles experienced a 110 percent increase in families demanding benefits. Inadequate funds forced three states (Arkansas, Mississippi, and New Mexico) and sixty-nine counties to eliminate their programs. "It is probable that less than half the counties with legal authority to aid dependent fatherless children in their own homes in 1934 were actually giving aid," noted the Children's Bureau. Reformers appealed to Washington for help, but President Herbert Hoover, reflecting widespread fear that government spending would undermine individual initiative, initially refused the request. "You cannot extend the mastery of government over the daily lives of the people without at the same time making it the master of their souls and thoughts," he declared. By 1932, with unemployment topping eight million and no relief in sight, Hoover reluctantly signed a bill that created the Reconstruction Finance Corporation (RFC), which offered states three hundred million dollars in federal funds. For most people, however, it was too little too late.[6]

Confronted with a deepening depression, massive suffering and unrest, and rising unemployment, the public turned to Franklin Roosevelt in the 1932 presidential election. Though he had been vague about his plans, Roosevelt had promoted extensive government relief programs as governor of New York, and he made it clear that his administration would be open to experimentation. "I pledge you, I pledge myself to a new deal for the American people," he told the National Democratic Convention in the summer of 1932. He was true to his word, and within the first one hundred days the new president proposed an ambitious agenda to deal with the pressing economic crisis. Along with signing legislation to save the banking system, Roosevelt moved to offer relief to the unemployed. Three weeks after assuming office, Congress authorized the Civilian Conservation Corps (CCC) to provide jobs for some of the fifteen million unemployed. In May it approved the Federal Emergency Relief Administration (FERA) to provide "sufficient relief to prevent physical suffering and to maintain living standards." The FERA administrator Harry Hopkins wasted little time, spending five million dollars his first two hours and distributing more than four billion dollars in federal aid before the agency was terminated in 1936. Later in 1933 Roosevelt created the Civil Works Administration (CWA), a work relief program that employed more than four million workers at its peak in January 1934. By then more than twenty-eight million people, or 22.2 percent of the population, were receiving aid from New Deal programs. Many states used the federal relief money to replace the depleted mothers' aid pensions. One study revealed that for every child receiving a mothers' pension, three were receiving money from federal emergency relief. In urban areas families with single mothers made up 20 percent of the relief rolls.[7]

By 1934 Roosevelt was under intense public pressure to move beyond the hodgepodge of relief programs and offer permanent solutions to deal with the economic crisis. Most of the pressure came from the left. The colorful Louisiana senator Huey Long, bringing his brand of southern populism to the nation, proposed a Share Our Wealth program that promised to use steeply graduated income and inheritance taxes to redistribute income. The mild-mannered Dr. Francis Townsend attracted widespread support for his plan to guarantee two hundred dollars a month to people over sixty. As many as twenty-five million people signed petitions in support of the plan, and Townsend clubs sprouted up across the country. Roosevelt was also feeling pressure from within his own party. In the 1934 elections the Democrats won what the *New York Times* called "the most overwhelming victory in the history of American politics," picking up twenty-five of thirty-five contested Senate seats. Many of the new senators were to the left of the president. FDR, observed the historian William E. Leuchtenburg, "was riding a tiger, for the new Congress threatened to push him in a direction far more radical than any he had originally contemplated."[8]

The pressure was not unwelcome. Roosevelt considered his relief programs temporary, and while he pressed for an ambitious work program, he also planned to develop a comprehensive package of social insurance that would include old-age pensions, unemployment insurance, and categorical programs to assist groups—children and the blind and handicapped—that could not help themselves. "He regarded social insurance, or, as it ultimately came to be called, social security, as his principal monument to domestic innovation," noted the historian Irving Bernstein. Even before the congressional election, on June 8, 1934, Roosevelt sent a special message to Congress calling for a program that would provide "security against the hazards and vicissitudes of

. .

life." A few weeks later he established the Committee on Economic Security (CES) to draft the legislation. The committee included Secretary of the Treasury Henry Morgenthau, Jr., Secretary of Agriculture Henry Wallace, Relief Administrator Harry Hopkins, and Attorney General Homer S. Cummings, and it was chaired by Secretary of Labor Frances Perkins. The real work, however, was done by a professional staff under the direction of Edwin E. Witte, a University of Wisconsin economist who served as the executive director. Witte organized the CES into sections to deal with each of the major issues. In addition, he created what one observer called "a rather bewildering cluster of advisory groups" and special committees on medicine, public health, hospitals, and public employment.[9]

The committee was so consumed with debates over unemployment insurance and old-age pensions that it devoted little time to welfare. Should the federal government operate the pension program and unemployment plans, or should it coordinate its efforts with the states? How much would it cost, and who was going to pay for it? By contrast, the proposal for mothers' aid seemed simple and required little of the committee's time. In September Witte asked Abbott to write the provisions of the law dealing with children. "We badly need your thought and experience in developing a program for mothers and children to be part of a general program for economic security," he wrote in 1934. By that time Abbott had left the Children's Bureau and was teaching at the University of Chicago, but she leaped at the opportunity, boarded a train, and headed back to Washington to confer with her old colleagues at the Children's Bureau.[10]

Over the next few weeks Abbott joined two other bureau officials, Katharine Lenroot and Martha Eliot, to draft a series of proposals designed to benefit children. "The chief aim of social security is the protection of the family life of wage earners, and the prime factor in family life is the protection and development of children," they argued. After some discussion they broke their proposal down into three categories: aid to dependent children, services for handicapped children, and maternal and child health services. While many states had established mothers' pensions programs, the bureau officials pointed out that many localities either failed to participate or could not adequately fund the programs and that wide variation existed among the states. "Development of provisions for the health and welfare of children has been uneven in both extent and quality," their report noted. The goal was to "attempt to make universally available throughout the United States certain minimum measures of public protection," by building "a foundation of Federal, State, and local cooperation which will not lead to any difficult administrative realms or to any unpredictable costs."[11]

The three officials argued that the federal government needed to assume a direct role in providing aid, developing national standards, and coordinating efforts in the states. But they were not interested in developing an elaborate Washington bureaucracy, believing that the states could administer effective social welfare programs. The memorandum stressed that the new programs "do not set up any new or untried methods of procedure, but build upon experience that has been well established in this country." The federal government was to provide money and enhance the ability of the states to administer programs. A federal program "would be an instrument for improving standards in backwater States and wound tend to equalize costs." How much would a program of federal aid to dependent children (ADC) cost? Not much, they contended. Estimating that no more than three hundred thousand families would receive ADC at a given time, they proposed that the federal contribution would be around twenty-five million dollars annually. "This grant might be increased to not more than $50,000,000 per year as the program develops to include all families eligible for aid to dependent children." All the funds were to be allotted on a local-state-federal matching basis with the Children's Bureau running the ADC program.[12]

. .

Abbott's hard work paid off. Years later Witte observed that "she, above everyone else, was responsible for the child welfare provisions which occur in the Social Security Act." While they spent weeks deliberating the wisdom of old-age pensions and unemployment compensation, the members of the CES barely discussed the ADC provision. Like Abbott, they viewed it as a small, noncontroversial part of the overall legislative package. Their final report adopted both the spirit and the letter of Abbott's proposal for aiding single mothers. The committee's only change was procedural, switching control of the program from the Children's Bureau to Harry Hopkins's relief agency, FERA.[13]

On January 17, 1935, the president submitted to Congress the sixty-three-page economic security bill. It called for a federal-state system of unemployment insurance; a mandatory, federally administered old-age insurance system financed by employer and employee contributions and federal grants-in-aid to the states for old-age assistance (for people who were too old to contribute to the old-age insurance system); support of dependent children, expanded health programs; and child and welfare programs. The bill called for creation of a new federal agency, the Social Security Board, to keep the records and make payments to the millions of workers covered by the old-age provisions and to oversee the many other programs in the bill.

Because the president demanded that Congress move swiftly, the House Ways and Means Committee and the Senate Finance Committee held concurrent hearings during January and February. While legislators fired ideological missiles at both the old-age and unemployment provisions, the ADC proposal garnered considerable support from the legislators. "As it turned out," Witte remarked, "the child welfare provisions brought to the bill most valuable support and they turned out to be among the most popular provisions." For most members of Congress, ADC appealed as a modest proposal to help a mother raising children following the death of her husband. "To support ADC was, literally, to support motherhood," observed the historian Linda Gordon. Witte described the welfare proposals as "among the most popular provisions of the measure." New York Congressman J. L. Pfeifer claimed that mothers and children were "the real foundation of our country," who were "entitled to that which is necessary for the welfare of this country." Massachusetts Representative John P. Higgins said that ADC was "so manifestly human that I cannot conceive anyone opposing these features of the bill." Even Republicans who were skeptical of other parts of the Social Security bill spoke in glowing terms about the ADC provision. "The Republican membership has unqualifiedly endorsed this Title," declared Congressman Thomas A. Jenkins of Ohio. "It is not legislation that belongs to any party."[14]

Rhetorical support for ADC did not prevent Congress from tinkering with some of the language. The changes tightened the regulations and lowered benefit levels, but they did not alter the spirit of the original Children's Bureau proposal. The administration bill required that state plans "furnish assistance at least great enough to provide, when added to the income of the family, a reasonable subsistence compatible with decency and health." Southerners, fearful that northern standards would undermine their control over black labor, had this phrase deleted from the final bill. "There was much objection to federal determination of adequacy on the part of Southern members who feared Northern standards would be forced on the South in providing for Negro and white tenant families," Abbott observed. Congress set a maximum ADC grant at eighteen dollars per month for the first child and twelve dollars for each additional child. It also tightened the definition of "dependent child" by specifying the reasons for dependency and the adults with whom the child could be living. The new language limited federal subsidies to needy dependent children under the age of sixteen who have "been deprived of parental support or care by reason of the death, continued absence from the home or physical or mental incapacity of a parent" but who were living in the homes of near relatives.[15]

Perhaps the most significant change concerned who would run the new program. The House Ways and Means Committee objected to giving any part of the act to FERA, which it viewed as a temporary agency, and transferred control of ADC to the new Social Security Board. Arthur Altmeyer, a CES staff member, recalled that "we were much more concerned about allying opposition to the inclusion of the various maternal and child health and welfare activities in the bill than we were in the question of who would administer ADC." The new Social Security Board lacked any experience in dealing with the problems of single mothers and dependent children. It had more interest in promoting social insurance than in social welfare. Katharine Lenroot speculated years later that if the Children's Bureau had retained control over the program, "ours would have been an approach directed as much as possible to a total service to children and families . . . and not primarily a program characterized . . . by an almost total emphasis on eligibility, fair hearings, etc."[16]

A remarkable consensus developed about the purpose of the ADC provisions. Everyone involved in the process—the Children's Bureau, the Committee on Economic Security, and the Congress—viewed it as a temporary program that would fade away as the economy turned around and as social insurance expanded. No one intended to create a welfare state. Roosevelt saw social insurance as an alternative to relief, which he called a "narcotic, a subtle destroyer of the human spirit." He promised to remove the federal government from the "business of relief" as soon as prosperity returned. In his view, "Continued dependence upon relief induces a spiritual and moral disintegration fundamentally destructive to the national fiber." Over the next fifty years the welfare population exploded, but public attitudes toward the poor, and toward the federal government's role in addressing the poverty problem, remained remarkably consistent.[17]

Program supporters believed a woman's place was in the home, not the workplace. All the participants saw the provision as a means of preserving the family by keeping mothers at home taking care of children. "The belief was that no woman who lost her husband should be forced to go on poor relief or give up her children to an orphanage," noted the sociologist Theda Skocpol. Moreover, contemporaries had no intention of giving money to all single mothers. Even the women reformers in the Children's Bureau accepted the widely held distinction between the so-called deserving and undeserving poor. Widows and deserted mothers were deserving; divorced or unmarried mothers were not. As a result, the legislation established lower benefit levels for welfare than for insurance, and it provided states with wide discretion in determining eligibility.[18]

Other provisions of the bill drew more opposition, but the administration managed to fend off attacks from both the right and the left. In both chambers conservative critics took aim at the provisions for old-age insurance. "The worst title in the bill," exclaimed a Republican member of the House Ways and Means Committee. Conservatives charged that it would discourage thrift, destroy initiative, and hurt the recovery effort. "It would take all the romance out of life," thundered New Jersey's Senator A. Harry Moore. "We might as well take a child from the nursery, give him a nurse, and protect him from every experience that life affords." The most serious threat, however, came from those on the left who complained the president's plan was not as generous as the proposals offered by Francis Townsend. Roosevelt, however, made clear that he wanted the bill passed intact with few changes, and most members of Congress were unwilling to oppose such a popular president. On April 19 the House passed the bill, 372 to 33. Senate passage followed in June by a lopsided vote, 76 to 6.[19]

Scholars have hailed the Social Security Act of 1935 for its lasting significance. "When future historians review the social legislation of the first two centuries of American history," observed the economist Henry Aaron, "they are likely to hail the Social Security Act as the most important piece of legislation in the entire period, with the possible exception of the Homestead Act." The law created a long-range old-age pension system to be financed by a payroll tax on employees and employers. It established a federal-state system of unemployment compensation based upon a payroll tax on employers. In addition to ADC, it set up funding for medical care of crippled children, rehabilitation of the disabled, and aid to the blind. On August 14, 1935, surrounded by lights and motion-picture cameras, Roosevelt signed the new act into law. The measure, he said, was "the cornerstone in a structure which is being built but is by no means complete—a structure intended to lessen the force of possible future depressions."[20]

Like everyone else discussing the legislation, the press underscored the importance of the old-age provisions and unemployment insurance but made only passing mention of ADC. The importance of the Social Security Act "cannot be exaggerated because in providing old-age health pensions and unemployment insurance this legislation eventually will affect the lives of every man, woman and child in the country," observed the *Washington Post*. While opinions were decidedly mixed about the constitutionality and wisdom of the social insurance provisions, most observers praised the ADC program. A writer in *Harper's* attacked the act as "not only of doubtful constitutionality but of questionable social and economic wisdom" but concluded that the ADC provisions were its "only sound part." The *New Republic,* which criticized most of the act, found ADC "rooted in traditional principles . . . and, on the whole, socially constructive."[21]

Whatever their feelings about the specific provisions, most observers complimented the president and Congress on the deliberative process that produced the new legislation. "In sharp contradistinction to most New Deal legislation, this program was prepared with real forethought and care," noted the *Washington*

Post. "Only partisan or uninformed criticism can say that this particular measure was stampeded through without the fullest opportunity for consideration of its implications."[22]

How little these observers knew! In fact, the Social Security Act was responsible for one of the great ironies of American social policy. "The program designed to take the government out of the relief business," observed the historian Edward Berkowitz, "proved to be the one that established the modern welfare system." The history of the Social Security Act, he noted, "underscores differences between outcomes and expectations" and "demonstrates that history alters the plans of policymakers." Over the next fifty years Congress and the nation repeatedly were to tinker with the system. Lawmakers promised to cut relief rolls and lower costs, but in time the welfare population grew and costs soared.[23]

THE ink had barely dried on the original act before critics began calling for changes. "Revisions in the social security program as now outlined will be necessary almost as soon as it gets under way," the *Washington Post* observed a few days after passage. From the moment Roosevelt submitted his proposal to Congress, critics had raised questions about the huge reserve fund needed to support old-age pensions, a fund that banked people's money at a time when many people were struggling to survive. In 1937 the government began deducting 1 percent from the paychecks of workers, even though no one was to receive benefits until 1942. Surpluses may have been financially necessary for the long-term future of the program, but they were politically unpopular. Roosevelt's enemies were quick to take the offensive. Alfred Landon, the Republican nominee in 1936, described Social Security as "unjust, unworkable, stupidly drafted and wastefully financed."[24]

In 1939 Roosevelt sought to shore up political support for his social insurance program by liberalizing benefits and moving up the schedule for paying benefits. The new amendments increased the federal share of ADC benefits, from 33 percent to 50 percent, up to a maximum of nine dollars in federal money per child per month. More important, the amendments extended old-age insurance to the wives and children of deceased workers and, under certain circumstances, to widows who had not reached retirement age. This change was consistent with a widely held belief that an expanded social insurance program could eventually replace relief. At the time, however, the reform weakened advocates of ADC by taking away the chief political weapon available to ADC recipients, their ability to generate public sympathy. Reformers in the 1940s maintained ill-funded mothers' aid programs only because the public associated them with aid to destitute and deserving widows. Without that image no political symbol could successfully connect the concerns of mainstream America with those in need. An absent father generated considerably less sympathy than a dead father.[25]

At the time, however, Congress readily embraced the new changes. Because most observers believed that widows with children would constitute the bulk of families on ADC, they happily predicted the withering away of welfare. The chairman of the Social Security Board told the Senate Finance Committee: "As this insurance system gets into operation . . . it ought to remove a large proportion of these dependent children from the State mother's pension rolls." Postwar economic expansion fed these hopes that ADC would eventually disappear. Between 1947 and 1967 average hourly earnings increased by 58 percent; median family incomes swelled by 75 percent. In his best-selling book *The Affluent Society* (1958), the economist John Kenneth Galbraith claimed that poverty existed "more nearly as an afterthought" than as a "massive affliction." His Harvard colleague Arthur Schlesinger, Jr., made the same point in a series of articles, suggesting that liberals needed to move beyond a quantitative liberalism "dedicated to the struggle to secure the economic basis of

life" and refocus on a "qualitative liberalism dedicated to better-
ing the quality of people's lives and opportunities." Since most
Americans had already secured the necessities of living, he encouraged liberals "to count that fight won and move on to the
more subtle and complicated problems of fighting for individual
dignity, identity, and fulfillment in a mass society."[26]

Welfare rolls, however, defied the optimistic predictions and
unrealistic expectations of liberals and policy makers. When the
first grants to states for ADC were made available in 1936, only
twelve states and the District of Columbia implemented the program. The combined expenditure for that first month was $1.7
million for 140,286 children in 56,836 families. By the outbreak
of World War II only 360,000 families had been enrolled in the
program. After a brief decline during the war the number of recipients surged to 2.2 million in 1950. Despite unprecedented
economic growth and a steep rise in social insurance payments,
the ADC rolls continued to expand, breaking the 3 million mark
in 1960. Cost for the program skyrocketed from $565 million in
1950 to $1.4 billion in 1962. Not only did the number of children
collecting welfare soar, but the makeup of the welfare population
had changed. A program designed with destitute widows in mind
was evolving into a system in which the majority of child beneficiaries had mothers who had never married or had been deserted.[27]

During the 1940s and 1950s the number of people collecting
welfare increased, and the costs soared, but only a minority of
those eligible for aid actually received it. As of 1940 nearly two-
thirds of eligible dependent children were not receiving benefits, a figure that remained fairly constant until the 1960s. Given
wide latitude by the Social Security Act, the states developed a
host of procedures designed to prevent "undesirables" from receiving benefits. Some states denied aid to mothers with criminal
records, while others imposed tough income or property qualifications. The two most common methods for denying benefits

were the "suitable home" standard—a euphemism for homes without illegitimate children—and the "absent father" clause, which disqualified dependent children whose father was suspected of visiting the home. Many southern states used the restrictive clauses to deny benefits to African-Americans. In 1960, for example, Louisiana removed 6,281 families with 23,489 children from its rolls because the mothers had given birth to one or more illegitimate children. Nearly 95 percent of the families cut were black.[28]

Scattered criticism of ADC exploded onto the national scene when the city of Newburgh, New York, decided to introduce tough new welfare policies designed to cut costs. In 1961 the town's manager, Joseph Mitchell, and council passed a series of reforms to force able-bodied men to work, discourage unwed women from having more children, and limit benefits to all except the aged and the disabled. "It is not moral," declared Mitchell, "to appropriate public funds to finance crime, illegitimacy, disease, and other social evils." The courts eventually ruled that most of Mitchell's plan was illegal, but not before his actions triggered a national debate about the relationship among poverty, crime, and illegitimacy. Republican Senator Barry Goldwater of Arizona endorsed Mitchell's actions. "I don't like to see my taxes paid for children out of wedlock," he said. Many newspapers carried sensationalized front-page stories about waste and fraud in the welfare system. Polls showed that a majority of Americans supported transferring authority for running welfare from the federal government to local officials.[29]

The Newburgh crisis also attracted the attention of the White House. President John F. Kennedy focused his economic policy during his first year in office on trying to relieve unemployment and sustain economic growth, but in 1962 he decided to make welfare reform a centerpiece of his domestic agenda. In February he sent Congress an unprecedented special message devoted to public welfare. "The goals of our public welfare programs,"

Kennedy said, "must contribute to the attack on dependency, juvenile delinquency, family breakdown, illegitimacy, ill health and disability." The recommended legislation provided federal funds to pay for rehabilitative and preventive services, established day care centers for children of working mothers, and extended a program providing funds to children whose parents were temporarily unemployed. The new emphasis required a new name, so Kennedy changed the title of the program from ADC to AFDC (aid to families with dependent children). The 1962 amendments reflected a subtle, though important, shift in government's attitude toward welfare. Reformers had designed the original 1935 legislation so that mothers could stay at home, insulated from the rigors of the workplace. The Kennedy administration devised its amendments to rehabilitate the poor so they could eventually move into the workplace.[30]

The administration told Congress that its proposals would decrease dependence and provide people with social services, including help in finding work. "The byword of our new program is prevention—and where it is too late—rehabilitation, a fresh start," declared the Health, Education, and Welfare (HEW) head Abraham Ribicoff. Congressional hearings were full of success stories of people leaving the welfare rolls because of the assistance of skilled social workers. "We have here a realistic program which will pay dividends on each dollar invested," Ribicoff told Congress. "It can move some persons off the assistance rolls entirely, enable others to attain a higher degree of self-confidence and independence, encourage children to grow strong in mind and body, train welfare workers in the skills which will help make these achievements possible, and simplify and improve welfare administration." Congress readily embraced the proposals, which sailed through the House by a vote of 320–69 and passed by voice vote in the Senate. At a signing ceremony Kennedy called the law "the most far reaching revision of our public-welfare program since it was enacted in 1935." The amendment, he declared, "marks a turning point in this nation's efforts to cope realistically and helpfully with these pressing problems."[31]

As was often the case in the history of welfare reform, the promises of reduced rolls and lower costs failed to materialize. In 1967 the House Ways and Means Committee concluded that "those [1962] amendments have not had the results which those in the administration who sponsored the amendments predicted." There were a number of problems. Neither the administration nor the Congress had adequately defined what was meant by "services." As states scrambled for money from Washington, they defined "services" as broadly as possible, using the money to pay for a variety of existing programs. One survey in 1967 concluded that "social service is little more than a relatively infrequent, pleasant chat. It is somewhat supportive. It is rarely threatening but also not too meaningful in the sense of either helping poor people get things they want or of changing their lives." More important, the emphasis on prevention failed to address structural causes of poverty—among them single parenthood, joblessness, and low wages—for which there were no cheap or easy solutions.[32]

By 1963 Kennedy had more ambitious plans to reform welfare. Perhaps inspired by the publication of Michael Harrington's passionate book *The Other America,* which claimed that one-third of the country was poor, the president asked his advisers to develop a comprehensive plan for fighting poverty. "I want to go beyond the things that have already been accomplished," he told Walter Heller, chairman of the Council of Economic Advisers. Heller established a working group in the White House and solicited ideas from Cabinet members that "might be woven into a basic attack on poverty and waste of human resources, as part of the 1964 legislative program." Initially the results were disappointing. Government agencies simply recycled old ideas that had been lying around since the New Deal. As they searched for creative new approaches, Heller's committee stumbled on to David Hackett, a close friend of Attorney General Robert Kennedy's, who had been organizing the administration's program for juvenile delinquency. Hackett had adopted the ideas of two Columbia University social scientists, Richard A. Cloward and Lloyd E. Ohlin, arguing that the source of poverty was not the individual but "the social systems in which these individuals or groups are enmeshed." People turned to crime and delinquency, they suggested, because society provided few incentives for legitimate activities. The solution was to reorganize slums by using coordinated and comprehensive government services to provide the poor with opportunities.[33]

Hackett's community action approach was largely untested, but he convinced Heller's committee that it was worth pursuing. "I was . . . sort of swept off my feet," recalled William Capron, a Stanford professor on loan to the Council of Economic Advisers, "because these guys were really way ahead of and had tremendous impact on the thinking of the Council." Events were moving rapidly, and the committee had little time to investigate the few pilot projects that Hackett had created. "We were going on faith," Capron recalled. The council accepted the idea "without really knowing what it would mean when it got translated." Since no one knew whether the approach would work, they decided to start small, spending a million dollars to fund ten local community action agencies, five urban and five rural. That was where the program stood in November 1963, when President Kennedy traveled to Dallas.[34]

Now it was Heller's turn to try to sell President Johnson on the program. Johnson had warmly endorsed the poverty initiative. "That's my kind of program," he told Heller the day after President Kennedy had been assassinated in Dallas. "Move full speed ahead." But told of the community action program, Johnson was skeptical. The concept was too fuzzy, too abstract for such a practical man. "His conception of the War on Poverty had this sort of concrete idea," Heller said. "Bulldozers. Tractors. People operating heavy machinery." He wanted something that would "be big and bold and hit the whole nation with real impact," Heller recalled. Johnson's doubts were shared by Cabinet members, most of whom were excluded from the deliberations of the White House working group. The most vocal dissenters were Wilbur Cohen, a former staff member of the original Committee on Economic Security (CES), which had drafted the Social Security Act, and now an undersecretary of HEW, and Daniel Patrick Moynihan, a Labor Department official. Both men argued that the poor needed jobs and income, not better social skills.[35]

In an odd twist of fate, Johnson's doubts about community action led to an expansion of the program. Neither the president nor the members of the White House working group had a clear grasp of what community action was or how precisely it would alleviate poverty. But Johnson wanted to announce a new initiative in his January State of the Union address, and community action seemed to be the only new idea on the table. Whatever its conceptual confusion, "a war on poverty" provided the president with the type of bold initiative he needed to distinguish himself from his slain predecessor, convince liberals of his commitment to reform, and rally Democrats for the upcoming presidential election. Johnson told Heller that he would accept the program only if it were greatly expanded so that any community in America would be eligible to set one up. "In one stroke," observed Allen Matusow, "Johnson escalated community action from an experimental program to precede the War on Poverty into the very war itself."[36]

In January Johnson used his State of the Union address to make public his new poverty initiative: "This Administration today, here and now, declares unconditional war on poverty in America." He used language that officially transformed a modest proposal into a moral crusade. Two weeks later, in his budget message, he announced the community action program and offered to fund it at five hundred million dollars in the first year. "I propose a program which relies on the traditional time-tested American methods of organized local community action to help individuals, families, and communities to help themselves," he said.[37]

In February the president appointed R. Sargent Shriver, a Kennedy brother-in-law who had earned his reputation as the head of the Peace Corps, to run the war on poverty. The new poverty czar and his small group of assistants faced the formidable task of translating the amorphous community action concept into a specific legislative proposal. Johnson had already announced that community action would be the centerpiece of his war on poverty, but no one had confronted a fundamental question: What was community action? Community action, recalled one participant in drafting the White House bill, "was a concept that had various ideas associated with it. But any two people you talked to about what a community action program was and what was important about it would grab hold of a different part of the elephant." Johnson, and many politicians, saw it as another way of funneling money into heavily Democratic urban areas and of reaping the political benefits. The president, however, was not directly involved in developing or writing the legislation. Hackett's initial idea was fairly modest: It offered a way for local officials to offer coordinated services on the local level. By January Hackett had been so disillusioned by Johnson's distortion of his original modest proposal that he had drifted away from the planning. His deputy, Richard Boone, who had his own radical definition of community action, took his place and redefined community action. Boone believed that government needed to empower poor people to challenge existing institutions. In order to guarantee that his definition found its way into the legislation, he insisted that the administration's proposal state clearly that the poverty effort would be organized with the "maximum feasible participation" of the poor.[38]

Like Johnson, Shriver was originally skeptical of the community action idea, fearing that it would be unable to generate public support. "It'll never fly," he said after hearing about it for the first time. But the idea had gained too much momentum to be scrapped, so Shriver scrambled to include in the proposal more concrete programs that he could sell to Congress and the public. "The resulting program sent to Congress," recalled one participant, "represented not a choice among policies so much as a collection of them." The administration's proposal called for creation of an Office of Economic Opportunity (OEO) to administer the poverty program, created the Neighborhood Youth Corps to provide local training and jobs in public service, provided money for work study to assist needy college students, and established a Volunteers in Service to America (VISTA), a domestic Peace Corps.[39]

The debates in Congress did little to help clarify the definition of community action. "Rarely has so sweeping a commitment been made to an institution so little tested and so little understood as the community-action agency," noted the political scientist James Sundquist. "It was reviewed by the Congress with the minimum of care, in the shortest of time, and with the least understanding of what was about to happen." By elevating the war on poverty to a moral issue, the administration effectively muted potential objections to specific provisions in the bill. " 'War on Poverty' is a terrific slogan, particularly in an election year," noted a skeptical Republican. "It puts doubters under the suspicion of being in favor of poverty." Just in case Congress failed to respond to moral appeals, the White House launched what one journalist called "some of the most intensive administration lobbying that Congress has ever encountered."[40]

Republicans screamed foul, charging that the legislation was politically motivated and designed to win votes rather than to help the poor. They condemned the community action provision for being "hastily drafted," for violating the principles of federalism, for duplicating existing programs, and for granting too much power to a poverty "czar." Arizona Senator Barry Goldwater, Johnson's Republican opponent for president, predicted that the poverty program would "encourage poverty" and bring "more and more people . . . into the ranks of those being taken care of by the Government." Representative William Miller of New York, Goldwater's running mate, claimed that the administration "in its haste to solve the ills of the poor in one fell swoop . . . is overlooking the fact that we very well could be paving the way, through this all-encompassing program, for even more dependence on the Government."[41]

Conservative Republicans were not the only politicians criticizing the measure. A number of powerful Democratic mayors of major cities complained that the community action programs bypassed city hall and created the potential for conflict. New York's Mayor Robert Wagner told the House that "the sovereign government of each locality in which . . . a community action program is proposed should have the power of approval over the makeup of the planning group, the structure of the planning group, and over the plan." Chicago's Richard Daley made clear that he wanted to control the funds. "We think very strongly that any project of this kind, in order to succeed, must be administered by the duly constituted elected officials of the areas with the cooperation of the private agencies."[42]

These well-founded objections failed to slow the poverty juggernaut. "We have been blackjacked, gagged, threatened and bulldozed to accept something that we know is not good," exclaimed New Jersey's Republican Peter Frelinghuysen, Jr. Convinced they had a winning political issue in an election year, Capitol Hill Democrats rammed the bill through a pliant Congress. "We are moving with maximum speed, not deliberate speed," announced a House liberal. The administration felt little need to respond to big-city mayors who supported the initiative despite reservations about community action. Johnson was much more worried about southern Democrats who complained about the possibility of racially mixed Youth Corps camps. A Georgia congressman complained to a White House aide that the bill was "cooked up . . . to foster racial integration without real regard for poverty." In response the White House made a few concessions—it gave governors control over OEO projects in their states and added a loan program for impoverished farmers—but the community action provision remained largely intact.[43]

Both houses of Congress passed the poverty program by surprisingly large margins during the summer of 1964. As expected, the Senate voted overwhelmingly for the legislation, 61–34. The surprise came in the House, where a handful of liberal Republicans abandoned their party and supported the measure, allowing it to pass by a comfortable 226–185 margin. The press hailed the victory. The *New York Times* compared the poverty program with the Civil Rights Act of 1964, calling it an "expression of national resolve in a cause that is as necessary as it is just." The *Washington Post* called the war "a cause that is wholly beneficent and against an enemy whose defeat nobody will mourn." But as the historian Allen Matusow has noted, there was one significant problem with the heralded legislation: No one still had any idea what community action meant. "Thus in August 1964, when the Economic Opportunity Act was enacted," he wrote, "neither the president who sponsored it, the director-designate who would administer it, nor the congressmen who passed it really knew what they had done." A legislative history of the poverty legislation, he concluded, "might well be entitled 'How Not to Pass a Law.' "[44]

The administration and Congress may not have been clear about what they were voting for, but they were explicit about what they intended the legislation to accomplish. "We are not content to accept the endless growth of relief rolls or welfare rolls," Johnson said in the signing ceremony. "We want to offer the forgotten fifth of our people opportunity and not doles." Secretary of Health, Education, and Welfare Anthony Celebrezze enthusiastically predicted, "Welfare costs can go down if our theories are right." The press joined in the celebration. The *New York Times* underscored the administration's determination to provide opportunity, not more relief. "The program," it editorialized, "stresses work and study instead of handouts, opportunity instead of charity." The *Washington Post* said the legislation "offers the first real hope in a generation of purposeful public action to raise . . . families up into self-dependence, to take youngsters off the street corners and train them for steady jobs, to encourage the uncertain to stay in the classrooms until they get their diplomas."[45]

Rarely has a public policy initiative produced results that were more dramatically the opposite of what planners had predicted. During the 1960s the unemployment rate was cut in half, but the number of AFDC recipients increased by two-thirds, and the cost of the program doubled. Between 1965 and 1975 the number of recipients of AFDC more than doubled, from 4.4 to 11.4 million. New York, which saw its unemployment rate drop to 3.2 percent in 1969, watched as the relief rolls swelled to over 1 million. "It becomes increasingly clear," the *New York Times* noted, "that the welfare rolls have a life of their own detached from the metropolitan job market."[46]

What happened? No one had realized that the community action provision was a time bomb waiting to explode. In many urban communities the community action program (CAP) funded storefront service centers designed to assist poor people in the neighborhood. A study in Baltimore found that the AFDC caseload increased by 36.6 percent in areas with community action centers while the total city-wide caseload rose by only 8.6 percent. A government study suggested that "CAP programs may have helped the poor understand their rights under existing public assistance policies and may have lowered the amount of personal stigma recipients felt. There is evidence showing that CAP programs are associated with reduced feelings of helplessness." The study concluded that the less helpless people felt, the more likely they were to seek welfare. The social scientists Frances Fox Piven and Richard A. Cloward, activists who led the drive to bring eligible poor people onto the rolls, concluded that "the rolls had risen primarily because families of long-standing eligibility had been led to apply for public aid in unprecedented numbers as a result of a greater variety of welfare rights activities."[47]

The individual service centers gave birth to a coordinated national welfare movement. In 1967 the civil rights activist George Wiley founded the National Welfare Rights Organization (NWRO), claiming that "the poor at the grass roots needed a new voice." By 1968 the NWRO had established chapters in thirty-five states and was representing about twenty-five thousand welfare clients. Its strategy was to overwhelm the existing system by registering as many poor people as possible and provoking a fiscal crisis that would force local governments to increase benefits. At first, the NWRO experienced tremendous success. A drive to require New York caseworkers to give recipients legally required but rarely authorized special grants for minimum levels of furniture, clothing, and housing equipment forced the city to increase special grants from twenty million dollars in 1965 to ninety million dollars in 1968. According to a legal services attorney in Newark, New Jersey, many clients who came into her office after reading NWRO pamphlets were "much more eager to stand up for their welfare rights than [clients] were" even two years before.[48]

The success of the welfare rights movement depended heavily on the work of legal aid lawyers, who were also funded by the community action program. In 1965 the administration convinced Congress to create the Legal Services Program as a separate division within the OEO, claiming that the poor needed special assistance overcoming legal obstacles. "The uneducated and uninformed poor are easy prey for the unscrupulous landlord, unfairly administered welfare regulations, [and] racial discrimination," the OEO noted in its annual report. Between 1966 and 1968 the OEO spent about eighty-five million dollars on legal services. Some 250 legal service projects were established, and they operated about 850 neighborhood law offices staffed by eighteen hundred attorneys. Lawyers had previously always worked on a case-by-case basis to address the individual needs of their clients. Beginning in the 1960s, however, welfare rights lawyers promoted long-term social change to improve the quality of life for all poor people. They advocated "institutional change through law reform" by taking "test cases" of class action suits.[49]

The legal strategy produced a number of important judicial victories. In 1967 a federal court in Connecticut struck down the state's residency requirement for welfare recipients. The court held that "the right of interstate travel also encompasses the right to be free of discouragement of interstate movement." The decision, upheld by the Supreme Court in 1969, forced more than a dozen states to end their residency requirements. In 1968 the Supreme Court ruled man-in-the-house and substitute parent rules were unconstitutional. "Destitute children who are legally fatherless cannot be flatly denied federally funded assistance on the transparent fiction that they have a substitute father," the Court noted. The decision forced eighteen states and the District of Columbia to alter their eligibility rules. Just as important were legal challenges to arbitrary administrative procedures that gave welfare officials wide discretion to decide whether to give aid. The Supreme Court ruled in *Goldberg v. Kelly* (1970) that "welfare guards against the societal malaise that may flow from a widespread sense of unjustified frustration and insecurity" and held that welfare recipients had a constitutional right to an evidentiary hearing before their benefits could be terminated.[50]

THE drive to protect the legal rights of the poor was part of a broader definition of citizenship and an expanding universe of rights that grew out of the civil rights movement of the 1960s. "Today there is a growing recognition of the legal right to the receipt of public assistance, a legal right to insist that it be fairly designed and fairly administered—and a legal right to invoke the

Constitution to assure the fairness of the system," HEW's Wilbur Cohen noted. "What lies ahead is the task of applying these rights, point by point, so that the poor may come to stand truly equal before the law." The expanded definition of legal rights, and the willingness of the federal courts to enforce them, ensured that states could no longer control the number of recipients by imposing arbitrary eligibility rules. By 1971 an estimated 90 percent of those eligible for welfare were receiving it. In the past this rate had been much lower, perhaps 33 percent in the early 1960s.[51]

Though successful in expanding eligibility, the welfare rights movement produced an unanticipated political backlash. Advocates for the poor, including the NWRO, hoped through confrontation to force states and Congress to liberalize benefits. But the strategy produced the opposite result: Even the nation's most liberal states, Massachusetts and New York, placed sharp restrictions on the special grants program, and many other states soon followed suit. The response in Congress was just as harsh. Angered by the demands of poverty advocates, Senator Russell Long, the powerful Louisiana Democrat who chaired the Finance Committee, charged that welfare mothers were "brood mares." According to Long, "If they can find the time to march in the streets, picket, and sit all day in committee hearing rooms, they can find the time to do some useful work." In 1967 Congress added tough new amendments to the Social Security Act that imposed a freeze on funding for cases attributable to desertion or illegitimacy and provided incentives for recipients to participate in workfare programs. The emphasis on workfare showed how much the program had changed since 1935, when the original goal was to keep mothers at home and out of the workplace. Now the emphasis was on job training so they could go out and find jobs.[52]

Like many of the social programs of the 1960s, the war on poverty was characterized by grand ambition and limited gains. "The social history of the 1960's is already littered with the wreckage of crash programs that were going to change everything and in fact changed nothing," Moynihan observed. "[T]he tendency was to oversell and under-perform." In submitting his bill to Congress, Johnson called for "total victory." "Conquest of poverty is well within our power," he declared. Sargent Shriver, the president's chief evangelist, predicted that the program "will in the end eliminate poverty from the United States." But deeply held conservative attitudes toward the poor, and toward government's role in promoting social welfare, limited the choice of weapons used to fight the war. With polls showing that large numbers of Americans believed that poverty resulted from "lack of effort" and that the poor were partly to blame for their plight, the administration developed a program that emphasized opportunity and promised to help the poor help themselves. "Perhaps the most striking characteristic" of the administration's view of poverty, noted Henry Aaron, "is the absence of any mention of the economic system in which it operates." From 1965 to 1970 OEO spent an average of $1.7 billion per year—less than 1.5 percent of the federal budget, or one-third of 1 percent of the gross national product. If all OEO money had gone directly to the poor, it would have amounted to between $50 and $70 per person.[53]

The administration camouflaged the conceptual problems with the program by wrapping it in language familiar to most Americans. Describing the effort as a "war on poverty" appealed to American faith in social progress, while the emphasis on community control and local initiative reassured a public leery of an enlarged federal presence. "Community Action is at the heart of the War on Poverty because its primary principles are individualistic," the OEO observed in 1967. "In the American tradition, community action depends on local initiative. Local problems demand fundamentally locally developed solutions." Underlying the initiative was a naive notion about the malleability of American society, a false faith in consensus, a belief that all groups in society—the poor, the middle class, and big business—shared a common agenda and could work together to achieve similar goals.

. .

Convinced of the healing power of economic growth, policy makers believed they could solve the age-old problems of poverty by tinkering with the welfare system. The problem, however, was that poverty was not a local problem, and "the people" were fragmented into competing groups that battled one another for limited social resources. "There was a gnawing question about the capacity of a structure based on 'consensus' to work effectively for broad social change," observed a member of the president's task force. "But none of us, in our euphoria over the opportunity to mount the program on a nationwide level, were really prepared to raise openly that question."[54]

The ultimate irony of the war on poverty was that a program launched as the result of renewed faith in the power of government was to undermine public faith in Washington's ability to solve social problems. "Perhaps no government program in modern American history promised so much more than it delivered," noted the historian James T. Patterson. "More than any other program of Johnson's so-called Great Society, the war on poverty accentuated doubts about the capacity of social science to plan, and government to deliver, ambitious programs for social betterment." The contrast between promise and performance infuriated some of the poor. In 1967, when rioting hit Detroit, Mayor Jerome Cavanagh blamed the OEO and other federal programs. "What we've been doing, at the level we've been doing it, is almost worse than nothing at all. . . . We've raised expectations, but we haven't been able to deliver all we should have." The experience also soured a generation of intellectuals who viewed the war on poverty as a metaphor for government ineptitude. "There are limits to the desirable reach of social engineering," observed the sociologist Nathan Glazer. Increasingly the public shared many of these doubts. By 1967 more than two-thirds of the public thought the administration had gone "too far." In 1969 a total of 84 percent agreed with the statement "There are too many people receiving welfare who ought to be working."[55]

While the flawed assumptions of Johnson's poverty warriors contributed to the unintended explosion of the welfare rolls, broad social and demographic changes also played a role by undermining many of the assumptions that had informed the original legislation. First, ADC had been based on a rigid view of gender roles: Men belonged in the work force, and women should stay at home and raise the children. The economic expansion that followed World War II created new demand for women to enter the work force, especially as elementary school teachers, salesclerks, and office workers. By 1950 half of all working women in America were married, and the percentage continued to grow each year. Thirty years after Congress passed its provision designed to keep women at home raising children, more than half of all mothers of school-age children were in the labor force.[56]

There was a corresponding shift in public attitudes toward working women. When the Gallup organization asked the public in 1936 if "you approve of a married woman earning money in business or industry if she has a husband capable of supporting her," only 18 percent of respondents approved, while 72 percent expressed disapproval. A 1945 poll that asked, "If there is a limited number of jobs, do you approve or disapprove of a married woman holding a job in business or industry when her husband is able to support her?" elicited a remarkable 86 percent opposition to women working. Since then, however, the set of beliefs that formed the moral foundation for the mothers' aid and aid to dependent children programs has utterly collapsed. By 1969 the situation had changed dramatically, so that 55 percent approved, while only 40 percent disapproved. "A program that started out saying stay-at-home motherhood is a service to the nation is really undermined culturally when you get to the point where most Americans think an adult woman should be in the paid labor force," said Skocpol.[57]

Second, the movement of African-Americans from the South to cities in the North with liberal benefits increased the cost of the

· ·

program. In the 1940s the mechanization of cotton pushed many blacks off southern farms at the same time that wartime production provided new job opportunities in northern industries. During the decade more than 1 million African-Americans boarded buses and trains and migrated to cities in the North and West. They were joined by another 1.5 million during the 1950s. Chicago saw its black population increase by 77 percent, from 278,000 to 492,000 during the 1940s. In the 1950s it swelled to 813,000. By 1970 more than 4 million African-Americans had left the South. By 1960 half the black populations of New York, Chicago, Philadelphia, Detroit, Los Angeles, and Washington, D.C., had been born elsewhere. Most of the increase in welfare occurred in the urban areas where blacks settled. While AFDC rose by only 17 percent during the 1950s, 80 percent of that increase occurred in the 121 major urban areas. In urban areas in New Jersey where the black population had increased, AFDC doubled or tripled. In Chicago the rolls rose 83 percent. The Great Migration thus added an explosive racial element to the welfare problem. In 1931 only 3 percent of women receiving state pensions were black. A half century later African-Americans, 12 percent of the population, were 38 percent of AFDC recipients.[58]

Third, and perhaps most important, no one in 1935 could have anticipated the breakdown of the nuclear family. In the early years the majority of recipients of ADC were made up of widows. By 1967, however, only 5.5 percent of AFDC dependency followed the death of the father; 94.5 percent resulted from illegitimacy or desertion. In AFDC the term "women-headed families" was no longer a "shorthand for widows and orphans," noted the social scientist Gilbert Steiner. "It was a euphemism for desertion and illegitimacy." The change in the AFDC population was part of a broader epidemic of divorce and out-of-wedlock births. Between 1946 and 1973 the proportion of single-parent households headed by divorced mothers rose from 26 percent to 49 percent. An upsurge in out-of-wedlock births—from 4 percent of all births in

1950 to 27 percent in 1989—increased the numbers of children who were judged eligible in the 1960s. The problem of family disintegration was especially acute for African-Americans. By the start of the 1980s almost 55 percent of all black children were born out of wedlock, compared with 15 percent in 1940; 85 percent of black teenage mothers were unmarried; and 47 percent of black families were female-headed, compared with 8 percent in 1950. The reasons for the breakdown of the family are complex, the combination of changing gender roles, sexual liberation, and liberalized divorce laws, but the result has been clear: an upsurge in poor, female-headed families collecting AFDC.[59]

By 1969 policy makers were confronting a fundamentally different environment from that facing Roosevelt in the 1930s. The initial goal of welfare had seemed simple: protect abandoned mothers so they could stay at home and raise their families. But now reformers encountered a host of dilemmas: How to provide support for poor families without reducing the incentive to seek employment? How to aid single-parent families without encouraging out-of-wedlock births and divorce or separation? How to help poor children without encouraging their parents to loaf? Finally, how to build consensus among the competing interest groups that make up the poverty debate? The questions may have grown more complex, but the American desire to develop solutions remained as strong as ever.[60]

SO it was that during the 1960s the once-noncontroversial welfare provision of Social Security had emerged as a major source of public discontent and partisan wrangling. Republicans used the Great Society and its supposed "giveaway" programs as symbols of a Democratic party out of touch with "mainstream America." California Governor Ronald Reagan in his first inaugural in 1967 announced: "We are not going to perpetuate poverty by substituting a permanent dole for a paycheck. There is no humanity or

charity in destroying self-reliance, dignity, and self-respect." A
few years later *Time* declared, "The failure of the United States
welfare system is in large measure a defeat for liberalism." Pundits and politicians of almost every stripe charged that the expanded welfare state disrupted families and undercut the work
ethic. Most of the public seemed to agree. In 1972, 61 percent
agreed (and only 23 percent disagreed) with the statement that
"many women getting welfare money are having illegitimate babies to increase the money they get." A poll five years later found
that 54 percent of Americans thought "most people who receive
money from welfare could get along without it if they tried."[61]

While attacking the welfare state became standard political
fodder for Republicans, they were unsuccessful in trying to reform it. "America's welfare system is a failure that grows worse
every day," Richard Nixon declared in 1969. Shortly afterward he
shocked nearly everyone by unveiling his own ambitious welfare
scheme: a family assistance plan (FAP) that would have guaranteed
all families with children a minimum of five hundred dollars per
adult and three hundred dollars per child per year. Nixon
promised that his plan would sustain the incentive to work and
supplant welfare dependency by allowing a poor family to keep
some of its earned income. "What America needs," he told the nation, "is not more welfare but more workfare." Some contemporary commentators applauded the plan. The *Economist* asserted, "It
may rank in importance with President Roosevelt's first proposal
for a social security system in the mid-1930s."[62]

In the highly charged partisan politics of the early 1970s the
measure failed to convince critics on the left or right. Liberals objected to the workfare provisions that required adult recipients to
accept "suitable" training or work or forfeit their subsidies.
George Wiley insisted that the proposal offered relatively little to
the North. With characteristic hyperbole, the NWRO asserted
that the plan was an "act of political repression." Conservatives
balked at spending so much government money, charged that the

FAP would magnify the welfare explosion, and worried about the impact of the plan on the supply of cheap labor. "I can't get anybody to iron my shirts," Russell Long exploded at one point. Nixon himself quickly tired of the struggle and withdrew support for his own bill. In 1977 Democrat Jimmy Carter attempted to pass a revised version of the Family Assistance Act. But a stumbling economy, in which the cost of living increased by more than 12 percent in 1980, unemployment had risen to 7.4 percent, and the prime lending rate was an astonishing 20 percent, soured the public on new social welfare initiatives.[63]

In 1981 former California Governor Ronald Reagan rode the tidal wave of public discontent into the White House. He galvanized conservative support with his simple but compelling message: love of country, fear of communism, and scorn of government. Preaching what the economist Herbert Stein called the "economics of joy," Reagan repudiated the traditional Republican economic doctrine of tight fiscal policy and balanced budgets and instead proposed massive tax cuts and huge increases in military spending. "In this present crisis," he said in his inaugural address, "government is not the solution to our problem; government is the problem." It was time, the new president declared, "to reawaken this industrial giant, to get government back within its means and to lighten our punitive tax burden."[64]

Clearly, Ronald Reagan was able to tap into public anger at Washington by charging that social programs were riddled with waste, fraud, and abuse and calling for cutbacks and outright elimination of some programs. Poverty programs were a frequent target. During his campaign he had poked fun at "welfare queens," poor women who drove Cadillacs while collecting relief. "In the sixties we waged a war on poverty and poverty won," Reagan said. Once in office, he forced through Congress a budget resolution that called for deep cuts in many social programs and increased spending for the military. Reagan discovered, however, that the major components of the welfare state were popular middle-class entitlements, such as Medicare and Social Security. He focused his attacks on programs aimed primarily at the poor. The administration tightened eligibility standards for AFDC, throwing nearly five hundred thousand people off the rolls and reducing benefits for other recipients. In addition to changes in AFDC, the administration cut the food stamp program, jobs and training programs, and housing subsidies.[65]

Conservative intellectuals provided the president with ideological ammunition for his assault on government. In the 1980s many of the most provocative ideas and the most influential writers were found on the right. Well-funded conservative think tanks, such as the American Enterprise Institute (AEI) and the Heritage Foundation, produced scores of studies purporting to prove that government-sponsored programs had failed to make a dent in the poverty problem. They charged that poverty rates in 1980 were only slightly lower than they had been before Johnson had launched his war on poverty. The face of poverty had changed: As poverty rates fell among the elderly, welfare increasingly came to be seen as a system for shelling out cash to a growing pool of young, unwed mothers. In 1984 Charles Murray's *Losing Ground* concluded that American welfare programs had increased the number of people in poverty. Murray called for "scrapping the entire federal welfare and income-support structure for working-aged persons." His book became the rage among conservative social policy makers in the White House and throughout Washington. The conservative economist George Gilder wrote that the book was "the most devastating, sustained attack ever made against the welfare state."[66]

Despite his repeated promises to scale back the size of government, Reagan waited until the end of his second term to offer a comprehensive welfare reform package. By that time his conservative coalition had frayed, public support for his assault against government had waned, and Democrats had made major gains by painting his administration as heartless and out of touch with mainstream Americans. Much to the dismay of his right-wing supporters, Reagan worked closely with Democrats on Capitol Hill to develop a plan that would build bipartisan support. The negotiations resulted in passage of the Family Support Act (FSA) in 1988—the first major reform of AFDC since its enactment in 1935. A mix of conservative and a few liberal provisions, the legislation called for increased federal funding for innovative state programs that encouraged mothers on public assistance to become more self-sufficient and fathers to provide more child support. The central feature was a program called JOBS (Job Opportunities and Basic Skills), which allowed states to run training and work programs for parents on welfare. Washington promised $1 billion a year, and the states were to provide matching funds and design their own programs. Supporters on both the left and right praised the new law as the most important reform of welfare since the original Social Security Act. "The Senate's passage of a welfare reform bill puts the nation on the threshold of a historic change from old policies that foster dependency to new ones designed to promote self-sufficiency," the *New York Times* editorialized. "That is cause for celebration," exclaimed Daniel Patrick Moynihan, who had earlier won a Senate seat in New York, declaring it "the most important legislation of its time."[67]

Once again, however, the legislation lagged behind expectations. Over the next five years the welfare rolls expanded more rapidly than at any time since the late 1960s. In 1988 there were 3.7 million families receiving AFDC; by 1992 the number had risen to 4.7 million. Nearly all adult recipients were single parents, and the great majority were female. "It hasn't worked," observed Kansas Congresswoman Jan Meyers. "Less than one percent of the welfare population is working today. And the program has cost us $10 billion more than expected—$13 billion instead of $3 billion." The reasons for the failure were all too familiar: Congress hyped the workfare provisions but failed to provide enough funds for training or for child care. The legislation provided only $1 billion a year over five years for job programs, which worked out to just $250 annually per adult AFDC recipient. An unexpected economic downturn complicated matters, leaving many states without the money needed to qualify for matching federal funds. A study of southern states found that "for most recipients the nature of receiving AFDC has not changed."[68]

Most of all, the legislation failed because it assumed that people were poor because they lacked skills to enter the workplace, an assumption that informed every major legislative effort to solve the poverty program. What was missing from this approach was an appreciation of the underlying structural causes of poverty. The previous twenty years had witnessed a dramatic shift in the economy: Low-paying service jobs had replaced high-paying union jobs. The shift was especially noticeable in older industrial cities, which had been home to the nation's leading manufacturing centers. As good jobs either dried up or fled to the suburbs, the poverty rate soared. At the same time, a combination of forces—rising energy prices, growing international competition, lower productivity, and government policies—contributed to a widening gap between rich and poor. "By almost all measures, the degree of income inequality between rich and poor American families has been increasing," *Fortune* magazine said in 1983. By ignoring these deeply embedded economic problems, the FSA never had a chance to make serious inroads into the poverty population. Workfare offered little relief if few jobs were available.[69]

The failure of the FSA contributed to a growing sense that the nation faced another "welfare crisis." In 1992 the nation was mired in recession, and the federal government and most states were struggling with crippling deficits. At the same time, the recession increased the number of poor people and produced greater demand for relief. In 1992, 13.5 million Americans (roughly 5 million families) were on AFDC. One in 7 children received government relief, and roughly 2,000 were joining every day. It was predicted that more than 30 percent of all children born after 1980 would spend at least a year on welfare; the figure was an astonishing 80 percent for African-Americans. Observers were especially alarmed by the skyrocketing rate of out-of-wedlock births: The number had increased by more than 400 percent since 1960 and showed no signs of slowing down. While evidence was flimsy, many scholars, and a large majority of the public, believed that welfare was a major cause of family breakdown. "From across the political and ideological spectrum, there is almost universal acknowledgment that the American social welfare system has been a failure," observed a critic.[70]

SQUEEZED by higher welfare payments and a middle class reluctant to pay higher taxes, many states searched for ways to trim the rolls. In 1991 thirty-one states froze AFDC benefits, and nine passed reform bills that trimmed benefits. Adjusted for inflation, AFDC maximum benefits for a family of three fell 42 percent since 1970. Michigan dropped ninety thousand people from its relief rolls. Most states experimented with methods for promoting self-sufficiency by providing incentives to work and preserve families. Dozens of states allowed recipients to retain assets over the federal limit and provided transitional funds—namely, Medicaid and some child care assistance—for mothers moving from welfare to work. The incentives were not all positive: States were willing to use the stick as well as the carrot to alter welfare behavior. California passed a proposal that reduced family benefits across the board for any family headed by an able-bodied adult who stayed on AFDC for more than six months. New Jersey passed a welfare revision that denied mothers additional payments if they had additional babies. It also mandated that those on welfare with children over the age of two must obtain job training or other education.[71]

The various state experiments with welfare reform provided

social scientists with valuable evidence for their theories about how to prevent poverty. "We're much better informed than we were," observed the liberal Urban Institute. "We know how much poverty there is, who is poor, what works and what doesn't." Conservatives agreed that new information allowed them to make more informed judgments about the poor. "Everybody now agrees you can't talk about poverty alone," said Michael Novak. "We used to talk about 'the poor' and 'the war on poverty'—the image was much too simple. We must desegregate them. There are different kinds of folks which are poor for very different kinds of reasons." Liberals and conservatives hailed a new "welfare consensus" that eschewed traditional liberal and conservative notions in favor of a "new paternalism" that stressed shared responsibility. A poverty program, noted the sociologist Christopher Jencks, "must strike a balance between collective compassion and individual responsibility." Among the chief tenets of the new consensus was a belief in tougher work requirements for welfare recipients and a conviction that fathers needed to take greater responsibility for their children. If welfare were to be a truly transitional program, government would need to "make work pay" by guaranteeing health insurance and increasing the earned income tax credit (EITC), a subsidy for low-income workers. Finally, there should be a strict time limit on AFDC, with last-resort public sector jobs for those unable to find work in the private sector.[72]

Arkansas Governor Bill Clinton emerged as an articulate spokesman of the new consensus during his 1992 campaign for president. Throughout the primary season Clinton professed his concern for "the forgotten middle class." To independent suburban white voters he campaigned as a cultural conservative who supported capital punishment, who promised to make the streets safer and the schools better, to provide "basic health care to all Americans," and to "end welfare as we know it." For traditional Democrats he offered a message of economic populism, promising to soak the rich and fight to preserve popular social programs.

He told the National Democratic Convention that he offered a "New Covenant" with the American people. "We offer opportunity," he declared. "We demand responsibility." He made it clear early in his administration that ending welfare would be a top priority. "There's no greater gap between our good intentions and our misguided consequences than you see in the welfare system," Clinton declared. "It started for the right purpose of helping people who fall by the wayside. . . . But for many, the system has worked to undermine the very values that people need to put themselves and their lives back on track."[73]

During his first two years in office, however, the president abandoned his "New Democrat" message and concentrated his energies on passing a complex health care proposal. Business leaders and Republicans launched a successful counterattack to convince the public that the plan was too costly and complicated, and the president too liberal. "It was a grand failure," observed a Democratic congressman. The failure of the health reform package, combined with the president's support for a controversial measure to allow gays in the military and a series of failed appointments to the post of attorney general, eroded public support for the Clinton presidency. After two years in office Clinton had the lowest poll ratings of any president since Watergate. Energized Republicans, led by Georgia firebrand Newt Gingrich, pounced on the helpless Democrats in the 1994 midterm elections. All three hundred Republican congressional candidates signed a ten-point Contract with America, a political wish list polished by consultants and tested in focus groups, pledging to trim government waste, cap welfare payments, raise military spending, and lower taxes. On election day Republicans made major gains, seizing control of both houses for the first time in forty years and defeating thirty-five incumbent Democrats. "We got our butts kicked," said the chairman of the Democratic National Committee.[74]

Clinton responded to the Republican triumph by moving to the center, co-opting Republican themes while at the same time stigmatizing them as extremists. Clinton's adviser Dick Morris called the strategy triangulation. By moving to the center and acting independently of both Republicans and Democrats, Clinton could occupy the high middle ground of American politics. His first move was to accept the Republican goal of balancing the budget in ten years or less. "The era of Big Government is over," he announced in Reaganesque language. White House liberals fought against the move, and many congressional Democrats complained afterward that the president lacked a clear ideological compass. "Most of us learned some time ago that if you don't like the president's position on a particular issue, you just have to wait a few weeks," complained a House Democrat.[75]

Welfare reform became a pawn in Clinton's strategy of triangulation. True to the terms of their Contract with America, congressional Republicans passed the Personal Responsibility and Work Opportunity Reconciliation Act, which ended the federal entitlement to welfare by collapsing nearly forty federal programs, including AFDC, into five block grants to the states. Clinton vetoed an early version of the bill, claiming that it would harm children. But six months later, in the heat of a presidential campaign, he signed a bill that maintained the central features of the original legislation. The 1996 welfare reform act eliminated the federal guarantee of welfare as an entitlement, replacing it with a block grant program that gave the states authority to develop their own plans. The most striking provision of the new law declared that the heads of most families on assistance must work within two years or the families would lose their benefits. Lifetime welfare benefits were limited to five years, and states could set stricter limits.[76]

Liberal critics were quick to denounce the president, but for Clinton welfare reform was more about politics than policy. "This bill simply says, we give up," said the journalist E. J. Dionne. Moynihan called it the "most brutal act of social policy since Reconstruction." Leading scholars charged that the act would "push more than a million additional children into poverty." Mayors of major cities predicted the law "would profoundly increase the nation's homeless population, leaving local governments ill-equipped to contend with a growing demand for services." The political response, however, was just as clear: Clinton's poll ratings soared, and he trounced his Republican opponent in the 1996 presidential election. Clinton's strategy of playing to the center lured back to the Democratic fold many white suburbanites who had defected in 1994. With his victory in 1996, Clinton became the first Democrat since FDR to win two terms in office.[77]

It is too early to judge the impact of Clinton's reform package. The laws of unintended consequences dictate that no planner can predict, and no politician can promise, what will happen when the new reforms go into effect. "We have no idea what the repercussions will be," declared a welfare expert. But if past reform efforts offer any clue, the measures will likely fall well short of expectations. Like many of its predecessors, the 1996 legislation promised to cut relief rolls and lower costs but failed to address underlying structural problems. The result is usually resentment, cynicism, and a new cycle of promises. "Welfare reform is its own biggest enemy," observed Theda Skocpol. Not only do politicians promise far more than they can deliver, but their efforts have usually backfired, producing expanded rolls and higher costs.[78]

Chapter 2

The Politics of Deinstitutionalization:
The Community Mental Health Act of 1963

MARCH 7, 1963: Robert Felix sat patiently at the Senate witness table waiting his turn to testify. It was a familiar position for the charismatic psychiatrist who, as head of the National Institute for Mental Health (NIMH), had been called dozens of times before Congress. This was a special day, however, because the Senate was debating legislation that Felix had helped craft and to which he had devoted much of his professional life, the Community Mental Health Act of 1963, an ambitious bill that called for emptying state hospitals and developing comprehensive psychiatric centers in communities across the nation. When it came time for him to speak, Felix did not need notes. "This has my blood, it has my life," he told the hushed committee room. "I wish to God I could live and be active for 25 more years, because I believe if I could, I would see the day when the state mental hospitals as we know them today would no longer exist."[1]

Felix, the son of two country doctors in rural Kansas, had developed his interest in mental health during the 1930s, when he served his medical residency in psychiatry under Dr. Franklin Ebaugh at the University of Colorado. "He constantly kept us aware of the community aspects of psychiatry," Felix recalled. The Depression dried up jobs in private practice, so Felix worked in public health positions during the decade, helping psychotic federal prisoners and drug addicts and later counseling cadets at the Coast Guard Academy. On May 29, 1941, his fortieth birth-day, he was sent to Washington, where he eventually earned appointment as the chief of the Division of Mental Hygiene. "Well, now you have the job, do you have any program?" he recalled the surgeon general asking one day. That night Felix scribbled nearly twenty pages of notes, which he later refined into a memorandum titled "Outline of a Comprehensive Community-Based Mental Health Program" and which he showed to Tennessee Congressman J. Percy Priest, powerful head of the House Labor and Public Welfare Committee. A few days later he read in the newspaper that Priest had introduced a mental health bill in Congress. "I read it," he recalled, "and it was my bill." The legislation, signed into law by President Harry Truman on July 3, 1946, authorized $7.5 million for research, training, and grants and technical assistance to states for "the improvement of the mental health of the people of the United States" and created the NIMH to oversee the programs.[2]

Four key assumptions informed Felix's faith in community mental health. First, he believed that the current system of "warehousing" mental patients in large, antiquated state hospitals was inhumane and that physicians needed to develop new methods of treatment. Second, the states had proved themselves incapable of managing mental illness; only federal intervention could produce significant improvement. Third, most mental illness was not biological but an outgrowth of unresolved tension, much of it caused by environmental stress. Since its roots were social, it made sense that the solution to mental illness could be found in manipulating the environment. "We have long known that if we drink polluted water we are likely to suffer intestinal infection and, consequently, we insist upon safe water supplies," he observed. "Now that we are beginning to recognize that an emotionally frustrating environment is a dangerous threat to mental health, we can hardly escape taking the next step—that of examining the factors of our civilization with a view to determining precisely how they are contributing to our mental health or illness." Fourth, believing that serious psychological problems start out as small ones, Felix reasoned that mental illness could be prevented if caught early. The mentally ill "get well much more rapidly and have a better opportunity of staying well permanently if they are identified early in their illness, treated energetically and according to the latest techniques, and if they remain in their home community." The key was "primary prevention," by addressing the causes of social neurosis before they developed into psychosis. "After all, as a tree is bent so it grows. And we like to do what we can while the youth is, figuratively speaking, a sapling."[3]

Though these assumptions were untested, they developed a large following among public health proponents who believed that local community centers would revolutionize the treatment of the mentally ill. Two energetic and generous philanthropists, Mary Lasker and Florence Mahoney, spearheaded the drive, creating the National Committee against Mental Illness. They hired Mike Gorman, an outspoken former reporter for the *Daily Oklahoman* who as a full-time lobbyist had written an exposé of the state's mental hospitals. "My hidden agenda," Gorman confessed, "was to break the back of the state mental hospital." He could usually count on a few allies on Capitol Hill, including Alabama's Lister Hill, the son of a prominent surgeon who had a dual power position in the Senate as chair both of the Labor and Public Welfare Committee, which authorized health programs, and of the Appropriations subcommittee that provided the money.[4]

World War II served as midwife to the community mental health movement. During the war nearly two million recruits had been rejected for service because of psychological disorders. "Mental illness," General Lewis B. Hershey, director of the Selective Service System, testified, "was the greatest cause of noneffectiveness or loss of manpower that we met." Public health officials used these figures to suggest that mental illness was far more widespread than most people imagined and that it therefore required the involvement of the federal government. They also discovered that the stress of combat could produce psychological problems in normally healthy individuals, underscoring the role of environmental factors in mental illness. Just as important, the great success in treating soldiers in small groups behind the front lines convinced many psychiatrists of the value of treatment in small, supportive settings. "Our experiences with therapy in war neuroses have left us with an optimistic attitude," reported a manual of military psychiatry. "The lessons we have learned in the combat zone can well be applied in rehabilitation at home."[5]

The emergence of a new philosophy of prevention came at the same time that the traditional state hospital was coming under assault. Muckrakers and reformers, many of them conscientious objectors who had been assigned to state mental hospitals during the war, exposed the horrible conditions they had encountered: overcrowding, staff shortages, and inadequate facilities. Shortly after the war *Life* magazine published a lengthy piece by Albert Q. Maisel titled "Bedlam 1946," calling on the public "to put an end to concentration camps that masquerade as hospitals and to make cure rather than incarceration the goal." In the same year Mary Jane Ward published *The Snake Pit,* which depicted the degrading conditions in state mental hospitals. In 1948 Albert Deutsch grabbed national attention with his exposé *The Shame of the States.* Mental hospitals, he argued, rivaled "the horrors of the Nazi concentration camps," and he asked, "Could a truly civilized community permit humans to be reduced to such an animal-like level?"[6]

The greatest challenge to the future of state mental hospitals, however, came from the discovery of new antipsychotic drugs, which raised hopes that mentally disturbed patients could live safely on their own. In 1954 a drug manufacturer introduced chlorpromazine, popularly known as Thorazine, the first effective antipsychotic drug. In its first year doctors wrote more than two million prescriptions, and New York and California made it available to all state hospitals. At the same time, a second class of tranquilizers, called reserpine, entered psychiatric practice. By 1956 the new drugs were followed by antidepressants, such as iproniazid. Popular magazines and newspapers hailed their development. "The treatment of mental illness is in the throes of a revolution," proclaimed *Time* magazine.[7]

Community mental health advocates also forged an awkward marriage between fiscal conservatives and social reformers by promising to improve conditions for the mentally ill while saving cash-strapped states millions of dollars in medical bills. Treating people in small community clinics, they suggested, was more cost-effective than maintaining a large and expensive state hospital system. This message was especially appealing to the nation's governors, who saw the hospital system as an enormous drain on resources. Between 1939 and 1949 the states saw their annual per patient expenses soar over 150 percent, and costs continued to accelerate during the 1950s. In 1955 New York State devoted 38 percent of its budget to support a hospital system that housed more than ninety thousand people. "[T]he cost of dealing with mental illness on the present basis is becoming too great to be borne," declared Michigan Governor G. Mennen Williams. "We simply cannot go on building more and more mental hospitals to house more and more patients."[8]

As head of the NIMH Felix was the key player in translating the high hopes of the community mental health movement into a viable political strategy. "No individual played a more prominent role than Felix," noted the historian Gerald Grob. A shrewd tactician, Felix worked hard to develop close ties with important congressional figures and was a constant presence on Capitol Hill, often volunteering his services to help troubled family members of key congressional leaders. "I was available day or night," he recalled. By the late 1940s he had emerged as Washington's mental health power broker, determined to expand the federal presence and to develop his community mental health ideas. "Over the years I have never lost sight of what I originally wanted to do," he reflected, "and everything I have done over the years . . . has been to develop a community-based program for the mentally ill." During his reign the NIMH's budget grew from $9 million in 1949 to $189 million in 1964. Although conceding that mental hospitals would be required for the foreseeable future, Felix insisted that the greatest need was for a large number of outpatient community clinics to serve individuals in the early stages of mental illness. "The guiding philosophy which permeates the activities of the National Institute of Mental Health," he told his American Psychiatric Association (APA) colleagues in 1949, "is that prevention of mental illness, and the production of positive mental health, is an attainable goal."[9]

By the mid-1950s Felix and other mental health advocates believed that a new federal initiative was necessary to raise public awareness about the issue. In 1955 they scored another legislative coup when Congress passed a resolution calling for a Joint Commission on Mental Health to offer "an objective, thorough, and nationwide analysis and reevaluation of the human and economic problems of mental illness." With thirty-six organizations represented, the commission had a difficult time reaching consensus, but its final report, released in 1960, showed the clear influence of community mental health advocates. Calling mental illness "the core problem and unfinished business of the mental health movement," the report acknowledged a major role for the state hospital, but its emphasis was clearly on developing community health clinics as the "main line of defense in reducing the need of many persons with mental illness for prolonged or repeated hospitalization." Perhaps its most controversial recommendation was its call for federal involvement in financing new initiatives. Charging that the states "have defaulted on adequate care for the mentally ill," the commission called on the federal government "to assume a major part of the responsibility." The commission promised that its recommendations, if accepted, would "revolutionize public care of persons with major mental illness."[10]

The report attracted the attention of newly elected President John F. Kennedy, who had a mentally handicapped sister and a strong interest in mental illness. In 1961 the president set up a White House task force "to analyze the report with a view to developing courses of action which might be appropriate for the Federal Government." The key players in drafting the report were Felix; Boisfeuillet Jones, special assistant to the head of the Department of Health, Education, and Welfare (HEW), and Daniel Patrick Moynihan, from the Department of Labor. "Felix," noted the historian Gerald Grob, "was strategically situated to create a legislative agenda that reflected his views and that of his staff." Determined to take full advantage of the moment, Felix told his staff that assisting the president's task force was the institute's top priority. At his direction the NIMH prepared two reports that became the focus of discussion for the task force. One report attacked the mental hospital system; the other called for the creation of a network of community mental health centers (CMHC) that would make it possible "for the mental hospital as it is now known to disappear from the scene within the next twenty-five years."[11]

Task force members enthusiastically embraced the NIMH proposals, accepting all the assumptions that informed the community movement: New medical knowledge offered the potential for revolutionizing treatment; state hospitals had outlived their usefulness; and most mental patients could be treated in local settings. On November 30, 1962, the task force made its recommendation to the president, concluding that the emphasis of any new initiative should be on "strengthening of noninstitutional services, rather than massive subsidization of existing, anachronistic, State public mental institutions." Such institutions, Kennedy was told, might be expected to "disappear from the scene" within twenty-five years. The time has come, the report argued, "when almost all the mentally ill could be cared for in treatment centers in their own communities."[12]

The president accepted the task force report and molded it into a major legislative package. In February 1963 Kennedy announced a "bold new approach" to attack the problem of mental illness. Using the language of the report, he called for dramatic reduction in the institutionalized population and the establishment of community-based treatment. To implement the initiative, he urged Congress to approve federal matching money for the construction and staffing of community centers. "If we apply our medical knowledge and social insights fully," he said, "all but a small portion of the mentally ill can eventually achieve a wholesome and constructive social adjustment." If the legislation is enacted, he said, the "reliance on the cold mercy of custodial isolation will be supplanted by the open warmth of community concern and capability." The *New York Times* hailed the president's message as "long overdue," claiming it "deserves the wholehearted support of the Congress and the American people."[13]

In March Congress took up the president's reform package. Administration witnesses in both the House and Senate underscored the same points: The state mental hospital system had to be abolished; community centers could care for the severely mentally ill and reduce the incidence of mental illness. HEW Secretary Anthony Celebrezze said the large state mental hospitals were "primarily institutions for quarantining the mentally ill, not for treating them." A spokesman for the American Medical Association said that psychiatric knowledge had progressed to the point where "it is feasible as well as desirable to treat the mentally ill patient in the context of his home environment." Boisfeuillet Jones repeated the president's promise that the program would reduce the population of state mental hospitals by 50 percent within a decade or two. But he also declared: "The prevention of mental illness is as important as the care and treatment of the mentally ill." The centers, said Jones, were designed "to bring order to the existing chaotic situation by providing a coordinated system of services which efficiently and effectively ministers to the mentally ill and to the entire community."[14]

Most of the representatives and senators were deferential to the witnesses, rarely challenging the assumptions that informed the legislation. In a classic case of what the sociologist Robert Merton had called "Imperious Immediacy of Interest," everyone had an incentive to support deinstitutionalization. Liberals applauded the involvement of the federal government and the concern for a neglected social issue; conservatives welcomed it as a cost-cutting measure. Even southern barons who blocked other Kennedy social legislation seemed swayed by the arguments that the initiative would save money. Members of Congress raised questions about whether there were enough psychiatrists to staff the centers and whether the centers could become self-sufficient, but for the most part Congress accepted the view that psychiatric knowledge had uncovered the keys not only to treating but also to preventing mental illness and that community care was infinitely superior to state hospitals. "What you ultimately hope to accomplish by the program," noted an agreeable committee chair, Oren Harris, "is to reduce the number of patients in the big state hospitals to a minimum, and ultimately down the line to more adequately take care of the patients in the local center. . . ."[15]

Since most members of Congress accepted the underlying assumptions that informed the legislation, much of the debate focused on extraneous issues. Discussion in the Senate revolved around an amendment by New York's Jacob Javits to deny funds to states maintaining segregated facilities for mental patients. Once that amendment was defeated by a 43–27 vote, the legislation sailed through the Senate by a lopsided vote of 72 to 1. In the House conservatives backed by the American Medical Association raised concerns about the provision calling for federal matching funds to staff the new centers, claiming that it would lead down the slippery slope toward "socialized medicine." Under heavy pressure from the AMA, the House voted to delete the staffing provision from the bill. With that issue out of the way, the House passed its version of the bill in September by a lopsided margin of 335 to 18. A House-Senate conference approved the measure without any initial staffing provisions and sent the legislation to the White House for the president's signature.[16]

On October 31, 1963, President Kennedy signed the Mental Retardation and Community Mental Health Centers Construction Act of 1963 (Public Law 88-164). The law authorized spending $150 million over three years for the construction of new centers. The goal was to reduce the population of state hospitals by 50 percent and to create a national network of community clinics that would provide needed services for the severely mentally ill and decrease the incidence of illness in the broader population. "Under this legislation," Kennedy predicted, "custodial mental institutions will be replaced by therapeutic centers. It should be possible, within a decade or two, to reduce the number of patients in mental institutions by 50 percent or more. The new law provides the tools with which we can accomplish this."[17]

SUPPORTERS hailed passage of the bill. Dr. William Mayer, head of the California Department of Health, called it "the healthiest development in mental care in 100 years." Abraham Ribicoff, who had left his position as head of HEW a year before passage of the law, predicted that "mental illness might be brought under control in a generation or so," thanks to the community mental health movement. Felix, who retired from the NIMH shortly after passage of the act, claimed that the centers not only would prevent mental illness but would also create "a climate in which each citizen has optimum opportunities for sustained creative and responsible participation in the life of the community and for the development of his particular potentialities as a human being." Enactment of the president's proposals, he announced, would allow physicians to "restore all but a small proportion of the mentally ill to a socially productive life."[18]

The community mental health act did accomplish its goal of moving people out of the large state hospitals. When President Kennedy announced his "bold new approach" to mental illness in 1963, about 504,600 people were residents of public mental hospitals. Over the next ten years the resident population declined by 57 percent to 215,500. By 1980 the population had declined to 138,000. Rhode Island led the way with a 98 percent release rate, while seven other states—Massachusetts, New Hampshire, Vermont, West Virginia, Arkansas, Wisconsin, and California—trailed slightly behind with a 95 percent decline in resident population.[19]

What happened to the released mental patients? Most were reintegrated into society. Some returned to families that cared for them; others were released into the care of new community centers that helped ease the transition back to normal life for the thousands of patients who did not need the formal structure of the state hospital. Many had suffered from mild forms of mental illness that could be controlled by medication and occasional supervision. Surveys have shown that the vast majority of released patients were happier outside the hospital and enjoyed the added privacy, the independence, and the close contact with families and friends. A study of discharged residents in Rhode Island found that a stunning 94 percent "expressed a preference for life in the community."[20]

It was a different story, however, for many of the chronically mentally ill. The National Advisory Mental Health Council defined as severely mentally ill people those with "disorders with psychotic symptoms such as schizophrenia, schizoaffective disorder, manic-depressive disorder, autism," as well as "major depression, panic disorder, and obsessive-compulsive disorder." According to some estimates, as many as 75 percent of the released patients suffered from one of these conditions; nearly half were schizophrenic. Many of these people required comprehensive treatment: constant supervision to make sure they were taking medication and assistance with housing, food, and jobs. People suffering from schizophrenia, for example, often exhibited irrational, paranoid behavior that made them difficult to manage and often unresponsive to standard forms of psychotherapy.[21]

Though they were in the greatest need of support services, many chronically ill patients were released into communities where no centers existed. The legislation provided that one clinic be built for each hundred thousand people. "It was explicitly understood that there would be 2,000 such centers by the year 2000," observed Moynihan, who along with Felix was one of the architects of the legislation. But building new centers proved problematic: Many local communities had difficulty providing matching funds; others were unable to find enough professionals to staff the centers. Many people objected to having mental health facilities in their communities. More important, political and economic circumstances changed as the Vietnam War and social unrest sapped public support and drained needed resources for new social initiatives. In 1969 Republican Richard Nixon, a tough critic of social psychiatry and community mental health, gained control of the White House and fought a constant battle with a liberal Congress to cut funding for the program. When Congress balked and approved new spending, Nixon impounded the funds. As a result of all these developments, a large gap emerged between money appropriated for community mental health and the amount actually spent. In 1980 only 768 of the promised centers had been funded. In New York City, which qualified for 73 centers, only 5 existed.[22]

By 1980 most Americans had rejected the premise upon which the entire initiative had been built: that the federal government should replace the states in making important decisions about social welfare. Conservative Ronald Reagan, who as governor had presided over the dismantling of the state mental health system in

California, won election in 1980 by promising to cut taxes and slash social spending. "Government is not the solution to our problems," he said. "Government is the problem." In 1981 he pushed through Congress the Omnibus Reconciliation Act of 1981, cutting funds for mental health by 25 percent and combining them into block grants to the states. Many states, facing fiscal problems of their own, chose to shave services and cut jobs. Funding for community mental health usually topped the list of things to be cut. In California the governor sliced seventy-one million dollars in state mental health aid to counties.[23]

For some people who had been involved in drafting the Community Mental Health Act the federal government's failure to fund the promised community centers represented a betrayal of the legislation's intent. "What if," Moynihan reflected, "on the occasion of the bill signing in 1963, someone had said to President Kennedy: 'Wait. Before you sign the bill you should know that we are not going to build anything like the number of community centers we will need. . . . The hospitals will empty out, but there will be no place for the patients to be cared for in their communities. . . .' Would he not have put down his pen?"[24]

Not only were too few centers built, but those that did exist often failed to provide the intensive services required by the severely mentally ill. Congress had passed sweeping legislation designed to improve the quality of life for the mentally ill, but it delegated to an administrative committee the responsibility for developing guidelines for realizing that goal. After a brief bureaucratic tussle within HEW, Felix and the NIMH seized control of the committee. In a classic case of how an administrative committee can redirect the intent of Congress, Felix chose to emphasize the "preventive" aspects of the legislation and largely to ignore the concerns of the severely mentally ill. Harry Cain, one of the six members of the committee, recalled years later: "I don't remember our having any fix on the chronic population in general. It was much more an orientation toward the new people."

The committee agreed that all centers were required to offer five services: inpatient services, outpatient services, partial hospitalization, emergency service, and consultation and education programs. The regulations relegated services for the severely mentally ill to a second tier of optional services.[25]

The mentally ill were caught in the cracks between a state hospital system determined to downsize and a community mental health movement committed to a new preventive approach. The leaders in community health considered the state system obsolete; hospitals viewed the community centers as a threat to their funding. Since community mental health centers (CMHCs) did not view reducing the use of state mental hospitals as a primary goal, they refused to devote resources to the effort. When asked to rank their top ten priorities, center directors placed the goal of decreasing hospital utilization next to last. As a result, thousands of patients were released from mental hospitals without being informed of potential follow-up services provided by the centers. There was in fact little relationship between the construction of community centers and the rate of hospital discharge; many hospitals simply opened their doors and let patients out without any provision for aftercare. In 1977 a major study of the problem concluded that "followup of released persons was generally haphazard, fragmented, or nonexistent."[26]

Financial pressures on CMHCs also worked against the severely mentally ill. Federal financing provided seed money to help establish the centers, but their long-term survival depended on support from local and state sources. The administration and most members of Congress expected that as hospitals withered, states would redirect money to community centers. Trimming the budgets of state hospitals, many of which were either heavily unionized or located in rural regions that depended on the jobs, proved more difficult than anyone had imagined. Many state hospitals continued to require a significant portion of mental health funding, even though their populations had been cut dramatically. By

1980, 63 percent of the nation's chronic mentally ill were living in the community, but traditional state mental institutions still received two-thirds of all state and local funding for mental health. In New York, for example, hospitals absorbed 90 percent of mental health allocations in 1983, even though the resident population had dropped from eighty-five thousand in 1965 to fewer than twenty-five thousand. That meant that most CMHCs had to survive with few dollars from state and local sources.[27]

With federal funding so precarious, many centers needed to attract patients who could pay for services. As one therapist put it, "Our staff meetings began to focus on reaching more clients who could verbalize their problems—and who could pay." In order to stay afloat financially, many centers focused on serving the troubled, not the seriously ill, with marriage counseling, family therapy, and seminars on midlife crises. One survey in the early 1970s found only twelve centers in the whole country that offered programs for the acutely sick, such as housing assistance, job opportunities, and access to medical care. The psychologist William Schofield referred to the CMHC clientele with the acronym YAVIS—young, attractive, verbal, intelligent, and successful. The shift in treatment led the American Psychiatric Association president Donald G. Langsley to charge that centers had "drifted away from their original purpose."[28]

Instead of responding to these concerns, Congress aggravated the problem by expanding the CMHCs' mandate. Beginning in 1968, it ordered the centers to provide programs for alcoholics and narcotic addicts. Amendments in 1970 added a new specialized program for children. In 1972 Congress required centers to provide services for drug addicts or users. As the services supplied by centers proliferated, the interests of the severely mentally ill receded further into the background. For example, the Fort Wayne CMHC in Indiana, which between 1977 and 1981 received $12.7 million in federal funds, changed its name in 1983 to the Park Center so that it could "better reach those persons who need counseling services for life adjustment problems such as marital, family, and personal problems." A congressional committee in 1990 found that centers in many cities built swimming pools and tennis courts with their construction money. With its $2.1 million in federal staffing funds, the Orlando Regional Medical Center hired a cosmetic and fashion counselor, a beautician, maids, a gardener, a lifeguard, and a swimming instructor.[29]

What happened to the severely mentally ill if they were not going to community centers? Many were caught in the crosswinds of social activism during the 1960s. Following his landslide victory in 1964, Lyndon Johnson pushed through Congress a cornucopia of social programs known as the Great Society. "Hurry, boys, hurry," he urged his aides. "Get that legislation up to the Hill and out. Eighteen months from now, ol' landslide Lyndon will be lame-duck Lyndon." Among the dizzying array of laws Congress passed that year none was more important than the amendments to the Social Security Act that created Medicare, a program that provided medical health insurance for most Americans over age sixty-five. Included in the act was a little-noticed provision, Title XIX, establishing Medicaid, which provided federal grants to states to cover medical care for the poor. Under the program Washington paid states between 50 and 78 percent of the costs for treating the eligible poor. In time Medicaid became, in the words of the comptroller general, the most significant "federally sponsored program affecting deinstitutionalization."[30]

The rules governing the Medicaid program provided a financial incentive for states to move the mentally ill out of state institutions and into facilities where the federal government would pick up the tab. The legislation specifically barred payments to state psychiatric hospitals and other "institutions for the treatment of mental diseases," which included CMHCs. In other words, if a poor person were treated in a mental hospital, the state would have to pick up the entire bill. If, however, the patient could be transferred to a facility that was not designated solely for the treatment of mental illness, the government would pick up as much as 70 percent of the bill. Nursing homes were the chief beneficiary of this fiscal shell game. Between 1960 and 1970 nursing home facilities increased by 140 percent, beds by 232 percent and patients by 210 percent. The movement of mental patients from state hospitals accounted for much of the change. A 1977 survey revealed that 87 percent of the 1.3 million residents of nursing homes suffered from chronic mental illness.[31]

Mental patients were rarely better off in nursing homes than in state hospitals. In many cases the homes were large, crowded, and impersonal. A study by the National Center for Health Statistics indicated that more than 50 percent of nursing home residents were in facilities with one hundred or more beds and about 15 percent in facilities with two hundred or more beds. Most lacked trained medical staff, and few offered the range of medical services—checkups, tests, diagnoses, or follow-ups on medication—that were essential for the seriously mentally ill. The comptroller general reported that most people were receiving only "custodial care." In 1975 an Oregon task force reported that a typical day for a mentally ill person in a nursing home was "sleeping, eating, watching television, smoking cigarettes, sitting in groups in the largest room, or looking out the window." Most homes were poorly regulated. In Michigan, according to the AFL-CIO, "standards for pet stores are more stringently enforced than for nursing homes."[32]

In 1972 Congress passed another social program that inadvertently had a profound and often detrimental impact on deinstitutionalization: Supplemental Security Income (popularly known as SSI). A modest federal program designed to consolidate and make consistent the numerous state disability programs, SSI provided a floor of $130 a month to the blind, the disabled, and the aged poor who were ineligible for other social security. To qualify, an applicant had to be poor and either sixty-five years or older, or disabled and unable to work, or blind. The small print, which stated that recipients could not collect other forms of welfare or live in public housing, was to have a major impact on the mentally ill. Since a recipient could not receive both SSI and welfare, the states had an incentive to move people from the AFDC program, where the state paid a percentage of the cost, to the fully funded federal program. Many states set up special programs to make sure that released mental patients applied for SSI. In 1974, the first year that people could receive SSI benefits, the resident population of state hospitals decreased by a record 13.3 percent. By 1994 mental illness accounted for 30.2 percent of all SSI disabilities.[33]

The rules created an opportunity for enterprising businessmen to make a few dollars by providing cheap private rooms to released patients who were not allowed to live in public accommodations. "Psychiatric ghettos" sprouted in cities and towns surrounding downsizing state hospitals, as people converted run-down hotels and old private houses into boarding homes for the mentally ill. A 1974 study found that one-quarter of those living in New York City's welfare hotels had once resided in psychiatric hospitals. Of a total of 378 community placement residences in Detroit serving the mentally disabled, 165 were in the inner city. One street housed 101 such homes, many of them old and dilapidated. New York City's twenty thousand chronically mentally ill persons converged in the city's 300 single room occupancy hotels. "They're turning this community into a mental ward," a frustrated resident of Ocean Grove, New Jersey, complained as he watched the two downtown hotels transform into boarding homes for discharged patients.[34]

Conditions in many boarding homes were reminiscent of the old state hospital system. In 1979 the *New York Times* described "the fetid odor of unclean bodies," large rooms where "the gray-blue haze of cigarette smoke hung like smog," where "ragged men with vacant eyes" sat for hours in plastic chairs. "This was not the kind of life envisioned for New York's psychiatric patients," the *Times* noted, when the state launched its deinstitutionalization initiative. Federal hearings found that at least 50 percent of all homes were substandard, defined as "with one or more life-threatening conditions." In 1973 alone sixty-four hundred fires killed 551 residents. In Chicago's thirty-block psychiatric ghetto called Uptown, the Better Government Administration found that mental patients were frequently robbed. In several boarding homes food fed to resident patients was rancid, and vermin and insects were commonplace. Boarding homes were not required to provide services to the chronically disabled. "The only service being provided to many released mentally ill persons was medication," the comptroller general reported. In many cases the residents received three meals a day but very little medical follow-up. Many spent the day just staring in silence in lobbies or wandering pathetically in the streets, where they were regarded by residents as nuisances and threats. A Senate subcommittee claimed that boarding homes provided a quality of life "ranking with prisons and concentration camps as prime examples of man's inhumanity to man."[35]

Reformers had viewed community care as a marked step forward, but the proliferation of boarding homes could hardly be viewed as a sign of progress. As Queens, New York, Borough President Donald Manes remarked, "the snake pits have been moved to the communities." What had occurred was not a deinstitutionalization movement but rather a lateral shift of patients among institutions, what critics called transinstitutionalization, which meant that "the chronically mentally ill patient had his locus of living and care transferred from a single lousy institution to multiple wretched ones." In 1978 Florida Senator Claude Pepper, head of the Select Committee on Aging, called the dumping of former mental patients a national scandal. The severely mentally ill, already abandoned by community mental health advocates, were further victimized by well-intentioned efforts to help the poor. Both Medicaid and SSI channeled patients away from community centers and into nursing homes and substandard housing. In 1965 two-thirds of discharged patients had returned to families or relatives; ten years later only 23 percent returned home. Nearly 50 percent went to federally financed nursing homes or boarding houses. In a classic example of unintended consequences, "Congressional desire to help these people by making them eligible for benefits backfired," observed a critic.[36]

A series of court decisions in the 1970s played a major, though also unintended, role in redirecting the original purpose of the legislation. In keeping with the expanded definition of individual rights that grew out of the civil rights movement, the courts began to consider institutionalization as a form of imprisonment and issued rulings that expanded the rights of patients to receive treatment, made it difficult to commit someone without his or her consent, and gave individuals the right to refuse treatment. In a landmark case, *Wyatt v. Stickney* (1971) U.S. District Court Judge Frank Johnson, Jr., ruled that the state must provide adequate staff and resources to ensure a patient a "realistic opportunity to be cured or to improve his or her mental condition." Johnson proceeded to outline, in minute detail, the precise staff to patient ratios for psychiatrists, psychologists, and other professionals. In 1972 a Wisconsin judge ruled in *Lessard v. Schmidt* that a person could be committed only if "there is an extreme likelihood that if the person is not confined he will do immediate harm to himself and others." In 1975 the Supreme Court decided in *O'Connor v. Donaldson* that mental patients cannot be confined in institutions against their will and without treatment if they are not dangerous and are capable of surviving on the outside. The same year a judge in the District of Columbia concluded that patients had the right to treatment in "the least restrictive setting."[37]

The combined effect of these judicial decisions was to improve conditions for the few patients who remained in the hospital, but to add to the burden of the many who had been released. In response to the rulings, many state systems upgraded facilities and provided residents with greater freedom. At the same time, how-

ever, they opted to lower hospital populations instead of invest-
ing the money needed to hire thousands of professional staff
members to meet the required patient-staff ratios. The rulings
also made it more difficult to commit new patients or to recom-
mit released residents who had encountered tough times. Before
the *Lessard* decision, courts could commit someone if it was determined he or she was in need of treatment; afterward lawyers
had to prove that patients represented a danger to themselves or
others. It was a hard case to make, especially since psychiatrists
were unable to make certain predictions about a patient's future
behavior. In addition, the courts chose to interpret narrowly the
criteria of "dangerousness to self or others," making it difficult to
commit people against their will. "In the end," noted the former
NIMH chief Dr. Bertram S. Brown, "it may be the legal profession
that will largely determine the fate of the chronic mentally ill."[38]

In a celebrated case in 1987 the New York State Supreme
Court ruled that Manhattan authorities had no right to hospital-
ize an abusive woman who had taken up residence on a hot-air
vent. Joyce Brown lived in front of a Swensen's ice cream shop on
Manhattan's Upper East Side for nearly eighteen months, urinat-
ing and defecating on the street, ripping up money she had pan-
handled, and running into passing traffic. City authorities
hospitalized her five times, but each time hospital authorities released her, claiming she did not fit the narrow criteria of "dangerousness." Undeterred, New York City's nonconformist Mayor
Ed Koch instructed the police to round up anyone who appeared
to be mentally ill and refused shelter and to transport that person
to a hospital for observation when the temperature dropped
below thirty-two degrees. The New York Civil Liberties Union,
which mounted a special patrol to advise the homeless mentally
ill of their constitutional right to freeze, used the case of Joyce
Brown to test the city's policy. The state supreme court agreed
with the ACLU, claiming: "Freedom, constitutionally guaranteed,
is the right of all, no less of those who are mentally ill."[39]

Released from the hospitals into communities without appropriate facilities, many former patients led precarious existences, collecting welfare, occasionally seeing caseworkers, searching for jobs, trying to create or rebuild relationships with family and friends. In many instances, however, they ended up decompressing: They refused to take medication and lost touch with their caseworkers. The sudden transition to freedom disoriented many released patients who had come to depend on the structure the institution provided. A typical patient, observed a New York health official, had been living in a ward with his friends where all his needs had been taken care of for twenty years. "Suddenly he's sent into a community unknown to him and placed in a single room in a rooming house" and forced to negotiate a bureaucratic maze of overlapping and uncoordinated agencies: interviews with welfare officials, job interviews, summonses to appear at SSI hearings, medication monitoring, and scheduling meetings with social workers and therapists. Without proper supervision the experience could be overwhelming. In many cases, noted two authors, "the term 'community care' has become a chilling euphemism for decentralized neglect."[40]

Many ended up back at state hospitals, where they were quickly treated and released only to begin the cycle again. While resident populations at state hospitals decreased after 1955, the number of people admitted to mental hospitals actually increased from 178,000 in 1955 to a peak of 414,925 in 1971. Readmitted former residents constituted a large percentage of the increase: Thirty-five to 50 percent were readmitted within one year; 65 to 75 percent within five years. "All we're good at," said a Los Angeles psychiatrist, "is processing people through a revolving door."[41] Two physicians in a general hospital in Boston recounted their experiences with the revolving door:

Time and time again we see patients who were released from state hospitals after months or years of custodial care; who then survived precariously on welfare payments for a few months on the fringe of the community, perhaps attending a clinic to receive medication or intermittent counseling; who voluntarily returned to a hospital or were recommitted . . . ; who were maintained in the hospital on antipsychotic medication and seemed to improve; who were released again to an isolated "community" life and who, having again become unbearably despondent, disorganized or violent, either present themselves at the emergency room or are brought to it by a police officer. Then the cycle begins anew.[42]

Jails and prisons became the asylum of last resort for seriously ill patients, producing what psychiatrists call the criminalization of mentally disordered behavior. National surveys estimate that nearly seven hundred thousand people with diagnosed mental illnesses are taken to jail each year, more than nine times the number found in public mental hospitals at any one time. A 1975 study of five California jails concluded that the number of severely mentally ill prisoners had grown 300 percent in the preceding decade. "We are the biggest mental hospital around," said a prison official in Dallas. Once in jail, the mentally ill are often mistreated, subject to physical and verbal abuse from the other inmates. "The bad and the mad just don't mix," observed one official. In Miami the county jail set aside a floor of its ten-story jail to house a hundred mentally ill inmates, who were stripped naked, isolated, and fed through slots in the door.[43]

During the 1980s many of the chronically mentally ill ended up on the streets as part of the homeless army of hollow-eyed, ill-clothed people who filled the nation's cities. The roots of homelessness are complex, the result of the convergence of a number of disturbing trends. In the 1970s and 1980s the average rent increased twice as fast as wages. A real estate boom led many developers to convert boarding homes—the housing of choice for

many mentally ill during the 1970s—into expensive condo-
minium complexes. According to some estimates, developers
eliminated nearly half of all boarding home rooms during the
decade. In many urban areas the once proudly held unionized
jobs at large manufacturing plants were replaced with openings at
McDonald's, where employees flipped hamburgers for minimum
wage without benefits. Of the 12 million jobs created during the
decade, more than half paid less than $7,000 a year. The Reagan
administration's cuts in social programs, including welfare and
housing subsidies, added to the problem. Nearly a quarter of a
million people lost welfare benefits during the decade; about
the same number saw their benefits reduced. The administration
cut expenditures for low-cost housing from $30 billion to $7
billion.[44]

The most vulnerable in society, including the mentally ill, were
the people most likely to fall victim to the social forces responsible for homelessness. Since they are notoriously difficult to count,
no one knows for sure how many Americans were homeless in the
1980s. "Even if you track 15 people under this bridge today, how
do you know they won't be under another bridge tomorrow?"
asked one official responsible for getting an accurate count of
homelessness in his city. Some people were homeless for a few
weeks; others were long-term street people. The Reagan administration's Housing and Urban Development Department claimed
only about 250,000 Americans had no place to sleep at night,
while advocacy groups put the figure at nearly 3 million. After an-
alyzing much of the data, the sociologist Christopher Jencks produced a more credible figure in 1994 of between 400,000 and
500,000. Many experts estimate that approximately one-third of
homeless adults are seriously mentally ill. In 1986 the NIMH
found that the percentage ranged from a high of 56 percent in St.
Louis to a low of 25 percent in New York City. Official studies
counted only the homeless living in shelters; estimates are even
higher among street people, some ranging up to 60 percent. A

study followed a sample of 132 patients released from Central Ohio Psychiatric Hospital in the first three months in 1985. Within six months of their release more than a third had become homeless. In 1991 the U.S. Conference of Mayors complained: "Homeless shelters and city streets have become the *de facto* mental institutions of the 1980s and 1990s." The problem, said Boston Mayor Raymond L. Flynn, had been caused by the "failed policy of deinstitutionalization," which "unleashed a tidal wave of homelessness onto our streets."[45]

The daily sight of homeless mentally ill wandering the streets underscores another unfortunate consequence of deinstitutionalization: Bringing the mentally ill in closer proximity to the general public has increased social fears. Studies have confirmed what most Americans observed in their daily lives: The mentally ill are more likely than the general population to commit violent crime. Police officers in suburban Philadelphia reported a 227 percent increase in "mental-illness–related incidents" between 1975 and 1979. Asked to explain the increase, an officer replied: "It's harder to get people into the hospital now, and once they're in, they don't stay long. You can turn around the next day and see someone back on the street." Stories of mentally ill individuals shooting, stabbing, assaulting innocent people fill the local news in cities and towns across America. "A simple visit to the local elementary school, post office or grocery store," observed a New Yorker, "can be a Dantean journey through the dark underside of our society."[46]

· In October 1985 a woman who had been committed twelve times to mental hospitals opened fire in a suburban Philadelphia shopping mall, killing three and wounding ten.

· In Atlanta in 1990 Calvin Brady, recently released from a mental hospital, shot and killed a man and wounded four others in a shopping mall.

. .

· Eleven days after being released from Western State Hospital in Seattle in 1997, Dan Van Ho fatally stabbed a man in an unprovoked attack.

These incidents, often sensationalized by the news media, produced a hardening of public attitudes toward the mentally ill. Homeowners and business groups organized in many cities and towns to fight the introduction of community centers into their neighborhoods, claiming they represented a threat to their quality of life. "We want to live among people like ourselves, and there ought to be a place for that," said a disgruntled homeowner in Denver. "It's like the racism of the 1960s," said a mental health advocate in Detroit. "No one wants to admit prejudice, but they don't want them living next door and dropping property values and raping their daughters." The constant scenes of the homeless have made many Americans numb to their plight. "Thirty years ago, if you saw a person lying helpless on the street, you ran to help him. Now you step over him," observed a journalist.[47]

TWO decades after the passage of the Community Mental Health Act many of its chief sponsors despaired at its consequences. In 1984 Robert Felix apologized for mistakes made and consequences unforeseen. "Many of those patients who left the state hospitals never should have done so," he told the *New York Times*. "We psychiatrists saw too much of the old snake pit, saw too many people who shouldn't have been there and we overreacted. The result is not what we intended." Many of the movement's other pioneers expressed similar feelings. Seymour Kaplan, who led the deinstitutionalization movement in New York, said that "it was the gravest error he had ever made." His California counterpart recalled that "those of us who were once so enthusiastic now weep a little as we look backwards at what has happened to the promising child of the 1960s and 1970s." In 1990 a public interest group was more blunt, calling deinstitutionalization "a disaster by any measure used."[48]

How could such a well-intentioned reform turn so sour?

The proposal came gift-wrapped in language congenial to most Americans. Who could argue with a reform designed to save money, replace an impersonal state institution with one governed by local control, and offer people greater freedom? Most Americans clung to a simpler vision of community as a relatively small and homogeneous group bound by a common moral code. "By community is meant home, work, and neighborhood," Felix observed. Since the concept was so familiar, there was little effort to clarify the meaning of community, even though it was the cornerstone of the legislation. Unable to develop a working definition of community, supporters used numbers, promising that each center would serve areas of one hundred thousand people. In the 1960s, however, American communities were deeply divided by race and class and growing urban-suburban divisions. For most of the mentally ill, the hospital was their community. Almost 75 percent of mental patients in 1960 were unmarried, widowed, or divorced, and few had meaningful relationships outside the hospital.[49]

The faith in the healing power of communities, a faith that echoes a historically powerful Jeffersonian love of the local and suspicion of the state, also blinded psychiatrists and public health advocates to the fact that little scientific evidence supported the claim that mental patients would receive better care in local communities. "There are at the moment, as far as I know, no American studies that demonstrate that, when the quality of care is held constant, community-based treatment facilities function any better than those located in large hospitals," a psychiatrist noted in 1963. There were, however, many prescient studies that highlighted the need for careful coordination between hospitals and clinics, made clear that effective community care required extensive support facilities, and advised against sweeping general-izations in discussing the varied needs of the mentally ill.[50]

A dearth of scientific evidence did not prevent supporters from making exaggerated claims about the benefits of community cen-ters in the 1950s and 1960s. Felix contended that modern psy-chiatry was in "transition from an era of primarily custodial care" to an "era of comprehensive treatment for all the mentally ill," when physicians could alter the social conditions that produced mental illness. By the late 1960s some experts were criticizing this notion. The political scientist Robert Connery, though generally sympathetic to the initiative, said the legislation "had all the ear-marks of a *coup d'état.*" According to the NIMH's Saul Feldman, advocates depicted community mental health centers "as the he-roes who would liberate the forlorn and hopeless victims from the clutches of the villainous state hospitals." In 1965 Dr. H. G. Whit-tington, the head of the Community Mental Health Services in Kansas, asked: "Why do community mental health programs tend to take on an evangelical, moralistic, crusade-like quality?" He answered his own question by speculating that psychiatrists lacked the "scientific knowledge" to deliver on their promises to pre-vent mental illness. "Perhaps we should recognize the partial phoniness in our claims," he suggested, "and see clearly how large the gap really is between future expectations and present ability."[51]

Convinced that they had found the medical holy grail, sup-porters pushed through a pliant Congress an ambitious nation-wide program before any of the ideas had been tried on a local level. Unfortunately most of the underlying assumptions of the movement proved false. "They had lovely ideas," observed the sociologist Morton Wagenfeld, "that had absolutely no basis in reality." Community facilities were not always preferable to in-stitutionalized care, and the most troubled patients could not sur-vive on their own without extensive assistance. "There was a widespread failure to recognize that after discharge, many former patients needed the same intensive support that had been provided for them in institutions," observed Governor Hugh Carey, who earlier presided over the emptying of state hospitals in New York. The centers failed to take over hospital functions. Not only did Washington refuse to build enough centers, but those that were operating preferred "to deal with mad housewives who hate their husbands rather than with old women who hear voices inside their heads." Communities were not prepared to take over responsibility for dealing with the mentally ill, and as a consequence, discharged patients were "resegregated" into run-down facilities in the poorest, most crime-infested areas. For tens of thousands of mental patients and their families, this combination of arrogance and ignorance produced tragic results. "To a very large extent we were caught up in a social movement— humanizing mental health care—and that was a good thing," noted Dr. Leona Bachrach. "But like a host of social movements, our zeal outstripped our readiness to deal with the consequences."[52]

Neither the Kennedy administration, which proposed the idea, nor Congress, which approved it, tried hard to ask or answer a basic question: How do you define mental illness and mental health? Though psychiatrists were far from understanding the causes of schizophrenia or depression, Washington passed legislation that promised to "prevent" mental illness. "How are we going to take the first preventive actions if we are still uncertain about the causes of mental disorders?" asked H. Warren Dunham, a psychiatrist. Advocates of the community mental health movement downplayed biological influences on behavior and instead emphasized the social roots of illness, arguing that poverty and a lack of opportunity, not genes, were the principal culprits. The desire to uncover the social roots of problems and to "empower people" formed the mantra of social reformers during the 1960s and 1970s but had little relevance for dealing with chronic mental illness. While the roots of diseases such as schizophrenia and bipolar disorder remain obscure, a growing body of scientific evidence indicates that biology, not the environment, plays the central role. New testing methods have demonstrated conclusively that the brain structures of the mentally ill are different from those of healthy people. "A condition like schizophrenia is an illness that is first and foremost a brain disease," noted a psychiatrist.[53]

In many cases the emphasis on manipulating the environment as a means of achieving mental health blurred the line between psychiatry and social reform. Felix said that community mental health must be "concerned with such problems as housing, unemployment, prejudice, and other sources of social and psychological tension in the neighborhood as well as in the home." His successor at the NIMH, Stanley Yolles, declared that "unresolved major social problems may be the unsanitary breeding grounds for chronic mental stress." With characteristic exaggeration, Mike Gorman said that "the community mental health center is part and parcel of a healthy revolt against the impersonal colossi of our age—big government, the vast military-industrial complex, enormous universities which have become insensitive diploma mills, and social welfare institutions of all kinds whose bureaucratic procedures violate and offend the dignity of the individual." In some areas, social reformers took this language to heart and tried to use the centers as vehicles for social change. When the professional staff resisted, activists seized control, demanding greater influence in the decision-making process. This power struggle, which crippled centers in New York and Philadelphia, was a direct outgrowth of a confused mission that viewed psychiatry as a means of social protest.[54]

The well-intentioned efforts of public interest lawyers who fought successfully to expand the definition of individual rights for the mentally ill compounded the problem. The American Civil Liberties Union viewed the mentally handicapped as another oppressed minority group that, like African-Americans, women, and prisoners, deserved redress under the law. Underlying the drive was a belief that the hospital environment contributed to mental illness and that freedom was its own form of therapy. A lawyer with the Mental Health Law Project stated in 1974: "They're better off outside of a hospital with no care than they are inside with no care. The hospitals are what really do damage to people." As many critics have pointed out, the obsession with individual "freedom" and "liberty," so central to American identity, are often counterproductive when applied to the mentally ill. "Freedom to be sick, helpless and isolated is not freedom," a New York psychiatrist said. "In the name of a liberty that illness does not allow them to enjoy," noted the essayist and psychiatrist Charles Krauthammer, "we have condemned the homeless mentally ill to die with their rights on."[55]

Once enacted, deinstitutionalization fell victim to poor planning and to the vagaries of federalism. In 1978 President Carter's Commission on Mental Health concluded that deinstitutionalization had "occurred without adequate planning . . . propelled by a desire to shift fiscal responsibility from the States to the federal Government and has proceeded on unverified assumptions that appropriate community care for these people exists." In Washington responsibility for deinstitutionalization was spread over eleven major agencies, which administered nearly 135 programs affecting the mentally disabled. Housing and Urban Development had responsibility for housing; the Labor Department set up programs to help with jobs; HEW supervised education and clinical care. The fragmentation of authority was compounded by the states, where overlapping jurisdictions were commonplace. There was little communication and coordination among agencies. In some states one branch of government discharged patients into housing that another agency had found to be substandard. The "convoluted array of federal, state, and local government programs with fiscal responsibility for the seriously mentally ill would make Rube Goldberg proud," the psychiatrist E. Fuller Torrey complained.[56]

The diffusion of authority often meant that no one was in charge. In 1973 an investigation revealed that many patients released from the Creedmoor State Hospital in Queens, New York, were living in dilapidated homes owned and operated by employees at the hospital. Conditions were horrible: Residents went days without food, were crammed into locked dark cellars at night, and lived in constant fear. In a fragmented system that the *New York Times* claimed was "worthy of Kafka," everyone publicly condemned the situation but washed his or her hands of responsibility. Hospital officials said that privacy rules prevented them from following patients after they were discharged; the city welfare department, which sent checks every week, claimed it lacked jurisdiction to investigate. Lawyers for the owners refused to talk. "Although the unmet needs of the chronically ill living in the community are more visible with deinstitutionalization, their care has become diffused among so many agencies that it is unclear whom to hold responsible," observed the *New England Journal of Medicine*.[57]

Critics on the left and right bicker about who bears the greatest responsibility for the deinstitutionalization catastrophe. Other Western European nations experimented with community mental health, but none pushed the program as far, or with such severe consequences, as the United States. In the final analysis it is a uniquely American tragedy, the result of a culture that combined liberal efforts to expand personal liberty and a conservative crusade to limit government spending and power. "We in the United States have tended to pursue programmatic changes with an almost unquestioned zeal, and our disappointments are proportionately profound," observed Leona Bachrach. As Daniel Patrick Moynihan, the Labor Department official who later won election to the Senate, has noted, deinstitutionalization serves as a metaphor of how good intentions can go astray. As a personal and painful reminder of that fact, he keeps on prominent display in his office the pen President Kennedy used to sign in the act. Nestled in red velvet and framed in gold, the pen is accompanied by a marker reading: "This pen was used by President Kennedy in signing Public Law Number 88-164, October 31, 1963, and presented to Daniel P. Moynihan." "We keep this as a reminder of the cost of good intentions," he said. "I look at it on occasion and wonder what ever became of our capacity to govern ourselves."[58]

Chapter 3

The Strange Career of Affirmative Action:
The Civil Rights Act of 1964

MARCH 30, 1964: An exhausted Hubert Humphrey stood on the Senate floor, his pockets bulging with notes, his suit rumpled, his resonant voice ringing through the chamber. He was in the middle of a three-hour-and-ten-minute monologue on the pending civil rights bill. Section by section, Humphrey explained the bill's eleven titles, offering striking examples of the evils of southern segregation that the legislation was designed to combat. "The time has come for America to wash its dirty face and cleanse its countenance of this evil," he proclaimed. Like many liberals, Humphrey worried that legalized segregation and persistent black unemployment would lead to social unrest and believed that rigorous antidiscrimination enforcement could help solve the problem. "This bill has a very simple purpose," he declared. "That purpose is to give Negroes the same rights and opportunities that white people take for granted."[1]

Giving impassioned speeches on civil rights was nothing new for Humphrey. A former political science professor and Minneapolis mayor, Humphrey won election to the Senate in 1948 after convincing the national Democratic party to adopt a strong civil rights plank. "[T]he time has arrived in America for the Democratic party to get out of the shadow of states rights and walk forthrightly into the sunshine of human rights," Humphrey declared in a speech that electrified the convention hall and established his reputation as one of the leading orators in American politics. Over the next fifteen years Humphrey emerged as the Senate's most outspoken supporter of New Deal liberalism and a champion of civil rights. Now, at fifty-two, he had grown to become the party's majority whip and one of the most influential men in Congress.[2]

The civil rights bill that occupied Humphrey's attention in 1964 had been born the previous summer, when televised images from Birmingham of Bull Connor's police dogs and fire hoses forced a reluctant President Kennedy to confront the politically sensitive issue of civil rights. Since Franklin Roosevelt's New Deal, the Democratic party had consisted of an uncomfortable alliance between southern segregationists and northern liberals. In the early 1960s civil rights protesters threatened the peace and promised to expose the fault line in the party. Forced to choose between politics and principle, Kennedy chose principle. "We are confronted primarily with a moral issue, as old as the scripture and . . . as clear as the American Constitution," the president told the nation in an eloquent address in June 1963. He followed up his strong rhetoric with a proposal to outlaw racial segregation in public accommodations—"in facilities which are open to the public: hotels, restaurants, theaters, retail stores, and similar establishments."[3]

In Congress an unusual alliance of liberals and conservatives worked to strengthen the Kennedy legislation. Liberals acted out of a conviction that the legislation did not go far enough to protect civil rights; conservatives acted out of a calculated hope that a stronger bill would be less likely to pass the Senate. Kennedy opposed any effort to alter the legislation. "What I want is a bill, not an issue," Attorney General Robert Kennedy declared. Liberals on the House Judiciary Committee, however, succeeded in strengthening the bill by adding Title VII, an employment clause, to make it unlawful "to fail or refuse to hire or to discharge any individual, or otherwise to discriminate against any individual with respect to his compensation, terms, conditions, or privileges of employment, because of such individual's race, color, religion, or national origin." To enforce the new provision, liberals called for creation of an equal employment opportunity commission (EEOC), modeled after the fair employment practices commissions (FEPCs) that already existed in many northern states. Most liberals viewed the FEPC as a tried and trusted model of efficiency and effectiveness for enforcing nondiscrimination. Like state FEPCs, the EEOC would screen complaints, negotiate conciliations, and, if persuasion failed, either hold public hearings or file suit in the courts.[4]

Three weeks after the Judiciary Committee approved the strengthened bill, President Kennedy was assassinated in Dallas. Many liberals felt suspicious of his successor, Lyndon Johnson, the first president from the Deep South since Reconstruction, because of his Texas background and his reputation as a compromiser. They underestimated the new president, who possessed a visceral concern for the disadvantaged and was looking for the opportunity to prove his liberal credentials. Five days after being sworn into office, Johnson told a joint session of Congress there could be no more eloquent "memorial oration or eulogy" to President Kennedy than "the earliest possible passage of the civil rights bill for which he fought so long." Later Johnson made it clear that he would use his legendary legislative skill to win passage. "It would be a fight to total victory or total defeat without appeasement or attrition," he declared.[5]

Johnson's outspoken support failed to intimidate critics, who developed ingenious methods of sabotaging the legislation. In the House the most serious threat came from Virginia's Howard Smith, who tried to divide liberals and burden the bill by adding "sex" to the list of classes protected by Title VII. "This bill is so imperfect," said the octogenarian Democrat, "what harm will this little amendment do?" The Johnson administration opposed the amendment, and its chief sponsor in the House, Judiciary Chairman Emanuel Celler, called it "illogical, ill-timed, ill-paced, and improper." Celler's appeal fell on deaf ears as an odd coalition of women representatives and southerners approved the amendment by a vote of 168 to 133. On February 10 an exhausted House, trying to adjourn before the Lincoln Birthday holiday, voted to approve the Civil Rights Act by the lopsided vote of 290 to 110.[6] It was, in the words of the *Congressional Quarterly*, "the most sweeping civil rights measure to clear either house of Congress in the 20th century."[7]

Now it was Humphrey's turn to push the legislation through a reluctant Senate. He faced formidable opposition in Georgia's Richard Russell, a master of parliamentary maneuvers and an outstanding debater. Calling the legislation a "vicious assault on property rights and the Constitution," the Georgian warned that his troops were "preparing for a battle to the last ditch —to the death." Russell had won his Senate seat in the same year that Franklin Roosevelt was first elected president and had led his first filibuster—he called it extended debate—in 1935, against FDR's attempt to outlaw lynching. By the 1950s Russell had emerged as the field marshal of southern forces opposed to ending segregation. Liberals had never succeeded in invoking cloture against a civil rights filibuster, and the Georgia Democrat had no intention of losing this battle. His strategy was to stall the legislation long enough to allow Alabama Governor George Wallace, a staunch segregationist, to tap into northern grass roots resistance to civil rights. His battle plan seemed prescient when the governor, who had once stood in the schoolhouse door to block the admission of blacks to the state university, scored nearly 30 percent of the vote in Indiana's May Democratic primary. Wallace's victory, the *New York Times* noted, proved that "grassroots resistance to effective civil rights legislation is disturbingly widespread."[8]

Humphrey had his work cut out for him, but he also possessed advantages that liberals had never before enjoyed. In order to end the filibuster, he would need two-thirds of the Senate, or sixty-seven votes, to impose cloture. The pro–civil rights forces could then produce the fifty-one votes needed to pass a civil rights bill. In order to invoke cloture, Humphrey needed to pick up an additional sixteen votes. This time, however, President Johnson had thrown his considerable support behind the legislation and Humphrey had organized his troops with military precision. He designated some senators as "floor captains" to discuss various titles, or provisions of the bill. Other senators were assigned to "military police" duties—namely, keeping check on the whereabouts of supporters so that a sufficient number would be present to answer quorum calls. "Give me your body," he exhorted colleagues. While organizing his forces in the Senate, Humphrey was mobilizing public opinion outside the chamber, meeting with religious and civil rights groups to bring moral and public pressure to bear on the deliberations.[9]

Conservatives began the debate complaining about the enlargement of federal power but quickly discovered the effectiveness of the "quota" issue. Republican Senator Barry Goldwater of Arizona, seeing opposition to civil rights legislation as a potent political weapon in his bid to unseat Johnson in 1964, predicted that the bill would "require the creation of a federal police force of mammoth proportions." As the debate progressed, conservatives focused their attacks on Title VII, claiming that it would inevitably lead to racial quotas and reverse discrimination. "The bill would discriminate against white people," said Senator James Eastland of Mississippi. Alabama's Lister Hill, a New Deal Democrat and strong supporter of organized labor, warned that the civil rights bill would undermine labor's seniority system by requiring racial preferences. Hill feared that civil rights bureaucrats might find violations on a construction site "because there were less [sic] carpenters, proportionately, of a given race than of another race, and that the job was not racially balanced."[10]

The Illinois Fair Employment Practices Commission had unwittingly provided ammunition for these charges by ruling aptitude tests invalid if they contributed to a racial imbalance in the work force. Leon Myatt, a twenty-eight-year-old African-American, had been rejected for an assembly line job at the Motorola Corporation in Chicago after he failed the company's standard ability test. The commission, in a decision that was later overturned, ruled for Myatt, holding the test unfair to "culturally deprived and disadvantaged groups" because it did not take into account "inequalities and differences in environment." The decision sent shock waves through the nation. Arthur Krock, writing in the *New York Times,* bristled that the ruling was "an example of the extent to which a politically-oriented Government agency could interfere with equitable hiring policies of private management." Furthermore, he warned that Title VII threatened "to project the rationale of the Illinois F.E.P.C. ruling throughout the free enterprise system of the United States."[11]

The *Motorola* decision and the attacks by southern opponents of the Civil Rights Act focused debate on a central question: What did affirmative action mean? In the context of civil rights the phrase had appeared for the first time in Executive Order 10925, signed by President Kennedy in March 1961. The phrase "affirmative action" lay buried in the forty-five-hundred-word decree calling for "equal opportunity in employment by the government or its contractors." This original definition of affirmative action required employers only to search aggressively for qualified minority applicants. Once found, minority applicants would go into the same pool with everybody else, and the final selection would be made on a color-blind basis. "The contractor will not discriminate against any employee or applicant for employment because of race, creed, color, or national origin," the president decreed. When asked at a press conference his opinion about racial quotas, Kennedy responded: "We are too mixed, this society of ours, to begin to divide on the basis of race and color."[12]

Most Americans, even leading African-American leaders, accepted Kennedy's definition of affirmative action and agreed with his rejection of quotas. The NAACP, the National Urban League, and Martin Luther King's SCLC all endorsed this view, as did the representatives of organized labor. Most commentators dismissed conservative charges that Title VII would lead to quotas. AFL-CIO lobbyist Andrew Biemiller insisted that the civil rights bill "does not give to any race the right of preferential treatment in hiring or terms of employment." In a memorandum sent to all its chapters the AFL-CIO noted that fair employment practices commissions existed in more than two dozen states and that none had "undercut unions, impaired seniority systems, or compelled the discharge of white workers because there were not enough Negroes on the payroll." The law explicitly disavowed "any requirement that unions or management grant preferential treatment to rectify racial imbalance or to establish quotas in line with community race ratios," noted A. H. Raskin.[13]

Leading news publications emphasized the "no quota" rule. The *New York Times* reassured its readers that the "misrepresentations by opponents of the civil rights legislation are at their wildest in discussing this title" and insisted: "It would not, as has been suggested, require anyone to establish racial quotas. . . . To the contrary, such quotas would be forbidden as a racial test." *U.S. News & World Report* informed its readers: "The law makes it clear that there is to be no 'quota system,' that employers will not be forced to hire a certain proportion of Negroes. Neither is the employer required to give preference to any one group to correct any imbalance that may exist in the makeup of his workforce."[14]

Humphrey too rushed to clarify the bill's language to avoid any ambiguity about the Senate's definition of affirmative action. In the opening speech of formal Senate debate, the Minnesota Democrat stated clearly that Title VII's language outlawed the use of racial quotas. "The truth," he declared, "is that this title forbids discriminating against anyone on account of race. This is the simple and complete truth about title VII." He continued: "Contrary to the allegations of some opponents of this title, there is nothing in it that will give any power to the Commission or to any court to require hiring, firing, or promotion of employees in order to meet a racial 'quota' or to achieve a certain racial balance. That bugaboo has been brought up a dozen times; but it is nonexistent. In fact, the very opposite is true. Title VII prohibits discrimination. In effect, it says that race, religion and national origin are not to be used as the basis for hiring and firing. Title VII is designed to encourage hiring on the basis of ability and qualifications, not race or religion."[15]

At one point, after listening to another speech about the legislation producing racial quotas, an exasperated Humphrey declared: "If the senator can find in Title VII . . . any language which provides that an employer will have to hire on the basis of percentage or quota related to color, race, religion, or national origin, I will start eating the pages one after another, because it is not in there."[16]

Humphrey's lieutenants on the floor underscored the point during deliberations. Edward Kennedy, in his maiden speech in the Senate, rejected as "groundless" conservative arguments that "Title VII can only make jobs for Negroes by taking them away from whites." New Jersey's Clifford Case assured his colleagues that a federal court could not read Title VII to require an employer "to lower or change the occupational qualifications he sets for his employees simply because fewer Negroes than whites are able to meet them." An employer "may set his qualifications as high as he likes, he may test to determine which applicants have these qualifications, and he may hire, assign, and promote on the basis of test performance." In April, Case joined Pennsylvania's Joseph Clark, a fellow liberal, in introducing a memorandum dealing with common criticisms of the bill, including the charge that racial quotas would be imposed under Title VII. The answer was simple and to the point: "Quotas are themselves discriminatory."[17] The memo continued: "There is no requirement in title VII that an employer maintain a racial balance in his work force.

On the contrary, any deliberate attempt to maintain a racial balance, whatever such a balance may be, would involve a violation of title VII because maintaining such a balance would require an employer to hire or to refuse to hire on the basis of race. It must be emphasized that discrimination is prohibited as to any individual."[18]

While the debate over quotas raged on the Senate floor, Humphrey was working behind the scenes to court the minority leader, Everett McKinley Dirksen, of Illinois. With his thatch of gray hair and heavy-lidded eyes, Dirksen possessed, in the words of one reporter, "the melancholy mien of a homeless basset hound." A master of the arcane rules of the Senate, he prided himself on his ability to make compromises and pass legislation. "I am not a moralist," he explained; "I am a legislator." Dirksen's support was crucial; he could bring with him enough moderate Republicans to end the filibuster. The path to passing civil rights, observed a Humphrey aide, "went through Dirksen." Along with relishing his role as broker, Dirksen had compelling reasons to support the bill. Despite Wallace's impressive showing in the Democratic primaries, polls showed that 60 percent of the public supported the legislation, and he feared that his party would suffer in the upcoming election if it played the role of obstructionist. "He knew that the majority of Americans were eager to see a civil rights bill become law," observed Georgia's Senator Herman Talmadge, "and he wasn't about to let the Republicans be on the wrong side of history."[19]

During the first two weeks of May, Humphrey and other supporters of the legislation met regularly with Dirksen. One Humphrey aide noted that "the battle for the Civil Rights Act of 1964 shifted into the rear of Dirksen's chambers on the second floor of the Capitol." Initially Humphrey was shocked by Dirksen's stack of notebooks full of research and possible amendments, but once he started wading through the materials, Humphrey realized that most of the changes were cosmetic. After four intense meet-

ings they neared an agreement. "The trick," recalled one participant, "was to be sure you got it agreed to before too much bour-
bon was drunk." On May 13, after weeks of negotiations, they
reached agreement on a substitute civil rights bill. "We have a
good agreement," Dirksen declared. "This bill is perfectly satis-
factory to me," said Robert Kennedy. "And it is to me," said
Humphrey. "We have done nothing to injure the objectives of this
bill."[20]

Most of Dirksen's amendments simply clarified the language
and procedures of the original legislation; there were, however,
two significant changes. First, the Dirksen substitute limited the
power of the EEOC by depriving it of the right to bring suits to
enforce compliance with the law. In place of this authority, the
substitute bill authorized the attorney general to bring suit where
there is "a pattern or practice of resistance to the full enjoyment"
of the rights secured by the law. Second, Dirksen insisted on
adding amendments that specifically addressed the issue of racial
balancing and preferential treatment of minorities[21]: "703(J)
Nothing contained in this title shall be interpreted to require any
employer . . . to grant preferential treatment to any individual or
to any group because of the race, color, religion, sex, or national
origin of such individual or group on account of an imbalance
which may exist with respect to the total number of percentage
of persons of any race, color, religion, sex, or national origin employed by any employer."[22]

Along with the change to 703(J), Dirksen insisted on adding
the word "intentionally" to Section 706(G), making sure that
proving discrimination required uncovering an evil motive and
could not be inferred by statistical distributions of employment
patterns. Humphrey did not consider either change threatening to
the legislation; in fact, he believed they clarified his own thinking
on the issue of quotas. The new 703(J) section, he said, was added
to "state . . . expressly" and as "clearly and accurately" as the power
of language would permit what the leadership had maintained all

along: "Title VII does not require an employer to achieve any sort of racial balance in his work force by giving preferential treatment to any individual or group." The emphasis on intent, he argued, "is designed to make it wholly clear that inadvertent or accidental discriminations will not violate the title or result in entry of court orders. It means simply that the respondent must have intended to discriminate."[23]

On May 26 Dirksen rose in the Senate, removed his tortoise-shell spectacles, and presented his revised bill. "Mr. President," he proclaimed, "I present an amendment in the nature of a substitute." Over the next few weeks Russell and his southern supporters made a desperate effort to sink the new compromise package, but they no longer controlled enough votes to continue the filibuster. On June 10 Majority Leader Mike Mansfield decided the time had come for cloture. "The Senate now stands at the crossroads of history, and the time for decision is at hand," he declared. Shortly afterward the motion of cloture was made, and the clerk started calling the roll. In ten minutes it was all over: The Senate voted 71–29 to close off the record-shattering southern filibuster, which had consumed, according to Russell's calculation, eighty-two working days, sixty-three thousand pages in the *Congressional Record,* and ten million words.[24]

With cloture enacted, passage of the bill was a formality. On June 17, one year after John F. Kennedy had submitted his proposal to the House, the Senate passed, 73–27, the most sweeping civil rights bill since Reconstruction. After a brief debate House members voted 289–126 on July 2 to approve the measure as amended by the Senate. Four and a half hours after the House had given final approval, Lyndon Johnson entered the East Room of the White House and, under the gaze of portraits of George and Martha Washington, signed what the historian Allen Matusow called "the great liberal achievement of the decade."[25]

Many of the participants in the great civil rights debate of 1964 believed they had passed a historic bill that would alter race relations in America. Emanuel Celler, the chief House sponsor, said the legislation would be like "the voice of Leviticus, 'proclaiming liberty throughout the land to all the inhabitants thereof.' " The legislators felt confident that the long, sometimes acrimonious debates would provide the courts with a clear sense of direction. "I doubt very much whether, in my legislative lifetime, there has been a measure that received so much meticulous attention," Dirksen declared. Observers of the debates reached the same conclusion. "Seldom has similar legislation been debated with greater consciousness of the need for 'legislative history' . . . to guide the courts in interpreting and applying the law," commented a legal scholar. It was not long, however, before they realized that many thorny questions remained unanswered.[26]

THE task of interpreting and enforcing Title VII fell on the shoulders of the newly created EEOC. The legislation mandated that the Equal Employment Opportunity Commission include five commissioners who were to serve terms of five years. Congress gave the administration a one-year grace period to get the EEOC up and running, but Johnson delayed, hoping to find a high-profile figure to head the agency. "There are plenty of technicians who could do the job," said a spokesman, "but the President wants a big name." Finally, in May 1965—only six weeks before the EEOC was supposed to start functioning—the president announced that Franklin Roosevelt, Jr., would be its first head. The long delay, not to mention the legislative compromises necessary to create the new commission, did little to dampen Johnson's ambition for Title VII. At a White House conference in August he called Title VII "the key to hope for millions of our fellow Americans. With that key we can begin to open the gates that now enclose the ghettos of despair."[27]

Roosevelt was acutely aware of the tension between the president's lofty ambition and Congress's limited mandate. "We will do the best we can with what Congress has given us," he told the *New York Times*. "Because of very limited enforcement powers we may have difficulty carrying out the full intent of the act." In keeping with the restrictive language of the commission's mandate, Roosevelt believed the EEOC should confine itself to using voluntary efforts to change the attitude of employers. "We have to bring the moral suasion of the commission onto employers to solve the education and training problem," he said. In the first few months abstract questions about the commission's role took a backseat to the daunting administrative task of setting up an office, recruiting a staff of three hundred, and creating regional offices in just a few weeks.[28]

One of these early recruits was a young professor from Rutgers University. Alfred Blumrosen joined the fledgling agency to coordinate federal-state relations but soon expanded his responsibilities to include all EEOC activities. Like many of the young lawyers hired to staff the EEOC, he had ambitious plans for the commission. In his work as a consultant in New Jersey he had been highly critical of the "administrative caution and ineptness" of that state's civil rights division. He concluded that the fair employment practices model upon which the EEOC was based had "little effect on overall patterns and practices of manpower utilization and employment discrimination." Convinced of the importance of "energetic administration," he was determined to see that the EEOC did not suffer from the same problems that plagued many state enforcement agencies. "As an administrator for EEOC, I attempted to bring my model of an aggressive and effective agency into reality," he recalled. Most of the problems confronting the EEOC, he concluded, "could be solved by creative interpretation of Title VII."[29]

Most of the EEOC staff shared Blumrosen's expansive view of the commission's administrative mandate. Its "philosophy," he reflected, "was to secure the maximum possible impact for the law by seeking the broadest interpretation of each of its substan-

..

tive and procedural provisions." All its decisions, he claimed, "emerged from a unified idea—that the statute should be read so as to maximize its impact on employer practices." He saw no difficulty in the EEOC's stretching the specific mandate of the law. He referred to the process as the law transmission system. "Administrators seeking to transform the social impulse into social change must take the broadest view of their law at the initial stages when all options are open," he wrote. [30]

The lack of effective leadership at the top of the EEOC allowed Blumrosen the power to implement many of his ideas. Roosevelt, who seemed more interested in yachting than running the agency, resigned after less than a year on the job to wage an unsuccessful campaign for governor of New York. Four months later Johnson appointed a new chairman, Stephen N. Shulman. He too served for a brief period, to be succeeded by the former White House aide Clifford L. Alexander, Jr., in August 1967. One of the results of the tumult at the top was, in Blumrosen's words, "de facto staff power" to be creative, to chart a new course through the "open water" of discrimination law. [31]

But how was the EEOC to maximize its impact? Congressional conservatives had specifically limited its mandate. Fearful of a muscular new enforcement commission, they had successfully constricted its powers, stripping it of both cease-and-desist power and prosecuting authority. The act limited the commission to using "conference, conciliation, and persuasion" in its assault on employment discrimination. What remained, in the words of one expert, was "a poor, enfeebled thing . . . [with] the power to conciliate but not to compel." Congress repeatedly cut administration budget requests for the new agency, even though an escalator clause increased its responsibility each year. The commission's $5.2 million budget in 1967 was smaller than that of the Office of Coal Research. Its staff of 314 was smaller than that of the Federal Crop Insurance Program. In 1967 the *Wall Street Journal* characterized it as "marked by administrative chaos and a revolv-

· ·

ing door personnel problem." A Brookings study conducted in the same year described the EEOC as "very new, very weak, and very small."[32]

At the same time, skeptical liberals were determined to prove that the commission lacked the teeth needed to take a bite out of discrimination. The left-leaning *Nation* called the EEOC "a jelly factory." The civil rights community decided to test the new organization by flooding it with complaints. "We think the best way to get it amended," said Jack Greenberg, head of the NAACP Legal Defense and Education Fund, "is to show that it doesn't work." Within its first hundred days, the EEOC received 1,383 formal complaints, although Congress had budgeted it to handle only 2,000 in its first year. "We are being overwhelmed," Roosevelt said, with an "uncontrollable complaint workload." By April 1966 it had received 5,000 complaints. The resulting backlog in processing them stretched to more than fifteen months by 1967.[33]

Blumrosen believed that as long as the EEOC drowned in individual complaints, it would never mount a successful drive to root out discrimination in the workplace. He and the other staff lawyers were convinced that the issues of discrimination found expression in far more subtle ways than Humphrey and Dirksen had ever considered. For example, legislators had called for a color-blind application of race, but what if the impact of past discrimination continued to hold back African-Americans? In many cases, seniority systems acted as grandfather clauses for white workers who had entered the systems before desegregation. What if testing procedures had the effect of limiting access to minorities, who were less likely to have received formal education, even if the tests were not openly discriminatory? The color-blind model, they believed, failed to root out institutional racism, which was the chief cause of employment discrimination. "During the first year, investigation revealed that discrimination was often inherent in the system of the employer," the EEOC concluded. "Thus it was necessary to change the system."[34]

· ·

Changing the system required the EEOC to take liberties with the language of Title VII. Responding to conservative fears about quotas and racial balance, Dirksen had specifically stated that evidence of discrimination must be based on "intentionality." Blumrosen and the EEOC staff, however, believed that using the legislatively mandated "intent" test would have "plunged Title VII investigations into an endless effort to identify an evil motive." Instead the EEOC decided to apply an "effect" test: Practices would be judged on the basis of their impact on minorities, regardless of the intent of the actor. "In its testing guidelines and in written reasonable cause decisions, and in *amicus* briefs to the courts, the commission propounded the notion that practices which adversely affected minorities were illegal, unless they could be justified." Without this broad "model of the world," Blumrosen noted, enforcement "of the statute would have been erratic and undirected."[35]

How did the EEOC justify the change? "The answer," observed the historian Hugh Davis Graham, "was a counter-appeal to a kind of higher-law doctrine." EEOC Commissioner Sam Jackson explained the "higher law" reasoning to a gathering of the NAACP. The commission "has taken its interpretation of Title VII a step further than other agencies," he said, by concluding that the law banned not only intentional discrimination but employer practices "which prove to have a demonstrable racial effect." "The underlying rationale for this position," he continued, "has been that Congress, with its elaborate exploration of the economic plight of the minority worker, sought to establish a comprehensive instrument with which to adjust the needless hardships resulting from the arbitrary operation of personal practices, as well as purposeful discrimination." Jackson confessed that "[t]his approach would seem to disregard intent, then, as crucial to the finding of an unlawful employment practice."[36]

The commission was fully aware that its interpretation of Title VII was contrary to the language of the statute. Blumrosen admitted that "use of the 'effect test' was not required by the statute or by the legislative history." The commission's official history noted: "Under the traditional meaning, discrimination must be one of intent in the state of mind of the actor." The EEOC's interpretation, however, "would seem to disregard intent as crucial to the finding of an unlawful employment practice." Realizing that its interpretation differed significantly from the wording of the statute and the history of discrimination law developed in the courts, the EEOC declared: "Eventually this will call for reconsideration of the amendment by Congress or the reconsideration of its interpretation by the Commission."[37]

The EEOC was not alone in its belief that the original legislation had underestimated the importance of institutional racism; many liberals were coming to a similar conclusion. Writing in 1965, civil rights leader Bayard Rustin claimed that the "classical" civil rights movement, which focused on individual rights and political access, had failed to change "the fundamental conditions of life for the Negro people." Noting that since the landmark Supreme Court decision in *Brown* (1954), the black unemployment rate had increased and the number of blacks attending *de facto* segregated schools had swelled, he urged a new strategy concerned "not merely with removing the barriers to full opportunity but with achieving the fact of equality." Echoing Rustin's views, Daniel Patrick Moynihan, then an assistant secretary of labor, wrote a 1965 government report on the black family. The political furor that engulfed Moynihan's controversial critique that racism and centuries of deprivation had created a "tangle of pathology" that was undermining the black family obscured its key policy recommendation: "The principal challenge of the next phase of the Negro revolution is to make certain that equality of results will now follow. If we do not," he predicted, "there will be no social peace in the United States for generations."[38]

In June 1965 President Johnson gave eloquent expression to Moynihan's ideas in a celebrated speech at Howard University.

The president recited the same statistics about black unemployment and the growing gap between black and white that troubled Rustin and Moynihan. The evidence demonstrated that the traditional liberal strategy of passing legislation and securing individual rights had done little to improve the lives of most African-Americans. Johnson suggested that true equality required more than the color-blind approach; aggressive steps were needed to redress the legacy of discrimination that continued to burden blacks. "You do not take a person who, for years, has been hobbled by chains and liberate him, bring him up to the starting line of a race and then say, '[y]ou are free to compete with all the others,' and still justly believe that you have been completely fair." The *New York Times,* commenting favorably on the speech, observed: "The cures for the social afflictions that hold the Negro in thrall lie in public and private programs that make the present War on Poverty and all its related undertakings for expanded education, urban renewal and improved welfare services seem incredibly puny."[39]

The urgency of the task came into sharp focus in August, just two months after the EEOC had opened its doors, when the Watts district of Los Angeles erupted in an orgy of racial violence. It raged for a week, left thirty-four dead, injured more than a thousand, and required the military occupation of forty-six square miles to halt the violence. Watts marked the beginning of a new, violent phase in the struggle for black equality. It was followed by 150 major riots and hundreds of minor ones that summer and the next three summers. In 1967 the black inner cities of Newark, New Jersey, and Detroit exploded in two of the largest of the urban riots of the century. At least seventy people were killed, nearly two thousand injured, and thousands arrested. Property damage left hundreds of families homeless.[40]

For many liberals the riots challenged the classic color-blind belief that America's "Negro problem" could be met through a combination of antidiscrimination laws, economic growth, and voluntary goodwill. Most disorders erupted in states and cities generally known for their liberalism and progressive views of race, and most had functioning fair employment practices commissions that had done little to alleviate oppressive social conditions. The residents of Watts already enjoyed equal rights before the law, but equal rights had done little to lessen the unemployment rate. The causes of the riots were complex, but in the highly charged atmosphere of the mid-1960s most liberals saw a clear connection between violence and lack of opportunity. "Bad conditions make for violence," observed Floyd McKissick, chairman of CORE. "You will have violence as long as you have black people suppressed." A. Philip Randolph added, "Teenagers with jobs don't throw Molotov cocktails." The Johnson administration shared the riot sociology of civil rights leaders. The war on poverty chief, Sargent Shriver, told Congress that the "social dynamite comes from discontent with joblessness, discontent with inhuman housing, discontent with money-hungry landlords and merchants, discontent with the raw differences between justice, health, and convenience for the poor and the rest of America."[41]

The riots put heat on the EEOC to add some teeth to the nation's antidiscrimination laws. A 1966 study conducted for the commission noted a "growing consensus" that "a significant segment of the Negro community is increasingly losing confidence in the effectiveness of these agencies" because of the "exceedingly slow" claims process and the "slight probability" of success. The following year Whitney M. Young, Jr., executive director of the National Urban League, charged that the EEOC's inability to enforce Title VII undermined confidence in the government's commitment to civil rights. "The actual agency experience, which has demonstrated that the Commission cannot enforce compliance, has given rise to disillusionment and lack of confidence." The "American Negro," he warned, "is rapidly losing faith in the democratic process to achieve his goal of equality of opportunity."[42]

If the rioting served to some as confirmation of the need for the EEOC's expanded definition of discrimination, the commission still confronted a serious practical obstacle in its plan to focus on impact rather than motive: It needed to find specific statistical information that would document patterns of employment in specific industries. But where could it find such information? In its early years the EEOC shared a building with an agency called PCEEO, a small, short-lived group that Kennedy had set up to oversee equal employment opportunity in companies under contract with the government. In the summer of 1965 Blumrosen had wandered into the PCEEO offices to ask a question and found boxes of "Form 40, which contained race counts ('zero lists' of employers with no black workers, 'underutilization lists' of employers with very low percentages of black workers) of the workforces of government contractors." Reviewing the forms, Blumrosen remarked that his "sense of outrage grew." He found that many of the largest firms in the country, including many that were part of a voluntary government program to promote minorities, "were on either the zero list or the low utilization list."[43]

The forms were a major find. They exposed the limitations of any voluntary program to end employment discrimination, and they provided the government with a statistical road map of large sectors of the economy. Blumrosen called them "a goldmine." The EEOC planned to use the statistical spotlighting of employment patterns as a sharp-edged weapon against discrimination. The official administrative history referred to the forms, and to the reporting system they helped create, as the agency's "calling card," giving "credibility to an otherwise weak statute." The forms gave the commission a path out of its predicament: Rather than be confined to a case-by-case "retail" handling of individual complaints, it could broaden its power into a "wholesale" approach to discrimination. Using an aviation metaphor, Blumrosen claimed the forms provided administrators with "sociological radar" that would allow them to pinpoint troubled areas. "I saw this as perhaps the most important tool in any program to eliminate employment discrimination. Here were lists of major employers excluding minorities in a massive way which outraged any reader of the statistics. . . . Here at last was a basis for government-initiated programs which were not based on complaints and which could focus on possible potential discriminators effectively. . . . There was a perennial shortage of manpower and money in antidiscrimination programs. If government could focus, through the reporting system, on those employers where underutilization was sharpest, there was a possibility of successfully combating discrimination."[44]

Not everyone in the EEOC supported using the forms, but in the end Blumrosen prevailed. An unlikely coalition of business groups and civil rights leaders opposed the reporting system, claiming that it would give tools to those who wanted to discriminate and that it "added a suggestion of police action to the activities of the Commission." Practical necessity, as much as reasoned argument, won the day. Many saw it as the only way for the EEOC, with its limited mandate and restricted funding, to get rid of its backlog. "The need to respond to the tremendous caseload," the commission noted, "made academic . . . the debate going on both inside and outside the Commission on the most desirable approach for eliminating employment discrimination."

Ironically the weakening provisions that conservatives had included in the EEOC's mandate helped produce a fundamental revision in discrimination law. Lacking the resources to investigate individual cases of discrimination, the commission used statistics as a shorthand formula for determining if a company practiced discrimination. Those statistics would push inevitably toward quotas, the result conservatives feared most and believed they had outlawed.[45]

In March 1966 the EEOC sent out its racial reporting (EEO-1) forms to every employer in its jurisdiction, requiring each to keep track of the race of every employee. The race-reporting EEO-1 form provided administrators with a bird's-eye view of entire industries and geographic areas. The goal was to document such large disparities in employment patterns that discriminatory intent might be legally inferred. The precision of these findings permitted the EEOC to zero in on troubled target areas. For example, the figures revealed that although blacks constituted 11.2 percent of the population of Kansas City, they made up only 2.1 percent of the white-collar work force in the city; in Cleveland the corresponding figures were 13 percent and 3.2 percent. The problem was not just geographical. Similar patterns emerged from national industry-wide comparisons. In certain industries blacks held a strikingly low share of white-collar jobs: 2.8 percent in the aerospace industry in Los Angeles, 1 percent in air travel in Atlanta, 0.7 percent in Cleveland railroads. Just as troubling, within those white-collar categories the great majority of blacks worked in low-paying clerical and sales positions. In Chicago, for example, where blacks held only 4.7 percent of white-collar jobs, 79.6 percent labored in low-status positions.[46]

The EEOC staff believed the figures would aid in its efforts to force business to accept conciliation agreements. "With these figures, we'll be armed to the teeth," EEOC Chairman Clifford Alexander, Jr., declared in 1967. "We can go to Mister X and say: 'Here's an employer in your industry who's doing twice as well as you are. Why aren't you doing better?' " With a few notable exceptions, however, most employers were reluctant to make major changes in the workplace based on EEOC recommendations and preferred to take their chances in the courts. The race-reporting forms then added a new weapon to the commission's arsenal: public relations. Since the EEOC could not bring suits, it decided to use publicity to embarrass companies into making changes by holding hearings (called forums) targeted at specific industries in specific areas. "The use of hearings for affirmative action," the commission noted, "proved to be a powerful weapon."[47]

A SIMILAR transformation took place at the Office of Federal Contract Compliance (OFCC), created by executive order in 1965 to enforce affirmative action among businesses working for the federal government. It required each federal contractor to agree that it "will not discriminate against any employee or applicant for employment because of race, color, religion, sex or national origin" and that it "will take affirmative action to ensure that applicants are employed without regard to their race, color, religion, sex or national origin." The order provided the enforcement mechanism for Title VI of the Civil Rights Act, which banned discrimination in programs receiving funds from federal grants, loans, or contracts. Unlike the EEOC, the OFCC had teeth: It had the power to "cancel, terminate, [or] suspend . . . any contract or portion thereof" that violated the order. With federal funds reaching 225,000 contractors involved in $30 billion in annual contracts, the agency wielded considerable leverage. The OFCC had another key advantage over the EEOC: effective leadership at the top in Edward Sylvester, Jr., an energetic and creative African-American engineer.[48]

As with the EEOC, those enforcing affirmative action in government contracts ran into murky rules dealing with seniority. The biggest problems occurred in the construction trades, notorious for shutting out blacks. Membership in the union locals of skilled trades often passed from father to son. Though union officials contended that their apprenticeships were open to all, blacks accounted for only a small fraction of union membership. In Philadelphia, for example, African-Americans made up less than one-half of 1 percent of trades even though blacks represented nearly 30 percent of the city's population. In 1963 an AFL-CIO Human Rights Committee condemned with "vigor the failure within our own family" to "break down the pattern of segregated locals." The pattern recurred in many other major cities.[49]

The Johnson administration confronted a difficult political question: How could it crack the white stranglehold in the construction industry without alienating key labor support? The OFCC made its first step in 1966, when it established the Philadelphia Plan, a program requiring contractors to present affirmative action plans before the awarding of a contract. Bidders submitted "manning tables" that listed by trade all the minority workers they planned to hire. The OFCC considered the manning table along with the bid price in determining awards. The administration moved cautiously. The plan applied to only a few cities—San Francisco, Cleveland, and Philadelphia—and the OFCC carefully avoided using specific quotas. "There is no fixed and firm definition of affirmative action," Sylvester said in January 1967. "We really prefer that the contractor determine himself what affirmative action he can take."[50]

The strengthened compliance program generated heated criticism from labor and business groups. Labor leaders dismissed the manning table requirement as "piles of nonsense and illegal." Many business leaders attacked the program not because it raised the specter of quotas but because it was too vague. Business groups hooted Sylvester for refusing to dictate actual quotas. "If I wouldn't tell them you need 10 percent of this or 10 percent of that, they'd start booing," he said. "Their tone was: We're in business to make money. Just tell us exactly what we have to do and then don't bother us." The legal branch of the federal government agreed with the critics, claiming that the program was too vague and therefore unenforceable. The problem with the administration's system, Comptroller General Elmer B. Staats ruled, was that it did not explain exactly what affirmative action required. Accordingly he advised the Department of Labor that pre-award negotiations on affirmative action were inconsistent with the rules of competitive bidding. Sensing political trouble, the administration backed away from the plan. Labor Secretary Willard Wirtz reassured anxious labor leaders that the manning table requirement "isn't right as a general policy and it won't work."[51]

Richard Nixon's election in 1968 seemed to dash any hope of salvaging the Philadelphia Plan, but as so many times in the past, Nixon surprised everyone. In 1969 the administration hired Arthur Fletcher, an African-American business leader and former professional football player, as assistant secretary of labor for employment standards. A fiscal conservative, Fletcher opposed efforts to expand government spending or to pass new laws and instead called for using existing machinery more efficiently. "My idea," he recalled years later, "was not to propose new civil rights laws, but to use existing government regulations—that little-recognized but powerful tool of the ingrained bureaucracy—to expand opportunities for people who had been shut out of the process."[52]

Sitting in his office one day, Fletcher came across the original Philadelphia Plan and liked the idea. If it was too vague, he reasoned, it could be fixed by clearly spelling out affirmative action goals. Employers, he thought, would simply ignore flowery but toothless presidential exhortations. As a company lawyer advised him one day in the mid-sixties, "When the government tells us what affirmative action is, then we'll comply." Fletcher thought that a revised plan would open jobs for blacks, while keeping Nixon's commitment to "helping people help themselves." Philadelphia, where craft unions were dominated by ethnic machines, made an ideal testing area for Fletcher. In some of the unions Italians with green cards, noncitizens unable to speak a word of English, worked on federal contracts while the unemployment rate for local blacks stood near 25 percent. "In essence, public taxes were being used to take care of a family clan called a union," Fletcher recalled.[53]

In making his case, a dynamic Fletcher "transfixed a Cabinet meeting," White House speech writer William Safire later wrote in *Before the Fall*. Fletcher succeeded in winning over the one person who mattered, Richard Nixon. The president's motives for supporting the plan were complicated. Though he came to office on a tough law and order platform, Nixon had always been a racial moderate, and in the tense political atmosphere of the late 1960s he was looking for ways to demonstrate his goodwill. As Tom Wicker noted, the plan appealed to Nixon's "usual preference for the middle course" between the NAACP's calls for tougher action and organized labor's resistance to any action. The president's motives were not wholly altruistic, however. Always a shrewd politician, Nixon saw racial preferences as an effective way to pit two Democratic groups—blacks and labor—against each other. In a long memorandum supporting the plan, White House adviser John Ehrlichman pointed out that the plan was both "anti-labor and pro-black" and would drive "a wedge between the Democrats and labor."[54]

On June 27, 1969, Fletcher traveled to Philadelphia to announce and sign the Revised Philadelphia Plan. The plan set specific percentage "ranges" for blacks and other minority groups for craft union jobs. For example, plumbers and pipe fitters, of whom only 12 out of 2,335 in Philadelphia were black, were given a hiring goal of 5 to 8 percent black in 1970, a range that was to rise to 22 to 26 percent by 1973. "The federal government," Fletcher said in the ceremony at First National Bank near Independence Hall, "has an obligation to see that every citizen has an equal chance at the most basic freedom of all—the right to succeed." He added that it was time to "quit looking at the civil rights movement without looking at the unemployment rate. This is an economic problem and we can use the economic genius of this country to solve it."[55]

The announcement sparked a fire storm of criticism, much of it revolving around the question of congressional intent and the Civil Rights Act of 1964. AFL-CIO President George Meany charged that the plan was an "illegal and un-American" application of "a quota system." Even Tom Wicker, who supported Nixon's initiative, said it "made a rather clever end-run around the legislative act of 1964." Potentially, the most damaging criticism came once again from Comptroller General Staats, a holdover from the Johnson administration, who took a literal interpretation of Title VII, concluding that the Philadelphia Plan violated the Civil Rights Act's prohibition against racial quotas. Staats quoted extensively from Hubert Humphrey to prove that the legislation banned any attempt to create "a racial 'quota' or to achieve a racial balance."[56]

Nixon's attorney general, John N. Mitchell, fired back, insisting that the plan was in keeping with the spirit of the legislation. Adopting the expansive interpretation of the EEOC, Mitchell maintained that the larger purpose of the law was to eliminate discriminatory practices and to promote employment equality for blacks. Nondiscrimination, he argued, required considering "the racial consequences" of "outwardly neutral criteria." The attorney general claimed that since the plan required only percentages, not specific numbers, it did not institute quotas, and was therefore not prohibited by the law. Asked to explain the difference between a "goal" and a "quota," Secretary of Labor George Shultz said that quotas "keep people out. . . . What we are seeking are objectives to get people in." The distinction was lost on Staats. "The obligation to make every good faith effort to attain his goal under the Plan will place contractors in situations where they will undoubtedly grant preferential treatment to minority group employees," he argued.[57]

The irony of the situation was striking. A partisan Republican defended quotas by adopting the expansive language of the liberal EEOC against a literal interpretation of the law. The Nixon Labor Department had adopted the same principles that had guided the activist staff lawyers of the EEOC: Both decided to ignore the issue of intent in determining whether discrimination existed and instead focused on racial "effect." Since documenting racial imbalance served as proof of discrimination, the OFCC, like the EEOC, used statistics to make its case, which in turn allowed for wholesale enforcement and dramatic expansion of government power. Both justified the change by appeal to a "higher law," claiming that the real intent of Congress had been to improve economic conditions for African-Americans and that the specific appeal to color blindness failed to appreciate the depth of institutional racism in America. The controversy played out in Congress, where Democrats attempted to pass legislation barring the administration from spending funds on contracts rejected by the comptroller general. Defending the Philadelphia Plan as an equal opportunity measure, the White House defeated the effort. "The Democrats are token oriented," Nixon noted; "we are job oriented." In the House a majority of Republicans voted in favor of the Philadelphia Plan; Democrats voted against it.[58]

Nixon never attempted to press for quotas in employment unrelated to federal contracts. But having cleared an important legislative hurdle, he extended the Philadelphia Plan to all federal contractors. Laurence Silberman, undersecretary of labor, wrote that the Nixon administration spread Philadelphia plans "across the country like Johnny Appleseed." In January 1970 Nixon's secretary of labor, George Shultz, signed Order No. 4 which required federal contractors to submit "affirmative action compliance programs" that set forth "specific steps to guarantee equal employment opportunity keyed to . . . the needs of members of minority groups." (A Revised Order No. 4 in December 1971 called for reports on women.) The regulation said bluntly: "The rate of minority applicants recruited should approximate or equal the rate of minorities in the population in each location." The executive order required a "utilization" study to determine minority representation in the work force and required employers to establish goals for hiring and promotion to overcome any "underutilization" found to exist. "By the end of the first Nixon Administration, a significant part of the 'civil rights' being enforced by the federal government could be described more plainly as a system of compensatory preferences for racial and ethnic groups," noted the legal historian Andrew Kull.[59]

Nixon proved to be a fair-weather friend of racial quotas, and as political winds shifted to the right, he repudiated one of his administration's major legacies. The pivotal event was the Hard Hat March in the spring of 1970, when thousands of New York City construction workers marched in support of Nixon's Vietnam policies. According to Safire, "Most of the zip went out of [the Philadelphia Plan] after the hard hats marched in support of Nixon and the war." Nixon saw an opportunity to win over the working class to the Republican party and now viewed his support of quotas as an obstacle. By 1972 Nixon was attacking the Democratic nominee, George McGovern, as "the quota candidate," claiming that a fixed quota system was "as artificial and unfair a yardstick as has ever been used to deny opportunity."[60]

"SCARCELY any political question arises in the United States," wrote Alexis de Tocqueville in the 1830s, "which is not resolved, sooner, or later, into a judicial question." Ever since Chief Justice John Marshall established the principle of judicial review in *Marbury v. Madison* (1803), the Court has assumed the role of determining if the actions of the other branches of government are legal. "It is emphatically the province and duty of the judicial department to say what the law is," Marshall declared. It was only a matter of time before affirmative action found itself on the Court's docket.[61]

The expanded EEOC interpretation of Title VII emboldened African-Americans to challenge practices they believed were discriminatory. At the Duke Power Plant in North Carolina the white employees were all supervisors or managers, while the blacks struggled as janitors. The most a black worker could make was $1.65 an hour. Whites started at $1.81. Willie Boyd, the son of a sharecropper, spent his days cleaning toilets that he was forbidden to use. The company had built a "colored" outhouse across the railroad tracks. It bothered Boyd that white men, with no more education than he had, were promoted to managers and supervisors, while he was stuck cleaning toilets. Boyd had been complaining about the situation for years to Jay Griggs, his local NAACP leader. Griggs tired of the endless carping and told his friend: "File your complaint or stop talking about it." In March 1966 the two men sat down and penned a letter, then persuaded a number of other black workers to sign it. "We the employees under the Civil Rights Act of 1964 feel justified in requesting the company for promotion when vacancies occur, in the following classifications, coal handling, shop, storekeeper, and general plant operation." The workers listed Willie Griggs—no relation to Jay—as the plaintiff since he was the youngest and would have the easiest time finding a new job if the company retaliated.[62]

The complaint bubbled up to the Supreme Court, which for the first time had the chance to review the EEOC's decision to define discrimination based on "effect" rather than "intent." Duke claimed to be complying fully with the Civil Rights Act: It had banned any discriminatory practices in 1965, and blacks who wished to be promoted could pass a qualifying test. Title VII permitted ability tests if they were not used to discriminate on the basis of race. The U.S. Chamber of Commerce submitted a brief on behalf of Duke, arguing that discriminatory motives were the *sine qua non* of a permissible legal challenge. It argued that "independent evidence of discrimination" must accompany the statistical disparate impact to make out a *prima facie* case. Lawyers for Griggs argued that the intent was irrelevant: The qualifying test failed to measure ability for the job and had the "effect" of perpetuating discriminatory patterns against blacks. The intelligence tests used by Duke, they charged, were "potent tools for substantially reducing Negro opportunities," which operated as "thinly veiled racial discrimination." Duke's tests, Griggs argued, "are being 'used' to discriminate even if not so intended."

In 1971 a unanimous Supreme Court decided in favor of Griggs and thus institutionalized the EEOC's definition of discrimination under Title VII. It held that "good intent or absence of discriminatory intent does not redeem employment procedures or testing mechanisms that operate as 'built-in headwinds' for minority groups and are unrelated to measuring job ability." The Civil Rights Act, the Court concluded, was passed to "achieve equality" and aimed at the "consequences of employment practices" and "not simply the motivation." The key was "business necessity." An employer needed to prove "that any given requirement must have a manifest relationship to the employment in question." If companies focused only on necessary job qualifications, Chief Justice Warren Burger opined, "race, religion, nationality and sex [will] become irrelevant." The Civil Rights Act "proscribes not only overt discrimination," Burger said, "but also practices that are fair in form, but discriminatory in operation."[63]

The EEOC itself could not have written a stronger decision. Blumrosen noted that the Court had accepted almost every argument the EEOC lawyers had made since 1965. "*Griggs* redefined discrimination in terms of consequences rather than motive, effect rather than purpose," he wrote. The Court gave legal sanction to the EEOC's definition of discrimination: It defined fair employment in terms of results, measured by statistics of minority group employment. Motive or intent to discriminate was irrelevant, and employment practices that did not alleviate racial imbalance could be justified only by business necessity. The Court insisted that the ruling did not require strict quotas, but by declaring suspect any employment standard that resulted in racial imbalance, the justices gave a powerful incentive to employers to use a proportional quota system.[64]

The *Griggs* decision was to employment discrimination what the *Brown* decision was to school desegregation, and it had a real effect much more quickly than the long-evaded *Brown* ruling. Lawyers used *Griggs* to attack a wide range of recruitment, hiring, assignment, testing, seniority, promotion, discharge, and supervisory selection practices. It helped abolish height and weight requirements in police and fire departments that disproportionately barred Hispanic, Asian, and female applicants. It forced airlines to abandon age cutoffs for flight attendants. With Court approval, the government expanded its affirmative action program. In 1977 Congress required that government contractors set aside 10 percent of their funds for minority subcontractors. Later in the decade the EEOC and the Office of Federal Contract Compliance Programs (the successor to the OFCC) developed tough and explicit new guidelines for employers who wished to avoid litigation.[65]

Inevitably the spread of affirmative action programs benefiting minorities and women in the mid-1970s produced a backlash from many white males, who called for a literal interpretation of the Civil Rights Act. In 1972 and again in 1973, Allan Bakke, a white honor student in college who had served with the Marines in Vietnam, was denied admission to the University of California Medical School at Davis. In the entering classes to which Bakke applied, the Davis Medical School accepted one hundred applicants; sixteen places were allotted to minorities. The university contended that it was not choosing between "qualified" and "unqualified" applicants but simply exercising discretion among groups of qualified students who differed by degree. Bakke sued.

The case attracted national attention as a test of racial preferences. Nearly sixty separate legal briefs were filed by "friends of the court"—up to that time the greatest number of *amicus curiae* briefs in Supreme Court history. Pundits lined up on opposite sides of the suit. "If the Supreme Court agrees with Bakke," said the NAACP general counsel Nathaniel Jones, "we will have to start over again with desegregation." Critics argued that guaranteeing minorities admission even when they appeared to be less qualified than whites amounted to "reverse discrimination." Philosopher Sidney Hook declared: "We are inconsistent as well as insincere if, in attempts to rectify the arbitrary and invidious discrimination of the past, we practice arbitrary and invidious discrimination in the present."[66]

In July 1978, after eight months of contentious debate, a divided Court issued its opinion. Four justices said the medical school had violated the color-blind principle of the Civil Rights Act by giving an explicit preference to black and Latino applicants. Four other justices claimed that "benign" discrimination was acceptable if it was intended to give minority applicants an equal opportunity. William Brennan, following the logic of *Griggs,* said that when Congress enacted the civil rights bill of 1964, it had not intended to stop "all race-conscious efforts to extend the benefits of federally financed programs to minorities who have been historically excluded from the full benefits of American life." The ninth and deciding justice, Lewis F. Powell, Jr., agreed that the university had violated the law by discriminating against Allan Bakke because of his race. He must be admitted, Powell said. However, he also agreed that universities might consider race as a "plus factor" in admissions so as to foster "diversity" in their classes.[67]

The Supreme Court had issued an ambiguous ruling in the *Bakke* case: It declared the university's racial quota illegal and ordered Bakke admitted. On the other hand, it approved using race as a consideration in selecting students. Many now were confused about what was permissible. Most observers predicted a flurry of lawsuits to test the limits of the *Bakke* decision. "It will take years and hundreds of reverse-discrimination suits before we know what direction we're going," said the commissioner of human relations in Philadelphia.

Attention turned to the next big reverse discrimination case making its way through the courts. In 1974 the Kaiser Aluminum Company had attempted to increase the number of black craft workers at fifteen plants. At its plant in Gramercy, Louisiana, twenty-five miles up the Mississippi River from New Orleans, fewer than 2 percent of the craft workers were black, while the local labor force was 39 percent black. Pressured by the OFCC, Kaiser agreed that "not less than one minority employee enter" apprentice and craft training programs "for every nonminority employee" until the percentage of blacks in craft positions equaled the percentage of blacks in the local work force. Workers would be eligible to enter the training program on the basis of seniority, but there would be separate seniority lists for whites and blacks. The slots would then be divided one for one by race. Inevitably some blacks would skip past more senior whites.[68]

Brian F Weber, the "blue-collar Allan Bakke," was one of those white workers who were overlooked. He complained to the EEOC and asked for a copy of the Civil Rights Act of 1964. After reading the language of Title VII, he was convinced his rights had been violated. "I didn't think it was lawful," he recalled. "I thought the civil rights law would cover everyone, not just one race." Weber charged that the plan violated the clear intent of Title VII, which forbade discrimination against "any individual" because of race.[69]

Weber scored two early judicial victories: The U.S. District Court judge and the U.S. Circuit Court of Appeals both ruled in his favor. In a two to one decision, the appellate court held that Title VII made affirmative action programs permissible only to remedy discrimination against individual employees, not as a response to general societal discrimination. The ruling created a dilemma for the company: In order to satisfy the requirement that an affirmative action plan be a remedy for past discrimination, an employer would have to admit that it had discriminated and thereby invite Title VII lawsuits from blacks. Failure to admit past discrimination, on the other hand, would invite reverse discrimination suits from whites.

The company decided to appeal the ruling to the Supreme Court, which issued its decision in June 1979. Ruling against Weber, the Court held that Title VII did not prevent the voluntary adoption of race-conscious affirmative action plans. Justice

William J. Brennan, Jr., writing for the five to two majority, concluded that a literal interpretation of Title VII was "misplaced" and ignored the real intentions of the legislators. Reading his thirteen-page opinion from the bench, Brennan stressed that Title VII was designed to improve economic opportunities for blacks. To rule that employers could not take steps to create places for blacks in jobs from which they had been traditionally excluded, Brennan suggested, would undermine the very reason for the act's passage. An interpretation of Title VII that "forbade all race-conscious affirmative action," he wrote, "would bring about an end completely at variance with the purpose of the statute and must be rejected." Racial quotas were legal, he declared, as long as they were voluntarily adopted and not required by the federal government.[70]

The two dissenters sharply disputed Brennan's interpretation of Title VII. Chief Justice Burger called it "contrary to the explicit language of the statute and arrived at by means wholly incompatible with long-established principles of separation of powers." In a sarcastic thirty-seven-page dissent, Justice William Rehnquist scoffed at the majority decision. Quoting from the legislative history of Title VII, he insisted that Congress had intended to prevent employers from discriminating against—or in favor of—a person on the basis of race. He compared Brennan's reading of Title VII with George Orwell's novel *1984,* in which public officials twist and alter meanings of policies without pausing for breath. "By a tour de force reminiscent . . . of escape artists such as Houdini, the Court eludes clear statutory language, 'uncontradicted' legislative history, and uniform precedent," he said. The Court had introduced "into Title VII a tolerance for the very evil that the law was intended to eradicate."[71]

Rehnquist was in the minority in the *Weber* case, but changes in the Court's membership in the 1980s soon repositioned him in the majority. Ronald Reagan and George Bush made the appointment of judicial conservatives a top priority. Responding to the concerns of "angry white males," both men promised to select judges committed to "protecting the rights of law-abiding citizens," defending "traditional values," and practicing "judicial restraint." Along with appointing more than half of the federal judiciary, the Reagan-Bush team tilted the political balance on the Supreme Court decidedly to the right. In 1981 Reagan appointed Sandra Day O'Connor of Arizona, the first woman to serve on the High Court. When Chief Justice Warren Burger retired in 1986, Reagan elevated Rehnquist to chief justice and named to the vacancy the conservative Antonin Scalia, a federal judge who had taught at the University of Chicago Law School. In 1988 Reagan sought to replace centrist Lewis Powell, author of the *Bakke* decision, with Robert Bork, a conservative judge, but a coalition of civil rights and women's groups helped defeat the nomination. The seat was eventually filled by Anthony Kennedy, a federal appeals court judge from California. Thurgood Marshall, a stalwart of the civil rights battles of the 1950s and 1960s and a reliable liberal vote for an expansive interpretation of civil rights laws, retired in late June 1991. His replacement, Judge Clarence Thomas, an African-American who had served in the Reagan administration, had made clear over the years his opposition to race-based preference programs.[72]

The new conservative bloc whittled away at affirmative action in employment. In *Wards Cove Packing Company v. Atonio* (1989), the Court scaled back on its *Griggs* decision by shifting the burden of justifying "business necessity" from the employers to the employees. In 1990 a divided Court further limited the reach of affirmative action in *Adarand Constructors Inc. v. Peña,* ruling that racial discrimination, whether against whites or blacks, is generally unconstitutional, except where the government acts to remedy a clear pattern of past discrimination. It ruled that any race-based affirmative action program must be "narrowly tailored" to further "compelling governmental interests." "There can be no doubt," declared Clarence Thomas, the deciding vote in the five to four ruling, "that racial paternalism and its unintended consequences can be as poisonous and pernicious as any other form of discrimination."[73]

THE convoluted history of affirmative action has helped make it vulnerable to criticism. For conservatives, affirmative action served as a case study of the evils of expanded federal power, which allowed unelected bureaucrats and judges to thwart the will of the people. "In less than a decade, federal bureaucrats and judges had cast aside Congress's rejection of preferential treatment for minorities and stuffed the pages of the 1964 Civil Rights Act down Hubert Humphrey's throat," commented Arch Puddington, head of the Civil Rights Commission in the Reagan administration. Even objective observers were struck by the irony of having important policy decisions implemented without popular approval. "A nation that had repudiated racial quotas at every legislative opportunity has cheerfully accepted them in practice," wrote the columnist Edwin M. Yoder, Jr.[74]

For many Americans, affirmative action violated the cherished faith in color blindness and equality. "[T]he law regards man as man, and takes no account of his color," Justice John Marshall Harlan declared in his 1896 *Plessy v. Ferguson* dissent. Martin Luther King eloquently described the idea in his famous "I Have a Dream" speech when he proclaimed that people must "not be judged by the color of their skin but by the content of their character." For many whites, racial preferences mocked the treasured belief that success should be based on merit and hard work, not on birthright or race. "Seldom," charged Puddington, "has a democratic government's policy so completely contradicted the core values of its citizenry as racial preference does in violating the universally held American ideals of fairness and individual rights, including the right to be free from discrimination." Florida Congressman Charles T. Canady argued that the public has reacted against affirmative action because "such policies are inconsistent with equality as most Americans understand that term." According to Canady, most Americans recognize that "preferential treatment" and "equal opportunity" are "fundamentally incompatible.' "We cannot claim to be treating Americans equally," he declared, "while at the same time we grant preferences or special advantages to some based solely on the fact that they happen to belong to certain racial or gender groups."[75]

Conservatives, however, do not have a monopoly on appeals to equality. Proponents of affirmative action have made a competing moral claim. For many African-Americans, racial preferences are a symbol of the nation's enduring commitment to racial equality. As the Swedish sociologist Gunnar Myrdal pointed out in his classic *An American Dilemma* (1944), there has always existed a tension between the American belief in "liberty, equality, justice, and fair opportunity for everybody" and the irrational prejudice that governed the treatment of African-Americans. This contradiction between belief and behavior—"a problem in the heart of the white American"—constituted, for Myrdal, the American dilemma. Despite enormous progress in addressing the most obvious manifestations of racial prejudice, the dilemma persists. Calls for color blindness often appear as a form of racial denial, an attempt to forget the nation's troubled racial history. "After two hundred fifty years of slavery, one hundred years of apartheid, and forty years of continuing discrimination, we cannot turn a blind eye to our past and now enact a 'color blind' code of justice," declared Jesse Jackson. Proponents see affirmative action as necessary to guarantee the promise of equality to a group that had long been excluded from flowery speeches about the American Dream. "In order to get beyond racism," Justice Harry A. Blackmun declared, "we must first take account of race."[76]

The competing claims on a cherished American belief in equality have exposed deep racial divisions in America. A *Los Angeles Times* poll in 1991 showed that nearly two-thirds of whites opposed expansion of affirmative action, while 60 percent of blacks called for more rigorous enforcement of antidiscrimination laws. By a margin of 65 percent to 30 percent, blacks blamed discrimination as the main cause of their having "worse jobs, income and housing"; whites disagreed by a nearly identical margin: 60 to 33.[77] A poll commissioned by the NAACP Legal Defense and Education Fund in January 1989 found blacks and whites "worlds apart" in their perception of race relations. Blacks by an overwhelming majority supported a larger government with many services; whites preferred a smaller government with fewer services. The authors of a major study of racial attitudes in America concluded: "The existence of this perceptual gulf helps define the context within which members of the two races consider the causes and solutions of racial inequality."[78]

The racial gap played havoc with political parties, alienating those Democrats who endorsed preferences from their traditional working-class constituency and energizing Republicans, who appealed to the racial anxieties of white men. During the 1970s rising unemployment and the decline in high-wage manufacturing jobs eroded public confidence that opportunities for minorities would not hurt white Americans. "As white Americans began to think of affirmative action as a fixture in a zero-sum game, their views began to shift," observed the political scientist Linda Faye Williams. A study by Democratic pollster Stanley Greenberg in 1985, investigating white male blue-collar defection from the Democratic party, found that affirmative action played a key role. "Quotas and minority preferences were a primary source of anti-government, anti-Democrat anger among white blue-collar voters," the report concluded. Republicans successfully tapped into the ideological gap between blacks and whites by creating "wedge issues," which allowed them to raise issues of taxation, welfare spending, and the general role of government that split the Democratic coalition along racial lines. "Direct appeals to racial prejudice may no longer be acceptable in American politics, but race, in an indirect and sometimes subliminal way, remains a strong undercurrent in presidential politics and a driving force in the battle today between Republicans and Democrats," concluded the journalist Thomas Edsall.[79]

The emergence of a Republican majority in Congress in 1994 and conservative gains in state legislatures across the nation helped push the issue of affirmative action to a prominent position on the public agenda. In November 1996 California voters by a 54–46 margin passed Proposition 209. This ballot initiative banned the use of race and sex in college admissions, contracting, and public employment. Echoing the language of the Civil Rights Act of 1964, the initiative declared: "Neither the State of California nor any of its political subdivisions or agents shall use race, sex, color, ethnicity, or national origin as a criterion for either discrimination against, or granting preferential treatment to, any individual or group in the operation of the State's public employment, public education, or public contracting." Men overwhelmingly supported the initiative (61 to 39 percent) while women disapproved (52 to 48 percent). Blacks and Latinos opposed it in large numbers.[80]

Opponents of affirmative action have received powerful support from an unlikely source, African-American intellectuals, many of whom have been beneficiaries of affirmative action programs. Unlike conservatives who view preferences in moral terms, black critics focus on the unintended consequences of a well-meaning program. Author Shelby Steele concluded that "affirmative action has shown itself to be more bad than good and that blacks . . . now stand to lose more from it than they gain." He argued that quotas undermined black morale, contributing to "an enlargement of self-doubt," by creating the perception that successful blacks have not earned their positions. According to black writers Jeff Howard and Ray Hammond, the self-doubt is rooted in "rumors of inferiority." Journalist Charles Krauthammer summarized their conclusion: "Affirmative action advertises and amplifies the rumor." Robert L. Woodson, Sr., a former Republican presidential challenger, contends that preferences not only have "failed in their intended purpose" but "have often provided opportunities for flagrant abuse." The "most devastating" unintended consequence of affirmative action, he argued, is a "culture of victimization" that "undermines the tradition of self-determination and personal responsibility that had long provided a foundation for the stability of the black community." Other scholars have pointed out that affirmative action has exacerbated white resentment, making a class-based coalition even less likely. "Many white Americans have turned, not against blacks, but against a strategy that emphasized programs perceived to benefit only racial minorities," sociologist William Julius Wilson has concluded.[81]

Unintended consequences such as these have indeed occurred, but they are not always bad, and a convincing case can be made that affirmative action has done more good than harm. While scholars disagree about the extent of the impact, probably a majority concede that affirmative action—together with changes in the economy—has helped open the doors of opportunity for minorities and women, increasing their representation in the work force. Both the gender gap and, to a lesser degree, the racial gap in median earnings have narrowed. Affirmative action has lifted the fortunes of many middle-class educated women, whose share of full-time professional and administrative jobs nearly tripled to 40 percent between 1960 and 1990. Blacks—mostly women— tripled their share of management, technical, and clerical jobs. The salaries of black male managers and administrators, who were paid twenty-five cents to every dollar that their white male counterparts earned in 1960, have climbed to sixty-nine cents on the dollar. A survey by Georgia State University said 87 percent reported interracial friendships, which commonly began at work.[82]

Critics of affirmative action are coming to realize that unintended consequences can have an impact on any effort to challenge the status quo. Fresh evidence from such states as California and Texas, which have banned using racial preferences in college admissions, suggests that color blindness, for all its moral and political appeal, may not be a practical option. In 1998 the University of California at Berkeley reported a 57 percent drop in the number of black applicants and a 40 percent decline in the number of Hispanic high school seniors who had been accepted for admission. For the University of California at Los Angeles (UCLA) the decline was 43 percent for African-American students and 33 percent for Hispanic-Americans. The figures shocked some conservatives and forced them to consider the possibility that widespread resegregation would follow from a rigid ban on racial preferences.[83]

The unintended consequences of abolishing affirmative action have led many conservatives to rethink their opposition. Harvard sociologist Nathan Glazer changed his mind because of the "unforeseen and unexpected" developments that followed the civil rights revolution. Like many liberals of his generation, Glazer believed that knocking down the legal walls that prevented blacks from participating in society would produce immediate and tangible economic benefits. Instead, he noted regretfully, the gap between black and white widened, inner-city schools continued to decline, and many black nuclear families unraveled. In the face of such evidence, Glazer reluctantly concluded, "an insistence on color-blindness means the effective exclusion today of African Americans from positions of influence, wealth, and power." For Glazer, it is a clear case of modifying views when principles meet reality. "It's the consequences," he told the *New York Times* in 1998. "It's one thing to fight for a principle, which is a very good principle, especially if you don't expect it to win. Then, as you come close, the consequences become a little larger."[84]

The strange history of affirmative action provides a striking example of the unpredictability of public policy. The greatest strength of the American political system occasionally can be its greatest weakness: Power is so diffuse and decentralized that it is difficult, if not impossible, for one branch of government to control the outcome of its actions. Unelected staff members of two key executive agencies—the EEOC and the OFCC—reinterpreted Humphrey's real intent. Unelected judges later codified their interpretation into law. Now that affirmative action is the law of the land, critics are finding it difficult, if not impossible, to abolish. "Perhaps the most important lesson I've learned is that there are no airtight, completely coherent, unassailable and holistic answers on the question of affirmative action that are not only theoretically perfect, but instrumentally practical," said John Bunzel, the former president of San Jose State University and an outspoken critic of affirmative action. "Any intelligent person who wrestles with it is going to be vulnerable and subject to the twists and turns of unintended consequences."[85]

Chapter 4

Still the Golden Door?:
The Immigration Act of 1965

❀

*T*HE grandson of German Jewish immigrants and a representative of one of the nation's most ethnically diverse districts, Emanuel Celler was the ideal person to lead the administration's fight to liberalize U.S. immigration policy. As a freshman representative in 1922, the peppery Brooklyn Democrat had devoted his maiden speech on the House floor to an attack on the national origins clause. Now, seven presidents and forty-three years later, Celler was the senior member of the House and the powerful head of the Judiciary Committee. Despite his grandfatherly figure—bandy-legged and stooped with only a thin patch of white hair covering his tanned head—he remained as colorful and combative as ever. In 1965 nothing was more important to him than passing President Johnson's immigration reform package. "The bill cures the evil of judging a man by his place of birth rather than his inherent worth," he declared from the House floor.[1]

The national origins clause had its roots in the xenophobic 1920s, when many Americans worried about the nation's ability to assimilate the millions of new immigrants who were flooding the nation's cities. "The welfare of the United States demands that the door should be closed to immigrants for a time," observed an influential congressman in 1920. "We are being made a dumping-ground for the human wreckage of the [world] war." The fears were widespread. Journalists complained that in cities like New

York, where three out of every four persons were foreigners or the children of foreigners, immigrants were responsible for rising crime rates; prominent scientists infatuated by new theories of eugenics, claimed that recent immigrants from southern Europe and Asia possessed more "inborn socially inadequate qualities" and were therefore unable to assimilate; business leaders fretted that the newcomers would swell the ranks of organized labor. In 1924 Congress responded to these fears by passing the Johnson-Reed Immigration Act. Under the law the government allocated visas to Eastern Hemisphere nations in ratios determined by the number of persons of each nationality in the United States in 1890. Not surprisingly, Europe consumed 98 percent of the quota, leaving only 2 percent for the rest of the world. Three countries—Ireland, Great Britain, and Germany—accounted for nearly 70 percent of the total. In addition to dramatically cutting immigration rates from southern Europe—Italians and Greeks were especially hard hit—the law almost completely excluded Asians. The quota did not apply to spouses or minor children of U.S. citizens or to residents of the Western Hemisphere, who could emigrate without restriction.[2]

For decades Celler and other reformers had struggled in vain to overturn the national origins formula. "My efforts were about as useless as trying to make a tiger eat grass or a cow eat meat," he told his colleagues. Celler argued that the clause, based on false notions about the superiority of white northern Europeans, was racist and damaged America's credibility in the Third World. It was also inefficient since it prevented unused quotas from being reassigned to nations with long waiting lists. Nearly half of all quota positions went unfilled every year while nations with low quotas, such as Italy and Greece, had long waiting lines. The rigid rules not only were discriminatory and racist but also prevented the United States from attracting the finest talent from around the world. Under the national origins system a construction worker from Britain or a bartender from Ireland had a far better chance of being admitted to the United States than did a scientist from Italy or a physician from Pakistan. Finally, Celler pointed out that the system was obsolete and Congress had regularly passed special legislation that allowed people to enter outside the quota system. Between 1953 and 1964 nearly-two thirds of those admitted to America came as nonquota family members, as refugees, or as a result of special legislation. In 1965 *Time* dismissed national origins as "an unworkable patchwork of discrimination and special dispensations."[3]

Despite the strong arguments against the clause, efforts to abolish it ran into a wall of opposition from conservative and patriotic groups. Defenders of the clause argued that basing immigration on national origins helped preserve the cohesiveness of American culture and kept out radical elements. In 1952 reformers pushed for a major revision of immigration policy but instead ended up with the McCarran-Walter Act. It represented a modest improvement over the old act, but it kept the national origins clause intact and added a few new objectionable provisions. The law created an Asian-Pacific Triangle that included most of east and south Asia, granted individual nations within the region a quota of one hundred, and capped the total for the triangle at two thousand. It also required immigrants with Asian blood to apply for admission against the quota set for the Asian-Pacific Triangle and not for the countries of their birth. A woman born in Canada who had a Chinese father, for example, would have to apply for admission using one of China's 105 annual visas, which were backlogged eighty-three years. In addition, the act restricted newly independent nations in the Western Hemisphere to quotas of 100. President Truman vetoed the measure, calling it "a slur on the patriotism, the capacity, and the decency of a large part of our citizenry." But Congress overrode the veto, and liberals lacked the votes during the 1950s to force major changes in immigration policy.[4]

In 1960 the election of John F. Kennedy offered new hope for breaking the logjam. A proud descendant of Irish immigrants,

Kennedy had been on record opposing existing laws and had authored *A Nation of Immigrants,* a paean to the contributions of immigrants to American society. Other forces combined to make the moment ripe for reform. The moral fervor of the civil rights movement made it difficult to justify a policy that based immigration on race. "Everywhere else in our national life, we have eliminated discrimination based on national origins," Attorney General Robert Kennedy told Congress in 1964. "Yet, this system is still the foundation of our immigration law." By the 1960s the Cold War between the United States and the Soviet Union had shifted from Europe to Asia and Africa, the nations most adversely affected by national origins. How could the United States present itself as a symbol of freedom in the ideological struggle with communism when it practiced discrimination based on race? Finally, the children and grandchildren of immigrants had attained considerable political power and influence, and most favored abolishing national origins quotas. By 1960 first- and second-generation immigrants made up more than 15 percent of the population in twenty-four states and were especially influential in many of the larger states that had become the backbone of the Democratic party: New York, Connecticut, New Jersey, California, Illinois, and Michigan.[5]

Despite the growing logic in favor of abandoning national origins, Kennedy moved slowly. He had won the presidency by a narrow margin and was reluctant to offend powerful congressional leaders who could jeopardize his other domestic legislation. He took the first tentative steps in 1962, when he directed Abba Schwartz, administrator of the Bureau of Security and Consular Affairs, to prepare an administration reform package. By 1963 Kennedy was looking for the right opportunity to unveil his new plan. That moment occurred in May, when Francis Walter, the powerful satrap of the House Immigration Subcommittee and staunch opponent of reform, died after a brief illness. Less than two months later Kennedy sent his proposals to Congress.[6]

The centerpiece of Kennedy's legislation was a phaseout of the national origins provision over a five-year period. "The use of a national origins system is without basis in either logic or reason," the president wrote. "It neither satisfies a national need nor accomplishes an international purpose." In place of the national origins system, he proposed that immigrants from outside the Western Hemisphere apply on a "first-come, first-serve" basis within specific preference categories. Half the visas would be allotted on the basis of skill or talent; 30 percent were reserved for the unmarried sons and daughters of U.S. citizens over twenty-one, and 20 percent for spouses and unmarried children of aliens admitted for permanent residence. The legislation called for abolishing the Asian-Pacific Triangle and for ending the 100-person cap on immigration from former British colonies in the Western Hemisphere—both key provisions of the 1952 amendments. It also added parents of U.S. citizens to the nonquota category. The president suggested that total immigration from outside the Western Hemisphere be limited to 165,000 annually, with no single country permitted to have more than 10 percent of the total.[7]

In making its case for reform to undecided lawmakers and an uncertain public, the administration argued that the national origins clause was racist and damaging to America's moral authority in the Third World. The "discriminatory nature" of the law "contradicts our world position as a defender of individual dignity and the equality of man," stated the administration's Blue Book, a thick briefing book created to make sure the administration spoke with one voice when testifying before Congress. "Our present immigration laws are obviously inconsistent with our professed ideals and needlessly provide ammunition for exploitation by our enemies." In public speeches and congressional testimony, administration spokesmen underscored the moral imperative of changing course. "This system is a blot on our relations with other countries," Robert Kennedy wrote in the *New York Times*. "It violates our basic national philosophy because it judges individuals not on their worth, but solely on their place of birth—or even where their ancestors happened to be born."[8]

The White House realized that moral appeals would have little impact on Americans—including many otherwise liberal blue collar-workers—who feared that abolishing national origins would produce an upsurge of immigrants, especially from Asia, Africa, and Latin America. The Blue Book advised spokesmen to emphasize that the new preference system "leaves the present authorized level of immigration substantially unchanged." According to the White House estimates, the legislation would produce a net increase of sixty thousand newcomers, but since fifty-five thousand of those would be authorized under existing law, there would be only five thousand more than the current law allowed. Reiterating the theme, Celler instructed his House colleagues that "the effect of the bill on our population [in numbers] would be quite insignificant." Edward Kennedy made the same point in the Senate. "Our cities will not be flooded with a million immigrants annually," he said. "Under the proposed bill, the present level of immigration remains substantially the same."[9]

The administration also insisted its proposal would not substantially alter existing patterns of immigration. The White House admitted "there will be some shift of immigration" away from northern Europe, but the chief beneficiaries of the new legislation would be those nations in eastern and southern Europe with the largest backlogs of applicants: Italy, Greece, Poland, Portugal, and Spain. Since new immigrants "will have to compete and to qualify to get in," they will "not be predominantly from Asia and Africa." Edward Kennedy told his colleagues that "the ethnic mix of this country will not be upset." The measure, he concluded, "will not inundate America with immigrants from any one country or area, or the most overpopulated and economically deprived nations of Africa and Asia." The Blue Book summed up the administration's position by arguing that "there would not be any horde or flood of immigrants from any country, any continent, or from all of them put together."[10]

If the reforms were to have any chance of passing, they would need the support of Ohio Congressman Michael Feighan, who took over as head of the influential House Immigration Subcommittee following Walter's death. At first Feighan was hard to read. Despite having close ties to conservative and patriotic groups, he had not been outspoken on immigration issues, and he represented a district with a high concentration of immigrants. In fact, during his twenty-six years in the House the Democrat had left few footprints, which at least left open the possibility that he could be swayed to follow the White House path. That hope soon proved illusory. In their first meeting White House officials described Feighan as "very cool" to their proposal. "He made us absolutely no promises about whether he would support it or whether he was sympathetic," recalled Norbert Schlei, an assistant attorney general and the chief architect of the administration's legislative strategy. Feighan also had a reputation for being temperamental and unpredictable, and his actions over the next few months added weight to the charges. He made headlines charging that Soviet spies had infiltrated the CIA and demanding that the State Department bar British actor Richard Burton from entering the country because of his extramarital affair with Elizabeth Taylor. According to *Life* magazine, Feighan was so incensed by the White House's decision to submit civil rights legislation that he publicly condemned the president as a "Communist sympathizer" and a "nigger lover."[11]

Perhaps even more troubling, an acrimonious personal feud between Celler and Feighan threatened to prevent congressional action on the legislation. As head of the parent House Judiciary Committee Celler had moved to consolidate control over the Immigration Subcommittee following Walter's death, stripping Feighan of many of the informal powers that had accumulated over the years. The Ohio congressman angrily denounced the effort and attempted to outmaneuver Celler by activating a defunct joint committee that he could use as a power base. In a close vote the House refused to endorse the move. The struggle consumed most of the legislative session and left Feighan in a sour mood and with little incentive to cooperate with the administration. The bill was still bottled up in his subcommittee on November 21, when the president left town for a trip to Dallas. "Immigration reform will just have to wait in the House until the differences between Messrs. Celler and Feighan are satisfactorily resolved," observed the American Jewish Committee.[12]

The 1964 elections changed the political calculus for Feighan. The veteran lawmaker received the scare of his political life when Ronald M. Mottl, a Democratic rival of Czech descent, made immigration the major focus of his primary challenge against him. "I do not understand," Mottl said, how Feighan, "representing a cosmopolitan district with a large population whose national origins are declared 'second class' by the present law, could oppose the administration proposal." Feighan managed to squeak out a narrow victory, but his opponent promised a rematch if the congressman continued to stall on immigration reform. President Lyndon Johnson, who promised to push the Kennedy immigration bill through Congress, used Feighan's political vulnerability to his advantage. He showered him with attention, invited him to travel on Air Force One, and assigned a staff member to respond to his concerns. At the same time he made clear that disloyalty would carry a heavy price. After his landslide victory in 1964 the president "packed" the subcommittee with administration loyalists and leaked to the press that he might be looking for a candidate to run against Feighan in 1966.[13]

As Congress convened in January 1965, Feighan faced a difficult political situation: The primary challenge suggested that his political survival required him to support some form of immigration reform, but he also wanted to appease his conservative followers and, perhaps most of all, deny Celler the legislative victory he desired. In February 1965 he floated a trial balloon in a speech before the American Coalition of Patriotic Societies. For the first time he publicly supported elimination of national origins quotas, but unlike the White House, which claimed the clause was racist, Feighan denounced it for being ineffective. "If the system was intended to restrict immigration to the United States it has failed," he asserted. The clever ploy allowed him to support reform by claiming that the old system was too permissive. The move, however, left him supporting the thrust of the administration's bill, even if for different reasons.[14]

The administration understood the political considerations that produced Feighan's change of heart, and over the next few months the White House worked closely with him to negotiate their differences in order to produce a bill that would satisfy everyone. The key stumbling block was the congressman's insistence on creating a worldwide system that would end the Western Hemisphere's nonquota status. "Feighan appears to be looking for a way to justify a vote to abolish the national origins system," Schlei wrote the president. "The justification has to make sense to the traditional supporters of the national origins system." The only way he can accomplish that is "to say that in return for scrapping the national origins system—which never really worked anyway—he has gotten a system that for the first time in our history puts a limit on all immigration, not just immigration from 'quota' areas."[15]

The administration refused to bend on the issue of nonquota status for the Western Hemisphere. Secretary of State Dean Rusk made clear that "he absolutely could not live with a numerical ceiling of any kind on the Western Hemisphere." He warned that Feighan's proposal would violate the "special relationship" that existed between the United States and its neighbors and "vex and dumbfound our Latin America friends." Not only would it be politically costly, but imposing a cap on immigration from the Western Hemisphere was unnecessary since demand was low and existing controls effectively curtailed unwanted immigrants. Attorney General Nicholas Katzenbach, who had replaced Robert Kennedy in 1964, told the House that "there is not much pressure to come to the United States from these countries," and Assistant Attorney General Schlei advised the president that labor, security, and health restrictions "can be so administered as to keep immigration from the Western Hemisphere at almost any desired level." By May, Feighan had relented, telling Jack Valenti, Johnson's special adviser, that "he was willing to go along with the State Department's views" and was "preparing substitute language to take care of non-quota countries in Latin America."[16]

On June 1 Feighan submitted his substitute immigration bill. Like the administration's proposal, the congressman's measure abolished the national origins quota system, ended the Asian-Pacific Triangle provisions, and allowed immigration from the Western Hemisphere to continue without numerical restrictions. Most of the differences were technical: the timing for phasing out national origins, restrictions on the president's power to reserve visas, and an increase in the number of refugees permitted. "In sum," Schlei advised Johnson, "the bill will create a fair, reasonable and nondiscriminatory system of immigration to the United States for permanent residence and will provide for the continuance of a reasonable limit on the number of immigrants."[17]

There were, however, two key differences between the Feighan and White House proposals. First, the congressman added a provision making it harder for newcomers to get work visas in the United States. It stipulated that applicants for admission—except for the immediate families of U.S. citizens—could obtain work visas only after the Labor Department had certified that there were not enough U.S. workers "able, qualified, willing, and available" to perform the jobs and that the aliens' terms of employment would not adversely affect prevailing wages and working conditions. The new rule applied to all immigrants, but the Ohio

Democrat designed it specifically to limit workers migrating from Latin America.[18]

Second, Feighan insisted on reversing the administration's preference structure, giving first priority to "uniting families of United States citizens and permanent resident aliens." In his proposal only two preference categories were reserved for those with professions, skills, occupations, or special talents needed in the United States. With little debate or discussion, the White House accepted the new preference system, thus transforming an immigration reform bill into a family unification measure. The change made the bill more palatable to conservatives, who believed that a policy based on family ties would be even *more* restrictive than the old national origins system. "Nobody is quite so apt to be of the same national origins of our present citizens as are members of their immediate families," declared a representative of the American Legion, "and the great bulk of immigrants henceforth will not merely hail from the same parent countries as our present citizens, but will be their closer relatives." Administration spokesmen picked up on the theme, reassuring lawmakers that family unification would favor nations already represented in the population. Celler announced: "Since the people of Africa and Asia have very few relatives here, comparatively few could immigrate from those countries because they have no family ties in the U.S." Even the staid *Wall Street Journal* noted that the family preference system "insured that the new immigration pattern would not stray radically from the old one."[19]

Much of the debate in the House and Senate revolved around Republican efforts to attach a provision that would have ended the nonquota status for the Western Hemisphere, the same provision that Feighan had voluntarily removed from his substitute bill. Many House members expressed concern about population explosions and hordes of newcomers flooding across the border in search of work. They had powerful evidence to support their fears. The population of South America was projected to swell from 69 million to 600 million by the end of the century, and migration from the south had already grown dramatically, from 95,701 in 1960 to 139,282 in 1964. These figures, noted the *Washington Evening Star,* "added substance to warnings that the time is ripe to erect a dam against a possible flood of immigrants."[20]

The president managed to twist enough arms in the House to defeat Republican efforts to impose a cap, but he had less legislative wiggle room in the Senate. Two powerful members of the Senate Judiciary Committee, North Carolina's Sam Ervin and Minority Leader Everett Dirksen, made support for a numerical limit on Western Hemisphere immigration a condition of their support. Worried that the bill would otherwise die in committee, Johnson reluctantly acquiesced. Even many conservatives who opposed ending the national origins quota hailed the new legislation. "This bill," claimed Republican Arch Moore from West Virginia, "is more restrictive than present law. It imposes even more rigid requirements, and it sets more specific limitations than does present law." On September 15 the Senate approved the new, tighter restrictions by an overwhelming 76–18 vote. The changes survived the conference committee, and on September 30 Congress sent the 1965 immigration reform bill to the president for his signature.[21]

The legislation represented the most important revision of immigration law in nearly fifty years. First, it abolished the Asian-Pacific Triangle and phased out the national origins categories over three years. During the transition the quota system would remain in place, but any unused slots would be redistributed to give preference to candidates in nations with long waiting lists. Second, it placed a ceiling of 120,000 visas from the Western Hemisphere, but there was no preference system established and no limit on the number of immigrants who could come from each country. Third, it added a labor certification procedure for immigrants planning to come to the United States for work. Finally,

· ·

it capped immigration from the Eastern Hemisphere at 170,000, with no country eligible for more than 20,000 visas. The government would distribute visas on a first-come, first-served basis within certain preference categories. Four of the seven categories, accounting for 74 percent of the total, were set aside for family unification; 20 percent were reserved for those with special talents or skills; and 6 percent were designated for refugees.[22]

First Preference: Unmarried sons and daughters (over age twenty-one) of U.S. citizens (maximum of 20 percent).

Second Preference: Spouses and unmarried children of legal aliens (20 percent plus any not required for the first preference).

Third Preference: Scientists, artists, and professionals of exceptional ability (maximum of 10 percent).

Fourth Preference: Married children (over age twenty-one) of U.S. citizens (10 percent plus any not required for the first three preferences).

Fifth Preference: Brothers and sisters of U.S. citizens (24 percent plus any not required for the first four preferences).

Sixth Preference: Skilled and unskilled workers in occupations for which labor is in short supply (maximum of 10 percent).

Seventh Preference: Refugees to whom conditional entry or adjustment of status may be granted (maximum of 6 percent).

In July, standing in the shadow of the Statue of Liberty, Johnson signed the Immigration Act of 1965. "The bill that we sign today is not a revolutionary bill. It does not affect the lives of millions. . . . Yet it is still one of the most important acts of this Congress and of this administration. For it does repair a very deep and powerful flaw in the fabric of American justice." The press hailed the new bill, emphasizing that it was both more humane and more restrictive than national origins. Most agreed with the assessment in the *Congressional Quarterly* that by making the Western Hemisphere a quota area, the new law would actually place greater restrictions on immigration. The legislation, it noted, "closed off the possibility of a very substantial increase in future immigration from the one area on which there previously had been no numerical restrictions." In this sense, it concluded, the act "foreclosed any long-term upward trend in the numbers of immigrants."[23]

IT was clearly Congress's intent both to maintain immigration levels and to continue to draw immigrants from Europe. Even during the transition period (1965–68), however, subtle but important changes began to emerge. Between 1953 and 1965 the United States welcomed almost 270,000 newcomers a year, and the administration had projected the reforms would add only 5,000 to that total. Yet in 1967 immigration jumped to 361,972, the highest in forty-three years. The following year an additional 90,000 people arrived, bringing the total to 454,448. As expected, European immigration shifted from northern to southern and eastern countries: In the first seven months Italy saw its number of visas climb from 9,987 to 24,967; Greece from 1,926 to 8,917; and Portugal from 1,698 to 8,719. There was a corresponding drop in the number of visas issued to previously high-quota countries that had no backlogs: Canada fell from 40,013 to 25,563; Britain from 28,698 to 20,831; and Germany from 25,171 to 18,595. What most surprised observers was the sharp increase in Asian immigrants. Three countries—China, India, and the Philippines—and Hong Kong were responsible for almost 80 percent of the increased migration.[24]

The numbers of new immigrants continued to climb after the new law went into effect in 1968. During the first few years the United States averaged nearly 400,000 newcomers. By the end of the 1970s the number had soared to 800,000. In the 1980s immigration, still theoretically limited to 270,000 a year, averaged more than 700,000. During the decade the nation absorbed 8.9

million legal immigrants and, by most estimates, at least 2 million illegal ones. In absolute numbers the 1980s saw more immigrants (legal and illegal) than any other decade in U.S. history.[25] By the early 1990s more than 1 million new legal immigrants were arriving in the United States every year, accounting for almost half of its population growth. By some estimates, over a thirty-year period (1965–95) the 1965 reforms were responsible for an additional 40 million people coming to the United States. The pattern is expected to continue into the next century. According to the National Research Council, if current immigration levels continue, there will be in 2050 in the United States 387 million people, 124 million more than in 1997. Immigration will account for 80 million, or two-thirds, of the increase.[26]

How could the forecast in 1965 have been so wrong? In 1982 the journalist Theodore White, looking back on a half century of liberal legislation, called the Immigration Act of 1965 "the most thoughtless of the many acts of the Great Society." The result, he observed, was "a stampede, almost an invasion," in which the "sources of fresh arrivals would be determined not by those already here, but by the push and pressures of those everywhere who hungered to enter." He had a good point, for neither Congress nor the White House had carefully analyzed the potential impact of the family preference system. Congressman Feighan had rewritten the administration's bill, bragging with some justification, "Anyone with sense knows that everything of substance in the bill is mine," but there is no evidence that anyone in the White House attempted to calculate how the change would affect immigration patterns. Feighan, with no vested interest in immigration policy, had proposed family unification as a way to save his political career. The administration, reflecting the equalitarian ethos of that liberal era, viewed abolishing national origins as a moral issue and was willing to compromise on specifics in order to achieve its ultimate objective. In the political brokering between Capitol Hill and the White House, which was absolutely central to the outcome, few stopped to consider that a policy based on blood could produce different results from one based on talent. Immigration policy is always unpredictable, dependent on many variables—population increase, natural disasters, international economics, changing expectations—that are beyond the control of policy makers. Legislators added to the uncertainty by adopting a major policy change without carefully calculating potential consequences.[27]

Legislators never considered how family unification could produce a chain of migration that would confound efforts to control immigration. Under the new preference system, an engineering student from India could come to the United States to study, find a job after graduating, get labor certification, and become a legal resident alien. His new status would then entitle him to bring over his wife, and six years later, after being naturalized, his brothers and sisters. They in turn could begin the process all over again by sponsoring their wives, husbands, children, and siblings. Within a dozen years one immigrant entering as a skilled worker could generate dozens of visas for distant relatives.[28]

Under the new system parents of U.S. citizens did not count toward the cap for each hemisphere, and the administration had assured Congress that even with this provision the total of all family members entering would be fewer than 40,000 annually. Yet in the first decade after the 1965 act passed the figures were about double the estimate, and they continued to grow. At the same time the liberalized family preference system produced a dramatic upsurge in the number of close relatives entering under the new system. In 1978 immediate family members topped 125,000, the vast majority from Asia, Mexico, or Central and South America. The next year immediate family members increased to more than 138,000. Just one nation, Mexico, sent almost 30,000 nonquota family members to the United States every year. In 1995, a typical year, relatives accounted for almost two-thirds of total admissions. Those admitted under employment-based preferences accounted for only 12 percent, but even among employment-based admissions, family ties were important: More than half the immigrants admitted in 1995 on employment preference visas were spouses or children of those entering for employment purposes.[29]

The family preference system was the chief source of the upsurge in immigration, but U.S. refugee policy also padded the numbers. The legislation designated 17,400 places in the annual quota of immigrants for refugees. On the day that he signed the act, Johnson used his parole authority to initiate an airlift to Cuba that brought about 360,000 Cubans to the United States between 1965 and 1979. The floodgates opened again in 1980, when Fidel Castro allowed thousands of Cubans, including many criminals and mental patients, to board creaky boats and head for American shores. By 1990 more than 800,000 Cuban refugees had entered the United States. The same month that he signed the legislation, Johnson made the fateful decision to send American ground troops to Vietnam. While no one at the time saw a connection between fighting communism in Southeast Asia and reforming immigration policy, the two became inextricably linked when the war effort faltered and a tidal wave of refugees fled Communist Indochina. In 1970 only about 10,000 Vietnamese were living in the United States. By the end of the decade that number had swelled to 400,000, and ten years later more than 1 million Vietnam War refugees and their children had settled in the country.[30]

Lawmakers not only had failed to anticipate the increased volume of immigration but had unwittingly produced a revolution in migration patterns. Congress and the administration accepted Feighan's two provisions—family unification and labor certification—believing they would preserve existing immigration patterns and discourage migrants from Latin America and Asia. In fact, they did just the opposite. Despite their large numbers in the United States, many northern European immigrants lacked the close family ties needed to benefit from the new system. Many came over as single men, applied for jobs, married Americans, and raised families. However, immigrants from southern Europe and especially from Asia emigrated as families and were therefore better positioned to take advantage of the family unification provisions. The tough new labor certification compounded the problem. Congress designed the provision to keep out unwanted immigrants from South America, but in practice it had a greater impact on restricting newcomers from Europe. The vast majority of migrants from Europe had been unskilled laborers, the very people who were locked out by the Labor Department's new certification process.[31]

Immigration from Western Europe plummeted in response to the changes. Ireland, which had one of the largest quotas under the National Origins Act, was perhaps hardest hit by the new rules. Historically, Irish immigrants had been low-skilled workers without close relatives in the United States. Usually only the eldest son would emigrate, leaving his brothers in Ireland to help the family. After 1968 Irish who wished to emigrate to the United States discovered that they were in occupations that the Labor Department would not certify or that they lacked the close kinship ties required by the family preference system. In 1968 the secretary of labor warned that under the new rules "Irish immigration will cease for 2 or 3 years." The same was true, he advised, of "other countries which have traditionally been under their quotas—England, Germany, France, and most of the Northern European countries."[32]

Asian emigrants rushed to fill the vacuum created by the downturn in European migration. In 1965 the administration and most members of Congress believed that immigration from Asia would increase only slightly. It seemed like a reasonable assumption at the time: Visa lines were small, and there were no visible signs that Asians were preparing to flood into the country. It soon became apparent, however, that lines were small because of

. .

dim expectations; quotas had been so low most Asians had had little hope of coming to the United States. Important changes in technology—the proliferation of television and the emergence of inexpensive jet airplanes—helped raise expectations and narrow the distance between Asia and the United States. By the 1970s American television shows were blanketing Asian nations with bountiful images of consumer goods. Almost 90 percent of all shows on Korean television were produced in the United States, and in the Philippines the figure was 50 percent. Attracted by the lure of good jobs and of American consumer culture, many immigrants decided to travel to the United States, and once here, many chose to stay. Unlike past generations of immigrants who had to endure the hardship of long boat rides, this generation could hop on a plane in Manila after breakfast and arrive in the United States before dinner.[33]

The wave of Asian immigrants following the 1965 act took advantage of the new labor certification process. Unlike the impoverished and often illiterate laborers who had once flocked to American shores, many of the new Asian migrants came from middle-class backgrounds and had professional or technical skills. From 1910 to 1930, a period of heavy immigration, only about 1.8 percent of the immigrants had professional or technical skills; by 1973 nearly 10 percent of the immigrants had such skills. About one-fifth of all Asian immigrants in 1973 were professional or technical workers. Many middle-class Asian professionals were either unemployed or underemployed in their home nations. India, for example, had twenty thousand unemployed physicians in 1970 and a surplus of a hundred thousand engineers in 1974. The educated middle class in such countries as India, the Philippines, and Korea realized that they could have better lives by finding employment in the United States. "Wages in Manila are barely enough to answer for my family's needs," said a Philippine immigrant. "I must go abroad to better my chances."[34]

Many of the new Asian immigrants used the labor certification system to gain employment in the health services. The same year that Congress changed the immigration law, it also passed Medicare and Medicaid, which created an enlarged demand for medical services, especially in inner-city hospitals. Growing private health insurance plans also stimulated a need for more medical services. American medical schools tried to adjust by admitting more students, but demand outpaced supply, and many strapped inner-city hospitals looked abroad for doctors and nurses. Between 1969 and 1973 more than fifty thousand doctors and almost forty thousand nurses were admitted on permanent or temporary visas. The Association of American Medical Colleges reported that 46 percent of all physicians licensed in 1972 were graduates of foreign medical schools. A large majority of the immigrant physicians—more than 70 percent—came from India, the Philippines, Korea, Iran, Taiwan, Thailand, Pakistan, and China. By 1974 Asian immigrants made up nearly one of five practicing physicians in the United States. The percentage was even higher in large urban areas. In some hospitals in New York City, Asian immigrants constituted more than 80 percent of staff doctors. Filipinos provided the largest percentage of foreign doctors; in 1970, 24 percent of all foreign physicians entering the United States came from the Philippines.[35]

Once here, many Asians used the family preference system to bring over close relatives. By 1980 the educational level of Asians had started dropping as the first post-1965 immigrants began bringing over in-laws and cousins. Among Chinese, for example, those who came before 1970 had a poverty rate of 2.8 percent, while of those who emigrated after 1975, nearly a quarter had lived in poverty. After 1980, noted the historian Roger Daniels, there was "a greater tendency for recent immigrants to be poorly educated, deficient in English, and to work in the low-paid service trades, such as laundries, restaurants, and the sweatshop enterprises typical of the inner city."[36]

The numbers were staggering and ran counter to the original intention of both Congress and the administration. In 1965 only 1 of every 14 immigrants was Asian; in 1973 the figure had risen to almost 1 in 3. In the twenty years following the 1965 Immigration Act, the Asian population in the United States soared from 1 million to 5 million; nearly four times as many Asians entered the country during that period as had emigrated in the previous hundred years. Most of these came from a handful of countries: the Philippines, China, Korea, and India. The largest Asian group in the country was Filipino. Between 1965 and 1985, 660,000 entered, averaging over 30,000 yearly in the 1970s and topping 41,000 in 1979; before 1965 Filipino immigration had averaged about 3,000 yearly. During the same period over 420,000 Chinese immigrants—almost as many as the 426,000 Chinese who had come between 1849 and 1930—entered the United States. Before 1965 New York's Chinatown had never had a population of more than 10,000 people; twenty years later it had become the home of 100,000. During the same time, the Korean and Indian population jumped from 10,000 to more than 500,000.[37]

The following table shows how dramatically the pattern changed in just the first years of the new law.[38]

FROM	1965	1973	CHANGE
Asia	20,683	124,160	Up 500%
Latin America	81,781	99,407	Up 22%
Southern and eastern Europe	40,106	68,322	Up 70%
West Indies	37,583	64,765	Up 75%
Northern Europe and Canada	111,645	33,499	Down 70%
Africa	3,383	6,655	Up 97%

In response to fears about hordes of immigrants from Mexico and South America flooding into the country, Congress had toughened the rules governing admission from the Western Hemisphere by adding a numerical cap and imposing a rigorous labor certification process. Much to the surprise and dismay of Congress and the administration, the new restrictions did little to hold back the surge of immigrants from the south. Forces beyond the control of any lawmaker—a population explosion, terrible economic conditions, and political instability—combined dramatically to increase the demand for entry. During the 1970s Cuba sent 200,000 people, more people than Canada and the United Kingdom combined. In 1960 only 17,000 people from the Dominican Republic were living in the United States, whereas the tiny nation sent 140,000 in the 1970s. The non-Spanish-speaking nations of Jamaica, Trinidad and Tobago, and Haiti saw their numbers swell from 30,000 during the 1950s to 130,000 during the 1960s and 271,000 in the 1970s. No nation sent more people here than Mexico, which was responsible for more immigrants than all South and Central American nations combined; their number swelled from 37,969 to 70,141 between 1965 and 1973. By 1978 Western Hemisphere immigration had reached a decade-high 262,542, more than double the mandated 120,000 figure.[39]

The new policy not only did not discourage legal entrants but may also have inadvertently produced a sharp upturn in illegal immigration. South Americans who were accustomed to practically walking across the border at will were now forced to meet stringent qualifications and wait in long lines for admission. Before 1965 a citizen of a country in the Western Hemisphere could emigrate to the United States by demonstrating that he could support himself without government assistance. The new rules were both more severe and more complicated, requiring the applicant to satisfy the Labor Department that his employment would not adversely affect the job market. By 1974 there was a two-and-a-half-year waiting period for emigration from anywhere in the Western Hemisphere, and many of those spots were already filled by high-priority persons, such as Cuban refugees or family members. "For the non-Cuban citizen in the Western hemisphere who cannot obtain labor certification and who does not have immediate relatives living legally in the United States, there is virtually no hope of legally emigrating—even if he were willing to wait more than two years," the *New York Times* observed.[40]

Loopholes in the law encouraged illegal migration. It was almost impossible for an alien to arrange for labor certification without coming to the United States since few employers would make a job offer without an interview. To get around the problem, many potential immigrants came on tourist visas and worked illegally. While living and working illegally, they could obtain labor certification based on their employment and apply for immigrant visas. Once a visa was approved, sometimes two or three years later, an applicant could return to his home country for a day, pick up the visa, and return as a legal resident entitled to hold any job available. According to the Department of Labor, half the twenty thousand annual requests for labor certification in the New York region involved aliens who were working illegally. "Under these conditions you'd have to be some kind of a fool to stay in another country and give up," a prominent immigration lawyer remarked. "At worst, if you're caught, they'll send you back."[41]

The United States unwittingly contributed to illegal immigration from Mexico by abolishing a program for importing Mexican workers at the same time that it tightened immigration rules. During World War II the government encouraged farmers to hire Mexican workers for seasonal agricultural work. The two nations spelled out the terms of the arrangement in a series of agreements known as the bracero program, from the Spanish word for agricultural laborer. By the late 1950s about 400,000 Mexican temporary workers were entering the United States each year under the program. Many small Mexican towns along the border depended on the seasonal work for their survival. In 1964, after withering criticism from labor and religious groups that the program exploited Mexicans and depressed U.S. wages, Congress ended the bracero program. By the time it ended more than 4.5 million Mexicans had come to work temporarily in the United States, and both American growers and entire Mexican border towns had become dependent on the program.[42]

No one knows for sure the number of illegal workers here, but the most reliable figures suggest that the numbers swelled from an estimated 23,000 in 1970 to 112,000 ten years later. Mexico topped the list of nations sending illegals: By the early 1980s an estimated 55 percent of all undocumented immigrants came from Mexico, and they accounted for around two-thirds of all Mexican immigration. They poured across the nation's 1,946-mile southern border, scrambling over fences, wading the Rio Grande, hiking through the desert, seeking menial jobs that paid ten times what they could earn at home. Said an agent in charge of the El Paso, Texas, Border Patrol station: "It's like trying to push the ocean back."[43]

While most of the early emigrants from Asia who entered under the new law were educated professionals, those who crossed the border in the south were less educated, made less money, experienced higher unemployment rates, and were twice as likely to be working in the crafts and laborer categories as previous generations of immigrants. The 1980 census revealed that only about 25 percent of Mexican immigrants had high school degrees; 25 percent spoke no English; only about 40 percent had a working knowledge of English. Fewer chose to become citizens. By 1980 only 21 percent of Mexican immigrants who entered during the 1960s had been naturalized, compared with 56 percent of those who had entered before 1950. These and other immigrants paid taxes, but because they had lower incomes and education, Mexican immigrants were also more likely to receive welfare.[44]

Congress has made a number of attempts to correct the patterns created by the 1965 amendments, but many of the efforts fell victim to the same unintended consequences that followed the original legislation. In 1986 Congress, worried about the large number of illegal immigrants, passed the Immigration Reform and Control Act (IRCA), which granted amnesty to all illegals who had entered the country before 1982 and imposed heavy fines on employers who hired illegal aliens. But the government was reluctant to impose sanctions, and most employers found ways around the restrictions. "We have found no evidence that the 1986 immigration law has shut off the flow of new undocumented immigrants," noted the scholar Wayne Cornelius after studying the law's impact. The law may, however, have had the unintended effect of keeping illegals in the United States since many were afraid to leave out of fear they would be unable to return. A decade later Congress tried to patch the holes in IRCA with the Illegal Immigration Act, which made it harder for illegals to use fraudulent documents and for the unscrupulous to employ them. It also stipulated that no American citizen could sponsor the immigration of a relative unless the sponsor could demonstrate an income at least 25 percent higher than the federal poverty level.[45]

Along with stemming the flow of illegals into the country, Congress attempted to restrain family-based immigration and to aid immigrants from Western Europe crowded out by the waves of newcomers from Asia and Latin America. The 1986 reform act contained a provision that set aside 10,000 visas for those countries adversely affected by the 1965 reforms. The visas were determined by lottery with nearly 40 percent going to Ireland. Two years later Congress passed another visa lottery with similar results. The primary goal of most reformers, however, was to substitute skills for blood by curtailing the family preference system and increasing the emphasis on attracting immigrants with needed labor skills. In other words, reformers wanted to return to the goals of the legislation that President Kennedy had submitted to

Congress in 1963. In 1988 Wyoming's conservative Senator Alan Simpson teamed up with Edward Kennedy to submit a bill that would have imposed a cap of 590,000 on total immigration, cut the preferences for brothers and sisters, and increased the number of visas based on economic considerations. "By redressing the imbalances in immigration which have inadvertently developed in recent years, America will open its doors again to those who no longer have immediate family ties in the United States," Kennedy declared. The House, however, objected to the efforts to restrain family-based immigration and made its support for an overall cap dependent on dropping the provision that curtailed family visas. In the end Congress refused to implement the provisions for reducing the number of immigrants admitted on the basis of family relationships and simply added positions for applicants from northern Europe.[46]

Why has American immigration policy been so unpredictable? To a large extent the forces that shape immigration are difficult to predict and impossible to control, especially when a nation shares a two-thousand-mile border with the Third World. Conflicting public attitudes toward immigration compound the problem. Supporters of restricted immigration often appeal to national security and respond to public concern about maintaining social order. "Every sovereign nation has the right and the duty to control its borders," noted William Bennett. Supporters of liberal immigration policy have equally powerful ideological weapons at their disposal and often counter with the invitation expressed in the Emma Lazarus poem engraved beneath the Statue of Liberty: "Give me your tired, your poor, your huddled masses yearning to breathe free." In recent years both opponents and supporters of restricted immigration have developed powerful interest groups that can mobilize quickly to defend their cause. On the anti-immigrant side representatives from organized labor and the environmental movement often work together with cultural conservatives. The pro-immigration forces include Hispanic advocacy groups, agribusiness, high tech businesspeople seeking skilled workers, free market conservatives, and old-fashioned liberals who champion cultural diversity. Alan Simpson described the political alliances as "the goofiest ideological-bedfellow activity I've ever seen." Illegal immigration has posed an especially thorny problem since many of the measures needed to control immigration run counter to American commitment to individual freedom. Courts have restricted the INS from searching workplaces without warrants, and they have restricted the police's ability to question suspicious persons in the street. The one idea that most people believe would be effective in controlling illegal immigration—a national identification card—raises the specter of Big Brother. "Perhaps that is why the legislative effort, however determined in tone, is so weak in practice," observed the *Economist*. "America has neither the money nor the will—nor, often, the heart—to keep people out."[47]

MOST Americans see daily reminders of the cultural impact of the new waves of immigrants. City streets are a babble of foreign tongues. Three-quarters of Miami's residents speak a language other than English at home. In New York City the figure is four out of ten, and of these, half cannot speak fluent English. In kitchens across the country salsa has replaced ketchup as America's favorite condiment. Phrases such as *"hasta la vista,* baby" and *"mi casa es su casa"* have become part of the American vocabulary. The faces of many popular icons, such as Andy Garcia and Jimmy Smits, have a tanned Hispanic look. During the 1980s Cuban-American singer Gloria Estefan emerged as the "queen of a new Latin sound with her dance-floor blend of rhythm and blues with Cuban polyrhythms." By the early 1990s mainstream business leaders were tripping over themselves to appeal to the growing Hispanic market, which spent $228 billion in goods and services in 1996, up from $94 billion in 1984.[48]

The social and economic consequences have been even more profound, though often overlooked. The emphasis on family unification, the centerpiece of the 1965 amendments, has produced a demographic revolution in America. Since most legal immigrants join family members already here, they have settled into a handful of states with large immigrant communities. More than two-thirds of immigrants arriving in the 1980s resided in only six states: California, New York, Texas, Florida, New Jersey, and Illinois. California and New York alone account for over 40 percent of new immigrants. Overall, California's foreign-born population, both legal and illegal, increased from about 9 percent to 22 percent of the population from 1960 to 1990 (1.3 million to 6.45 million).[49]

The movement of new ethnic minorities into the cities is part of a broader demographic revolution that is transforming the American landscape. According to the 1990 census, 93 percent of the foreign-born population resided in metropolitan areas. About half the immigrants who entered during the 1980s lived in eight metropolitan areas, what demographers call gateway cities: Los Angeles, New York, Miami, Anaheim, Chicago, Washington, D.C., Houston, and San Francisco. In 1930 almost one of four residents in gateway cities had been foreign-born, but by 1990 more than one in three were immigrants, almost five times the national average. By 1998 more than a third of New York City's residents were foreign-born, and about 60 percent were either immigrants or their children, the vast majority black, Latino, and Asian. Nearly 33 percent of the population of Los Angeles County is foreign-born, up from 11 percent in 1970. The influx of new ethnic minorities and African-Americans into the nation's cities accelerated the exodus of native-born whites to the surrounding suburbs. Between 1960 and 1990 the white population of New York fell by half. Between 1990 and 1995 both New York and Los Angeles lost more than one million native-born residents, even as their populations increased by roughly the same numbers with immigrants. "For every Mexican who comes to Los Angeles, a white native-born leaves," observed the demographer William Frey.[50]

Urban-suburban divisions reveal only part of the story, for sharp lines of ethnic segregation exist within many cities. Immigrants in the early twentieth century initially clustered tightly together, but rising income levels and the passage of generations blurred residential segregation within a few decades. Though it is too early to tell whether the recent immigrants will experience the same social mobility, there is evidence that the lines of segregation, both residential and occupational, are strong; Hispanics in Los Angeles were more segregated residentially in 1990 than they were in 1970. In the workplace immigrants are disproportionally represented in service industries, especially restaurants, hotels, and hospitals, and as private household help—low-paying jobs that require limited English-language skills. The low-paying service economy is further segmented by ethnicity. In California, for example, Mexican immigrants are employed overwhelmingly as gardeners and domestics, in apparel and furniture manufacturing, and as cooks and food preparers, while Koreans open small businesses and Filipinos are heavily represented in the medical professions.[51]

Economists are divided over the benefits of immigration. A few scholars, such as Julian Simon, author of *The Economic Consequences of Immigration,* argue that immigrants stimulate the economy and improve the American standard of living. "The more immigrants that come, the brighter our economic future is across the board," he declared. On the other side of the debate are restrictionists such as George Borjas, who argues that immigrants drain public resources, depress wages, and undermine American competitiveness. According to the National Research Council (NRC), "immigration produces net economic gains for domestic residents" because immigrants increase the supply of labor and help produce new goods and services. But the NRC also pointed out that even when the economy as a whole gains, "there may be

losers as well as gainers among different groups of U.S. residents."
High-skill workers, the owners of capital, and consumers benefit
from having cheap labor, while the losers tend to be those on the
economic margins of society, less skilled domestic workers who
compete with immigrants.[52]

Even scholars who disagree on the overall impact of immigration acknowledge that it has imposed a heavy burden on the handful of states that have absorbed most of the newcomers. On
average, immigrant-headed households include more school-age
children than native households, are poorer, receive more welfare,
and, since they own less property, pay less in taxes. Local governments provide many of the services immigrants need, yet the
federal government collects most of their tax dollars. "At the federal level, it appears that immigrants are a fiscal plus," noted a sociologist. "They pay more in taxes than they use in services. It's the
local governments that are most adversely affected." The NRC estimated that each illegal immigrant household in California consumed on average $1,178 more in public services than it
contributed in taxes. Multiply that by the estimated 2 million undocumented aliens in the state, and it adds up to a significant
drain on public resources. If averaged out across the nation, the
net burden would be much lower, between $166 and $226 per native household.[53]

During the 1990s public anxiety about supporting millions of
illegals stirred a potent public backlash against immigrants. A
1993 Gallup Poll found that 65 percent of those surveyed favored
more restrictions on immigration, double the percentage saying
the same in 1965. Another survey found that while most Americans thought immigration was a good thing historically, 68 percent said that immigration was "bad for this country." More than
half the public believed that immigrants were a burden because
they took jobs away from others and used health care and welfare
services. "There is a notion that we are 'full'—that there are not
enough opportunities to go around," Democratic pollster Mark

Mellman said. "Today the notion is [that] the pie is shrinking and that each new person who arrives not only takes a piece of the pie, but takes it from me." The backlash has been strongest in California, the state most affected by illegal immigration. On November 8, 1994, California voters endorsed the Save Our State ballot, known as Proposition 187, which prohibited the use of public social services and programs by those who could not prove legal residence. It also required police, school administrators, social service agencies, and public or private health care workers to report to the Immigration and Naturalization Service anyone they reasonably suspected of being an illegal immigrant.[54]

Added to the economic worry were anxieties about the nation's ability to absorb and assimilate so many different cultures. The large number of immigrants, and their concentration in a few states, have raised fears that this generation of migrants will avoid assimilation into mainstream culture. Hispanics have become so concentrated in some California and Texas communities that only Spanish is spoken. Even in large cities like Los Angeles and San Antonio, Mexican immigrants can go about their daily business without knowing English. Conservatives have been particularly vociferous in charging that the new wave of immigrants from the Third World has eroded America's common culture, fracturing the nation into separate ethnic enclaves. "Is it really wise to allow the immigration of people who find it so difficult and painful to assimilate into the American majority?" asked Peter Brimelow, author of the best-selling *Alien Nation*. The worry about social fragmentation was not confined to a few fringe voices on the right. Liberal historian and former Kennedy adviser Arthur Schlesinger, Jr., gave powerful expression to the cultural fears in his influential book *The Disuniting of America,* which lamented the "cult of ethnicity" that had arisen "to protect, promote, and perpetuate separate ethnic and racial communities." Like many social commentators, Schlesinger worried that the melting pot was losing its ability to forge a national identity that transcended ethnic and racial appeal. "One wonders," he wrote. "Will the center hold? Or will the melting pot give way to the Tower of Babel?"[55]

Nowhere was that concern more acute than in the debate over bilingualism. Beginning with Florida in 1960, a number of states with large Hispanic populations began offering young Spanish-speaking students the option of studying in their native tongue to ease their transition to English. Congress encouraged the development of new programs with passage of the Bilingual Education Act in 1968 and the 1975 Bilingual Voting Rights Amendment. By the early 1980s fears about the swelling populations of minority-language speakers had produced a powerful English only movement. "The language of American government is English," said a Connecticut Republican. "The language of American business is English. We are not a dual-language society." In 1986 California spearheaded the drive for English only by voting overwhelmingly for a referendum outlawing bilingualism and defending "English as a unifying force in the United States." The proposition, which instructed the legislature "to take all steps necessary to insure that the role of English as the common language of the State of California is preserved and enhanced," received 73 percent of the vote. Representatives of Hispanic groups condemned the movement as "fundamentally racist in character," but before the end of the decade seventeen other states had joined California in passing English only laws. A bill to designate English as the official language of the U.S. government gained 101 congressional sponsors in 1991 but failed to become law. "Language," the *Economist* noted, "symbolizes the United States' fear that the foreign body within its borders is growing too big ever to be digested."[56]

In most cases the concerns about the failure of immigrants to assimilate are misplaced; similar fears about earlier waves of immigrants have proved unfounded. The public has always looked favorably on past generations of immigrants and unfavorably on contemporary migrants. In the nineteenth century Americans complained about the "lazy and hard-drinking Irish" who were "polluting" the cities; later waves of newcomers from Italy and Poland confronted similarly hostile attitudes. Over time, however, those groups became acculturated and now swell the mainstream that fears the addition of new migrants from Mexico, Iran, and Haiti. Increasingly strident affirmations of identity actually mask the waning of real ethnic differences. Higher education, consumerism, movies and television, professional sports, and popular culture work to make Americans more alike, whatever their ethnic origins. According to the scholar Russell Jacoby, all ethnic groups "partake of a larger American industrial society." America's "multiple cultures define themselves by their preferences within a consumer society, not by a rejection of it." The rising rate of intermarriage between ethnic groups, especially Asian-Americans and non-Asians, also suggests that ethnic differences may soften over time. In the 1980s more than one-half of all Japanese-Americans and 40 percent of Chinese-Americans married outside their ethnic groups.[57]

There is some evidence, however, that recent immigrants are less willing than past newcomers to embrace American culture. Thanks to the marvels of technology, modern immigrants from all parts of the world are more likely than their predecessors to straddle two worlds, establishing U.S. residences while staying connected, on a day-to-day basis, to their home countries. Fax machines, direct-dial telephones, videos, foreign-language broadcasts, and relatively cheap jet travel allow newer immigrants to avoid making decisive breaks with their birthplaces. The most revolutionary change has been the inexpensive direct-dial phone call. In 1965 it cost $10.59 to call the Dominican Republic for three minutes, and $15 to call India. In 1998 it cost $1.71 and $3.66 respectively. "If the ability to call home cheaply connects immigrants to their families, the ability to click on the homeland's news or soap operas connects them to the society they left behind." In Queens, New York, Koreans can watch the twenty-four-hour Korean Channel that comes as part of basic cable. "For modern immigrants," noted the *New York Times,* "the homeland is no longer something to be forsaken, released into a mist of memory or nostalgia."[58]

Ironically, while it was the civil rights movement that helped motivate Congress to abandon national origins, African-Americans have perhaps been the group most adversely affected by the new immigration. Over the past two decades the population increase of the new immigrants has dwarfed the black rate of increase. During the 1980s the Asian population increased by 107 percent, the Hispanic by 53 percent, and the black by only 13.2 percent. In a democracy, demography is destiny, and the new immigrants have been flexing their political and economic muscle. Between 1992 and 1996 the Hispanic voting pool grew by nearly 30 percent nationally and by an astonishing 45 percent in California. In many urban areas Hispanics have been muscling African-Americans out of the local labor market. According to one study, the number of unionized black janitors in Los Angeles office buildings fell from twenty-five hundred in 1977 to six hundred in 1985, although total employment of janitors went up by 50 percent. They were displaced by immigrants who recruited others of their ethnic group. In the past black leaders argued for more representation in government and on police forces by claiming that blacks were the people being served by those institutions. But in many cities, especially in the Southwest, blacks are no longer the largest minority. At Martin Luther King Hospital in the Watts section of Los Angeles, Hispanics, who make up a majority of the patients, have been clamoring to replace black doctors and staff with Latinos. In the nation's capital Hispanics make up 10 percent of the population but less than 2 percent of municipal workers and less than 1 percent of the police force. The city's Hispanic leadership wants greater representation and complains that the black leadership has been unwilling to share power.[59]

Not surprisingly, the battle for scarce urban resources has aroused racial tensions. "The more diversity and burgeoning minority groups we have," observed the National Conference of Christians and Jews, "the more prejudice we must overcome." Many blacks, Hispanics, and Asians, it seems, feel as much animosity toward one another as they do toward whites. The Los Angeles riots following the Rodney King trial were the most visible demonstration of this new tension. "The riots were not carried out against Blacks or Whites, they were carried out against the Latino and Asian communities by the Blacks," the Mexican-American newspaper *La Prensa* claimed. "Faced with nearly a million and a half Latinos taking over the inner city, Blacks revolted, rioted and looted." According to an African-American commentator, the clash should "shatter, perhaps for good, one of the most enduring myths of our time: The myth of black-brown solidarity."[60]

The expressions of violence have not been limited to the West Coast. Confrontations between blacks and Koreans have flared since the early 1980s in New York, Atlanta, Chicago, and Washington, D.C. At the root of the conflict, exacerbated by language and cultural differences, is resentment of Korean immigrants' success in running small businesses in economically depressed black neighborhoods. "There are a lot of black people you pass on the streets who have been dreaming for years about opening up businesses in some of those boarded-up buildings," said the Reverend Fred Lucas, pastor of the Bridge Street AME Church in Brooklyn. "They are systematically denied access to insurances and capital and denied access." In Spike Lee's movie *Do the Right Thing,* set in Brooklyn, a Korean shopkeeper averts a confrontation with black residents of the neighborhood by shouting in desperation, "Me no white. Me no white. Me black." The appeal to a common experience of oppression worked in the movies, but it failed to dampen the hostilities in New York.[61]

The Immigration Act of 1965 was a product of liberalism at high tide, the powerful New Deal coalition flexing its political muscle. The result of the new waves of immigration, however, has been to fracture the old coalition. The law was "a momentous civil rights victory," observed the journalist Peter Schuck. "That it also contributed to the coalition's future decline is an arresting political irony." Historically, blacks and Hispanics had joined forces to effect groundbreaking political gains. They elected David Dinkins, New York City's first black mayor, and Harold Washington, Chicago's first black mayor. In recent years, however, serious cracks have emerged in their respective political agendas. In 1989 Hispanics gave white Democrat Richard Daley more than 80 percent of their votes in his successful bid for mayor in Chicago; his African-American opponent won 94 percent of the black vote. In 1997 Republican Richard Riordan won election as mayor of Los Angeles with 60 percent of the Hispanic vote, while three-quarters of the blacks supported his liberal opponent. Similar patterns often emerged in gubernatorial elections in New Jersey, Texas, and New York. "Taken together," observed the *New Republic*'s Peter Beinart, "these results represent a structural shift in the political alliances that define many of America's largest cities and states."[62]

Polls show that blacks tend to be more liberal on economic issues than either Asians or Hispanics. By large margins, African-Americans support more expansive government, especially on issues of affirmative action and social welfare. Hispanics and Asians appear more skeptical about government. A California poll showed that while a majority of blacks supported affirmative action (56 percent), only 36 percent of Hispanics supported it, and Asians overwhelmingly opposed any hiring preferences (81 percent). When asked in 1995 if they personally suffered from discrimination, 42 percent of blacks but only 19 percent of Hispanics and 15 percent of Asians responded affirmatively. According to the *Los Angeles Times,* 47 percent of black voters in California supported a 1994 ballot initiative to restrict benefits to illegal aliens, and 48 percent backed another voter initiative to curtail bilingual education.[63]

Not only have the new immigrants grown farther apart from blacks politically, but they are often too diverse to work among themselves for a common agenda. Hispanics include immigrants from Mexico, Puerto Rico, Cuba, and South and Central America. The conservative Cuban-Americans in Miami gave their "Hispanic" vote to George Bush in 1988; Michael Dukakis won the "Hispanic" vote among the more liberal Mexicans of Texas. "It would be disingenuous to argue that we think exactly alike on the same issues," said Lisa Navarette, of the National Council of La Raza. The same cultural differences separate many of the Asian immigrants, who speak a variety of languages. A Vietnamese boat person has little in common with a Sony executive from Japan. "It's hard enough to get a coalition of Democrats together on something, let alone people whose language and customs and political alliances in their own worlds are vastly different from each other," noted a political observer.[64]

In 1965 no one could have predicted that President Johnson's "modest" reform bill would have such a profound impact on American society. For most legislators the bill allowed them to make a strong moral statement without producing tangible changes in immigration policy. In practice the law fundamentally altered immigration patterns and produced ripples that affected nearly every aspect of American life, from the food we eat to the taxes we pay. As the historian Roger Daniels has noted, "Much of what it has accomplished was unforeseen by its authors, and had Congress fully understood its consequences, it almost certainly would not have passed."[65]

Chapter 5

The Politics of Campaign Finance Reform: The Federal Election Campaign Finance Reform Act of 1974

●

JOHN W. GARDNER'S tall, trim figure, Roman features, and impeccable social credentials made him appear the embodiment of the eastern establishment. A lifelong Republican, Gardner broke party ranks in 1965 to serve as Lyndon Johnson's secretary of health, education, and welfare. Over the next few years he fought to increase spending for new social programs, only to watch helplessly as the Vietnam War sapped needed resources. Frustrated by Washington's failure to respond to public pressure to end the war and to address pressing domestic needs, Gardner resigned his post in 1968. His experience left him obsessed with the belief that money was at the root of America's political crisis. "Unless you get at the capacity of money to buy political outcomes and at the secrecy which makes it possible, you've missed it all," he declared. "That's the point at which the system is placed at the disposal of the monied interests." Two years later Gardner formed a "people's lobby" of like-minded reformers to change the way "the system" worked. He called his new army Common Cause, and by 1973 the ranks had swelled to more than three hundred thousand soldiers. Composed largely of educated middle-class members, the organization lobbied lawmakers on a range of issues, from sunshine laws to ending the seniority system in Congress, but none was more important than campaign finance reform. "Common Cause believes that the root of campaign financing [abuse] can never be eliminated until candidates are assured of adequate funds to run a credible and competitive campaign without having to rely on big-money contributors," Gardner told the House Administration Committee, which was drafting campaign legislation. "This can never be accomplished until a comprehensive system of public financing is adopted."[1]

Americans have always worried about the possibility of powerful moneyed interests corrupting democratic institutions, and accusations of wrongdoing have dogged many of the nation's most respected leaders. "To pay money for securing it directly or indirectly," John Quincy Adams said of the presidency, was "incorrect in principle." But even George Washington was accused of buying an election. In 1757 he won a seat in the Virginia House of Burgesses after purchasing twenty-eight gallons of rum, fifty gallons of rum punch, thirty-four gallons of wine, forty-six gallons of beer, and two gallons of cider royal for his constituents— roughly a quart and a half of spirits for each eligible voter. Andrew Jackson created the spoils system to reward his supporters with Cabinet positions. After the Civil War large corporations, and the new industrial barons who led them, were rarely shy about flexing their monetary muscles. In response, Congress made feeble attempts to limit corporate contributions, tighten procedures, and force candidates to file financial disclosures. The laws, however, were filled with loopholes, and no candidate was ever prosecuted. "Inadequate in their scope when enacted, they are now obsolete," Lyndon Johnson declared in 1967. "More loophole than law, they invite evasion and circumvention."[2]

Initially Congress resisted Johnson's plea to tighten the nation's campaign finance laws, but by the end of the decade new forces had added momentum to the calls for change. A series of scandals involving political money shook Capitol Hill, leading to the ouster of two senators, Thomas Dodd of Connecticut and Daniel Brewster of Maryland. Most major newspapers and magazines ran sensationalized stories about wealthy candidates and "special interests" buying both influence and elections. The stories tapped into deep-seated American suspicion of government and politicians and drew on the general reform spirit of the 1960s, which attempted to make institutions more responsive to the public will. Americans learned that the seafarers' union had pumped a hundred thousand dollars into Hubert Humphrey's 1968 campaign a few days after the Johnson administration had ruled in its favor in a dispute with the Canadian government; that the truckers' union had showered members of Congress with twenty-nine-thousand-dollar gifts during a critical vote facing the trucking industry; that meat-packers had established a special fund to discourage members of Congress from tightening plant inspection procedures. Coverage of the 1970 congressional elections expressed uneasiness about rich telegenic candidates who appeared to be using their personal fortunes to buy elections.[3]

John Gardner tried to mold the general sense of apprehension and outrage into a blunt instrument for reform. In 1971 Common Cause spearheaded a drive by an army of reform groups determined to alter the way the nation funded its elections. In that year it pressured Congress into allowing taxpayers to volunteer $1 contributions on their annual income tax forms to create a pool of money for presidential candidates. A few months later the same reform coalition worked closely with congressional leaders to pass the Federal Election Act of 1971, which called on any candidate for national office to report and disclose financial information on all contributions of more than $100. Common Cause used the new disclosure information to build public support for tougher measures. It published reports showing that expenditures for all nominations and election contests at the local, state, and national levels had risen from an estimated $300 million in 1968 to about $425 million in 1972. Nixon's 1972 campaign managers spent a staggering $56 million, more than double the previous high of $25 million in 1968. The McGovern-Shriver ticket was not far behind, spending $49 million, more than four times Hubert Humphrey's costs in 1968.[4]

In 1973 the effort to rewrite the campaign finance laws received a big boost from an unlikely source, Richard Nixon. Congressional investigations into the Watergate affair produced the most alarming information about campaign abuses and the most powerful case in favor of reform. The Senate Watergate committee, chaired by North Carolina's Sam Ervin, revealed that the Committee to Reelect the President (CREEP) had obtained $5.4 million from officials of the 100 largest defense contractors and almost $5 million from officials of 178 leading oil companies. Corporate executives told Senate investigators that they had made the contributions to gain access to the administration and out of fear of White House retaliation. Circumstantial evidence indicated that the payoffs worked. The Milk Producers Association pledged $2 million to President Nixon's reelection campaign the same year the White House increased milk price supports. Many of the biggest donors were rewarded with ambassadorial appointments. In 1974 the secretly recorded Nixon tapes revealed that the White House had used campaign contributions to pay for the cover-up of the burglary of the Democratic National Committee. "Watergate is not primarily a story of political espionage, nor even of White House intrigue," Gardner declared. "It is a particularly malodorous chapter in the annals of campaign financing."[5]

The shocking revelations inspired widespread calls for election reform. Lawmakers fretted over polls showing an alarming drop in citizens' confidence in the Congress. Pollster Louis Harris told a Senate committee that "public confidence in government generally must be reported as being lower than a constituent democracy can afford." Surveys revealed a dramatic upsurge in support for public financing of presidential elections, from 11 percent in 1964 to 67 percent in 1974. For many people, both in and out of government, reforming the nation's campaign laws was necessary to restore public faith in the system. "Money, money, money is what has got the people of this country disgusted with politics and politicians," lamented Republican Senator Hugh Scott.[6]

Common Cause and its liberal allies on Capitol Hill had more ambitious goals for campaign reform. They believed that Washington's failure to address a host of pressing social issues, from poverty to pollution, was the direct result of a flawed campaign system that allowed powerful special interests to thwart the will of "the people." There were many reasons for the impasse—a Republican-controlled White House, a potent political backlash against liberalism, and a public mood soured by racial unrest and the war in Vietnam—but liberals focused on one villain, the corrupting influence of special interest money. "Who really owns America?" asked Senator Edward Kennedy. "Is it the people or is it a little group of big campaign contributors?" In his mind Congress had failed to solve the energy crisis because of "the campaign contributions of the oil industry." The "campaign contributions of the American Medical Association and the private health insurance industry" sabotaged plans for national health insurance. The National Rifle Association prevented gun control; the highway lobby cut off efforts to conserve on fuel. Only through public financing of campaigns, Kennedy claimed, could the nation "guarantee that the political influence of any citizen is measured only by his voice and vote, not by the thickness of his pocketbook."[7]

In February 1974 Senate liberals rallied around a proposal providing candidates for national office with public funds for both primary and general elections. In return for receiving the funds, candidates would have to accept strict spending limits determined by the number of voting-age residents in each state or congressional district. The legislation also imposed tough restrictions on national and state political parties and placed caps on the amount of money individuals and independent groups could contribute to campaigns. Individuals could contribute three thousand dollars to each primary and each general election campaign, but no more than twenty-five thousand dollars a year in all federal elections. Political action committees (PACs) and other independent groups could spend no more than a thousand dollars a year to advocate the election or defeat of any one candidate. The Federal Election Commission (FEC), a powerful watchdog organization, would enforce the new regulations. Supporters claimed that the bill would end the "misuse and corruption of power and a misguided dependence on the influence of large political contributors." While it may not "eradicate future Watergates," Rhode Island's Claiborne Pell said, it would "discourage the perpetuation of a climate in which power is abused by the clever at the expense of the unwary." Kennedy said enactment could "end the corrosive and corrupting influence of private money in public life."[8]

Critics raised a number of prescient questions about the wisdom of campaign reform. Since challengers needed to raise greater sums of money, would public financing inadvertently provide incumbents with an unfair advantage? Could it lead ultimately to government interference by manipulating grants to some candidates and parties over others? Skeptics fretted that public funds would encourage frivolous candidates to run for office and would weaken the political parties. Would not the rich and powerful always find methods of funneling money into politics? Watergate hero Lowell Weicker, a GOP senator from Connecticut, complained that public financing "is not magical Clorox guaranteed to end forever the dirty laundry of Watergate. It does not cut the cost of campaigns; it just shifts the cost." Republican Senator Howard Baker of Tennessee, another popular Watergate figure, worried about the constitutionality of a law that used taxpayers' money to fund candidates they did not support. Public subsidies, he charged, could "abridge the individual's First Amendment right of freedom of political expression." Many Republicans had more practical concerns. They feared that the new provisions would undermine the GOP's traditional fund-raising advantage by equalizing the amount of money each party could raise. "Political experts agree that Democrats would be the major beneficiaries of the bill," opined the *New York Times.*[9]

While most of the mainstream press, depicting the legislation as a classic struggle between good and evil, lined up behind the bill, a few skeptics continued to raise their voices in opposition. "Outlawing large private contributions will reduce, or at least make more perilous, the domination of the political marketplace by well-heeled individuals and special interests," the *Washington Post* editorialized. "Now is the time for a full and fundamental cleansing of the nation's outmoded, corrupt system of financing public elections with private money," observed the *New York Times.* But *Washington Post* columnist David Broder warned legislators to pay heed to the "total system impact" of the changes they were contemplating. In the current mood, he observed, "anything that is called a political campaign reform bill is automatically deemed deserving of applause." He reminded his readers of unforeseen consequences of the legislation. Unless Congress realized it was proposing "a fundamental alteration in our politics," the results would likely "be opposite what the reformers intended." The *New Republic's* editor Walter Pincus agreed with many conservatives that money would always find its way into politics and reforms would plug some holes but create new ones. "If campaign contributions helped someone get a government contract before, honorariums or some other financial reward to a willing legislator would be helpful under the new system."[10]

Senate opponents used every available obstructionist method to block voting on the measure, but in the frenzied post-Watergate atmosphere, nothing—not reasoned objections or parliamentary maneuvers—could derail the reform train. After failing to include a number of weakening amendments from the floor, conservative Republicans and southern Democrats filibustered the bill. On April 9 moderates and liberals from both parties joined forces to choke off debate by a 64–30 vote. Two days later, following thirteen days of debate and fifty-one roll-call votes, the Senate passed S. 3044 by a 53–32 vote. Kennedy said that passage of the bill "is one of the finest hours of the Senate in this or any other Congress."[11]

All attention turned to the House Administration Committee, the graveyard of all previous campaign reform efforts. Its autocratic chairman, Ohio Democrat Wayne Hays, used his positions as chair of the House Democratic Campaign Committee, which doled out money to party candidates, and as head of the Administration Committee, which controlled congressional office allowances and other perks, to bully members to vote against campaign finance reform. Irascible and sarcastic, Hays, once described as "the Archie Bunker of Capitol Hill," looked scornfully on self-identified political "do-gooders." "My knees do not start to dance and to jerk when the word 'reform' is mentioned," he remarked. "Common Cause is just trying to raise an issue so it can bilk the suckers who subscribe to it for more funds." Like other House Democratic leaders, Hays hailed from a safe one-party district and feared that the lure of guaranteed funds would encourage competition from Democrats in the primaries. If the government guaranteed every challenger ninety thousand dollars, Hays complained, "500 candidates would run in every district. It would be a travesty for every rip-off artist in the country."[12]

Hays may have opposed campaign finance reform and felt contempt for the John Gardners of the world, but he was shrewd enough to know that the public demanded that he produce something. In July, after months of delay, his committee reported a bill that included strict limits on campaign contributions and expenditures. Unlike the Senate version, the Hays bill provided public financing of presidential elections but not congressional races, and it watered down the proposal for an independent Federal Election Commission. Common Cause, which called the House bill "loophole-ridden legislation," tried to organize supporters to strengthen the legislation on the floor. They lost the fight for public financing of congressional elections by a wide, 228–187, margin but managed to force minor concessions on the makeup of the FEC. A few hours before President Nixon announced on August 8 that he intended to resign as a consequence of his involvement in the Watergate cover-up, the House approved the slightly revised version of the Hays bill by a vote of 355–48.[13]

House and Senate negotiators battled in a conference committee before coming to terms on a compromise package. Edward Kennedy led the Senate delegation, which lobbied hard for public financing of congressional races and for a tougher FEC. Hays, who led the House forces, refused to budge. On October 7, after weeks of partisan wrangling, both sides made concessions: The Senate dropped its insistence on public financing of congressional races while the House agreed to give the FEC the power to issue subpoenas and seek injunctions. The Federal Election Campaign Finance Reform Act Amendments of 1974 established a Federal Election Commission consisting of six voting members—two appointed by the president and four designated by congressional leaders. All six voting members had to be confirmed by both House and Senate. The law provided a complicated system of public financing for presidential elections. In order to qualify for federal funds in both the primary and general elections, presidential candidates had to accept contribution limits on individuals (one thousand dollars per candidate, not to exceed twenty-five thousand dollars to all federal candidates) and on political committees (five thousand dollars per candidate). Candidates for president and vice president could use up to fifty thousand dollars of their own money. Party nominees for House and Senate seats would not receive public funds, but they were required to abide by spending limits based on a complicated formula determined by the number of eligible voters in their districts or states.[14]

The compromise legislation sailed through the House and Senate by large margins. Howard Cannon of Nevada, floor manager of the Senate bill, said the "new law will constitute the most significant step ever taken in the area of election reform and one of the most important legislative actions taken by the Congress this year." The legislation, supporters argued, would eliminate the money advantage of conservative corporate interests. Most of all, it would clean up politics and reinvigorate public faith in government. "The measure's historic advance," declared the *New York Times*, "is that it offers for the first time the possibility that a man or woman may pursue the presidency without becoming seriously beholden to any person or organization in the land." Liberals were disappointed that Congress had refused to extend public financing to House and Senate races. "We got more than we had expected," Gardner remarked, "other than in the area of public financing of congressional elections." Most reformers, however, saw the bill as a necessary first step and predicted that public subsidies would soon be extended to include all national contests. [15]

On October 15 a reluctant President Gerald Ford signed the legislation into law. Like many other critics, he objected to the public financing provisions of the law, but he believed that something had to be done to reassure the public about the soundness of the electoral process. "The times demand this legislation," he declared. "The unpleasant truth is that big-money influence has come to play an unseemly role in our electoral process," and the 1974 law "will help right that wrong." [16]

ON January 2, 1975, an unorthodox coalition of liberals and conservatives challenged the law in the courts, charging that the limits on campaign contributions and expenditures violated the First Amendment rights of contributors and candidates to express themselves in the political marketplace. The following year, in *Buckley v. Valeo* (1976), the Supreme Court agreed, ruling that government-imposed limits on campaign spending violated free speech protection. "The First Amendment denies government the power to determine that spending to promote one's political views is wasteful, excessive or unwise," the justices declared in a 137-page opinion. "In the free society ordained by our Constitution, it is not the government but the people, individually as citizens and candidates and collectively as associations and political committees, who must retain control over the quantity and range of debate on public issues in a political campaign." The justices argued that any limitation on political communication "necessarily reduces the quantity of expression by restricting the number of issues discussed, the depth of their exploration and the size of the audience reached." Although the Court threw out any restraint on how much a candidate or campaign could spend, it upheld provisions that limited contributions to a candidate to one thousand dollars from individuals or five thousand dollars from political action committees. In addition, it ruled that the Congress had played an unconstitutional role in appointing four of the six members of the FEC, stating that the statute violated the Constitution's appointments clause by encroaching on the president's authority to appoint the "Officers of the United States" with the advice and consent of the Senate.[17]

During oral arguments Justice Potter Stewart articulated the central question in *Buckley:* Is money speech and speech money? The Court said yes; since limiting campaign money decreased campaign speech, any spending limit was a form of censorship. Using what the legal scholar Ronald Dworkin called "an individual-choice" model of politics, the justices stated that people had an absolute right to spend as much money as they wished to make their views known, even if doing so produced gross inequities by giving the rich an unfair advantage in advancing their electoral interests. An individual's right to expression took precedence over society's interest in establishing a fair electoral system. Critics took a much different view, suggesting there existed a "compelling governmental interest" to develop an election process that equalized the electoral influence of rich and poor. The

Court's emphasis on individual rights, they charged, produced unequal results. "Many lack the good fortune to possess a good fortune," Common Cause noted in its legal brief, "and this handicaps both their ability to run for office, and their ability to communicate their views to their elected representatives on an equal basis with large contributors." Constitutional scholar Burt Neuborne complained: "At some point, money stops being speech, and it becomes an oppressive force, reinforcing disproportionate power."[18]

With the 1976 presidential campaign already under way, Congress scrambled to produce a new law. Many liberals tried using the opportunity to rewrite and strengthen the entire bill, but President Ford threatened to veto any new provisions that went beyond responding to the Court's ruling. After three months of partisan negotiations Congress passed new amendments designed to achieve the same goal by different means. They maintained the system of public financing for presidential contests, reconstituted the FEC as a six-member panel appointed by the president and confirmed by the Senate, removed all limitations on spending, and adjusted rules governing contribution limits. The 1976 legislation raised from one to five thousand dollars the amount an individual could contribute to a political action committee and increased the contribution a PAC could make from five to fifteen thousand dollars. Once again the president resisted pressure from conservatives and signed the legislation into law, despite expressing "serious reservations" about some of its provisions.[19]

So how successful was the new legislation?

In 1978 the House Administration Committee asked the Harvard Institute of Politics to examine the impact of the campaign finance amendments. Declaring the amendments "successful in alleviating many of the perceived problems which stimulated congressional action," the Harvard study also noted that the act "has had consequences unanticipated and unintended by its authors and supporters." Most of the unintended consequences, it found,

stemmed from a single flawed assumption that informed the legislation, the belief that Americans spend too much money on
elections. "Contrary to popular impression," the report claimed,
"congressional campaigns spend surprisingly small sums," especially when compared with modern corporate advertising campaigns. It noted that in 1976 candidates for federal office spent
under $212 million. That same year corporations spent $33.6
billion advertising their products. "In a very real sense, electoral
politics is in competition with corporate advertising for the attention of American citizens," it concluded. "Limited campaign
funds often mean limited campaign activity, which, in turn, means
a poorly informed and apathetic electorate."[20]

The authors stated that by setting individual contribution limits too low, the legislation produced two obvious unintended consequences: It encouraged candidates to turn to political action
committees, and it gave an advantage to wealthy candidates who
could write checks to themselves while forcing poor challengers
to raise money in small chunks from numerous sources. "In effect,
the current law forces candidates to turn to corporate and labor
PACs as well as to their personal bank accounts for the needed
funds no longer available through the parties and from individual
contributors." According to the political scientist Frank J. Sorauf,
the legislation highlighted one of the immutable laws of campaign
finance: "Available money seeks an outlet, and if some outlets are
narrowed or closed off, money flows with increased pressure to
the outlets still open." Money will always find its way into campaigns, the Supreme Court decision outlawing spending caps
guaranteed there will be plenty of channels for the new money,
and political action committees were the most immediate beneficiaries. "By limiting individual contributions to candidates, the
1974 law almost certainly diverted giving to PACs," said the journalist Robert Samuelson.[21]

The story of the emergence of political action committees as
a major electoral force is itself a twisted tale of unintended con-

sequences. By the 1970s the AFL-CIO's Committee on Political Education (COPE) was the most effective and powerful PAC in Washington.[22] Under the watchful eye of its chief lobbyist, Andrew J. Biemiller, COPE not only raised and distributed funds but it led voter registration and get-out-the-vote drives that were the envy of most political operatives. In 1970, after an appeals court had ruled a union PAC in St. Louis illegal, AFL-CIO officials worked closely with House Democrats to incorporate language into the 1971 campaign reform bill that explicitly permitted labor unions and corporations to establish "separate segregated funds" for establishing and administering PACs. In the short run the clause served as a basis for the Supreme Court decision overturning the appeals court, but it also carried long-term risks by giving business a legal foundation to create PACs. The following year Common Cause filed a lawsuit against a major corporation charging that the new campaign law prohibited campaign contributions by groups that had contracts with the government. Though ostensibly aimed at corporations, the lawsuit worried labor officials who had secured government contracts for training workers. Once again Biemiller rallied House Democrats to include a provision specifying that unions and companies with government contracts were not barred from creating PACs. The 1974 amendments not only protected those unions but also permitted corporations that held large defense and other government contracts to use corporate funds for establishing and administering their PACs and for fund-raising purposes.[23]

Since corporations had never pursued the PAC strategy in the past, organized labor and its allies among House Democrats believed they would continue to shun PACs in the future. Thanks to the 1974 law, they were wrong. Before 1974 wealthy individuals and business interests could contribute unlimited amounts to campaigns in the form of private donations; thus they had little incentive to form PACs. The new legislation placed tough restrictions on the amount of money that individuals could funnel directly to candidates at the same time that it legalized PACs with looser requirements. The next twenty years witnessed an explosion in the number of groups forming political action committees. There were 608 PACs operating when Congress passed the campaign reform legislation in 1974. By 1977 the number had nearly doubled to 1,146, and it continued to grow at 20 percent a year for the rest of the decade. By 1990 there were more than 4,100 PACs dispensing money to candidates. More important, PACs provided a growing percentage of all campaign funds for House and Senate races. In 1978 PACs accounted for only 13 percent of contributions to Senate candidates. Ten years later that percentage had swelled to 22 percent. The increase was even more dramatic in the House, where PAC contributions rose from 24 to 40 percent. "At a time of general economic stagnation, PACs have become a truly remarkable growth industry," Common Cause observed.[24]

Ironically, organized labor was the big loser in the PAC wars. Labor had pushed for the legislative changes to preserve its electoral clout, but it found itself increasingly overwhelmed by the new corporate PACs. Beginning in 1975, when the FEC confirmed that corporations could use voluntary contributions from stockholders and employees to support candidates, the business community mobilized. In the six months following the FEC decision, more than 150 companies established PACs. In 1974 labor owned up to a third of existing PACs and accounted for half of all PAC spending. By 1984 labor unions constituted fewer than 10 percent of PACs and spent only 17.9 percent of the total PAC outlays. By 1982 business-related PACs were outspending labor in direct contributions to congressional campaigns by nearly three to one. Labor leaders then ruefully appreciated that business had access to greater resources and could easily outspend them. "That was certainly a mistake," confessed a labor lawyer who had lobbied for the 1974 changes that sanctioned PACs. "The way things

have turned out since, the labor movement would have been better off politically with no PACs at all on either side."[25]

A convincing case may be made that labor's miscalculation also
damaged the Democrats. Since the days of the New Deal the Democratic party had identified with the economic interests of the
poor and working class. During the 1970s, under the leadership
of Representative Tony Coelho of California, chair of the Democratic Congressional Campaign Committee, Democrats aggressively pursued business-sponsored PAC money. Indeed, Coelho
was so successful that by the end of the decade these PACs were
contributing far greater sums to congressional Democrats than to
Republicans, even though the GOP was more likely to support
their probusiness agenda. By 1988 House Democratic incumbents were getting 52 percent of their funds from PACs, compared with 38 percent six years earlier. The fund-raising success
placed many Democrats in a difficult political situation: Their
constituency was largely poor and working class, but in order to
get elected, they needed to raise money from groups that represented business interests. The result was a confused message and
a divided coalition. "Because Democrats and Republicans take
money from the same sources, it's harder to differentiate between
the parties," noted a member of Congress.[26]

The passage of campaign finance laws coincided with broader
changes that accentuated the power and influence of PACs. The
most significant change was the spiraling cost of campaigning.
Congress decided to regulate campaign contributions at the same
time that television and sophisticated new computer technology
drove up the cost of running for office. By 1996 the average campaign for Senate cost $4 million; the House $500,000. A typical
senator needed to raise $15,000 a week, every week, for six years
in order to run a competitive reelection race. PACs offered large
sums of money to candidates to pay for advertising, media consultants, and pollsters. In 1960 Democratic and Republican can-

didates for national office spent $14.2 million on radio and television commercials. By 1990 they were spending nearly $1 billion. One study found that a typical Senate campaign in 1988 spent 43 percent of its funds on buying television time. "The hard fact of life for a candidate is that if you are not on TV, you are not truly in the race," said South Carolina Senator Ernest "Fritz" Hollings.[27]

PACs also expanded in response to increased government regulation, which exploded in size during the 1970s. The *Federal Register,* which lists all laws, expanded from 20,036 pages in 1970 to 77,497 pages in 1979. Congress created a host of new regulatory bodies: the Environmental Protection Agency (1970), the Occupational Safety and Health Administration (1970), and the Consumer Product Safety Commission (1972). In addition, many executive agencies established subagencies to monitor enforcement of federal statutes: HEW depended on the Office for Civil Rights (OCR) to enforce fair housing; Labor had the Office of Federal Contract Compliance (OFCC) to monitor the Civil Rights Act of 1964; and the Justice Department relied on the Voting Rights Section to enforce the Voting Rights Act of 1965. As the historian Huge Davis Graham has noted, the new agencies adopted a more expansive definition of social regulation that went far beyond the economic rules of the New Deal era. In the past federal regulatory bodies had responded to specific complaints of wrongdoing, but the new social regulation was "provocative, emphasizing future compliance to reduce risk and eliminate hazards." During the 1970s the federal government shifted from an "administrative state," in which agencies provided money to states with few strings attached, to a "regulatory state," in which Washington established elaborate rules governing private behavior.[28]

In response to the new regulatory state many corporations and trade associations opened Washington offices, hired Capitol Hill law firms, and retained legions of political consultants to keep track of pending legislation and to develop strategies for promoting favorable policies and killing those considered bad. By 1980 nearly 500 corporations had Washington offices, up from 250 in 1970, and the number of lobbyists had tripled. Trade associations opened national headquarters at a rate of one per week, increasing from 1,200 to 1,739 during the decade. Procedural changes in Congress, which abolished the seniority system and led to a proliferation of subcommittees, increased the influence of PACs, which focused large amounts of money on small committees.[29]

Finally, the growth in the number of PACs coincided with the emergence of the New Right, a powerful conservative movement that used loopholes in the campaign finance system to raise money and mobilize fundamentalist voters. The 1970s witnessed an explosion in the number of self-identified evangelical Christians who had "born again" conversions, accepted the Bible as authority for all doctrine and Jesus as Savior, and felt an urgent duty to spread their faith. The number of Americans who identified themselves as born again increased from 24 percent in 1963 to nearly 40 percent in 1978. More than 45 million—one of every five Americans— considered themselves fundamentalists by the end of the decade. Introduced to the faith by television preachers like Jerry Falwell, Pat Robertson, and Jim Bakker, the converts reacted against the cultural revolution of the 1960s and the challenge to traditional gender roles. Like the old right, they believed in small government, low taxes, and free enterprise. Unlike the old right, they viewed politics through the prism of morality. Believing that America was in decline, suffering from the twin evils of political liberalism and loss of Christian faith, leaders of the New Right promised to save America's soul with born again religion and conservative politics.

The new conservatives made two significant contributions to the evolution of PACs. Since large individual donations were no longer legal, political entrepreneurs like New Right disciple Richard Viguerie developed massive computerized data banks of individuals who could contribute smaller sums to campaigns. Direct mail, he said, "allows a lot of conservatives to bypass the liberal media, and go directly into the homes of the conservatives in this country." The direct-mail appeals were designed to provoke. "Our purpose," said a New Right leader, was "to organize discontent." Liberals had hoped that campaign financing reform would remove the political obstacles that prevented Congress from acting on a long list of liberal issues. But direct mail, the weapon of choice for the modern conservative movement, polarized the political debate, increased Republican strength, and produced more stalemate. In addition, the New Right was the first to take advantage of the independent expenditure loophole in the reforms. The *Buckley* decision had made clear that organizations advocating a cause could legally spend limitless amounts on political advertising as long as the ads did not specifically urge voters to vote for or against a specific candidate. These were called issue ads. By 1980 the New Right had used the loophole to spend more than nine million dollars to defeat liberal candidates and elect conservatives. The most aggressive of the independent groups, the National Conservative Political Action Committee (NCPAC), developed a "hit list" of six liberal Democrats running for reelection to the Senate. When four of them lost, NCPAC took credit. In 1988 another conservative group, the National Security Political Action Committee, produced the controversial Willie Horton advertisement used against Democratic presidential challenger Michael Dukakis. The ad used the story of a black inmate who raped a woman while on leave from prison to attack the state prisoner furlough program that existed while Dukakis was governor of Massachusetts.[30]

There is no clear consensus among scholars or political observers about the proper role of PACs or about their influence in the political and legislative process. Opponents, led by Common Cause, continue to believe that PACs distort the political system, allowing powerful special interests to use money favors to buy elections and votes. "It is increasingly clear that PAC participation represents a threat to the public trust in the integrity of our electoral and congressional decision-making processes," Common Cause told the Senate Rules Committee. Supporters, on the other hand, see them playing a healthy role in a pluralistic democracy. The emphasis in this study is not on whether PACs are good or bad but on the fact that the results of the "reforms" in 1974 and 1976 were far different from what anyone at the time expected. Even organized labor and its Democratic allies in the Congress who drafted the clause that gave PACs legal sanction never imagined that PACs would dominate the political landscape and so dramatically influence the way political institutions functioned and, perhaps more important, the way the public viewed those institutions. "I'm not sure any of us knew what PACs meant," recalled a member of Congress who supported the 1974 amendments. "It sounded wonderful—a lot of little people coming together so their money means something. In practice, it became distorted."[31]

IF the purpose of campaign finance reform was to limit the influence of special interest money and restore public confidence in the system, the results were far different. Armed with figures made available by new disclosure laws, public interest groups showed that PACs were not in the charity business. They expected, and often received, something in return for their largess. Reformers never could show a direct relationship between money and legislative votes, but the public often made the logical leap. Many lawmakers reinforced that impression. "We are the only people in the world required by law to take large amounts of money from strangers and then act as if it has no effect on our behavior," said Congressman Barney Frank of Massachusetts. Polls showed that the vast majority of Americans believed that special interests controlled the system and that Congress and elections were bought by the highest bidder. "If one of the original intentions of campaign finance reforms was to limit the appearance of influence of special interests in the political process, the law has, in practice, had the opposite effect," the Harvard study concluded.[32]

Growth of PACs was not the only unintended consequence of the new legislation. By making it harder to raise money at the same time that campaign costs were soaring, the law forced candidates to devote much of their time to fund raising. Representatives and senators complained bitterly that they were spending many of their days searching for money. Senator Robert Byrd of West Virginia grumbled that his colleagues were becoming "full-time fund-raisers and part-time legislators," producing a Congress run by unelected staffs and part-time legislators. If anything, the scramble for money made lawmakers more susceptible to special interest money. "During hearings of Senate committees, you can watch Senators go to phone booths in the committee rooms to dial for dollars," said a Democratic senator. "In both the executive and legislative branches of government, public officials are consumed with the unending pursuit of money to run election campaigns, to fund party organizations, to help colleagues raise campaign funds," noted Senate Majority Leader George Mitchell in 1990.[33]

The Federal Election Commission was helpless to respond to many of the abuses that stemmed from the legislation. Congress had given the agency an even number of seats, equally divided between Democrats and Republicans, without another vote to break ties. On most major decisions the FEC divided on partisan lines, preventing it from taking action. In an effort to keep it weak, Congressman Hays had also intentionally restricted its mandate: It could not launch criminal investigations, impose penalties, or get court injunctions to halt illegal activity. As a result, the commission spent most of its time focusing on responsibilities that were within its mandate: keeping records and forcing campaign

staffs to fill out mountains of paper. Commissioners had to operate with a small budget, limited staff, and an explosion in campaigns searching for every loophole available. "We're underfunded
and overworked," said FEC Chairman John Warren McGarry.
"We have our hands tied behind our backs." Said a Democratic
party strategist: "It's a joke. Nobody takes it seriously."[34]

The Harvard study also confirmed what many critics had said
all along: The legislation contributed to the "deterioration of our
political parties." There were many reasons why parties had lost
their clout, but the new law added to the problem by limiting "the
services and resources they can provide to their candidates." In
1972, 17 percent of the money available to House candidates
came through their political parties. By 1978 that had declined to
4.5 percent. In those six years party contributions to Democrats
fell by 77 percent, to Republicans by 58 percent. In addition,
complicated regulations and burdensome reporting requirements
"had the effective consequence of discouraging local party leaders from becoming involved in the campaigns of Federal candidates."[35]

By the end of the decade Democrats who had widened the
PAC loophole were condemning the system of campaign financing as "scandalous" and "a paralyzing obscenity" in need of reform. Republicans seemed entertained by the change of heart.
"I'm a little amused that suddenly our opponents have developed
a real conscience about political action committees," said Ronald
Reagan. "I don't remember them being that aroused when the
only ones that you knew about were on their side." In 1979, liberals introduced another public financing bill for congressional
elections that placed strict limits on campaign contributions from
PACs. "It is threatening to the democratic process if more and
more of the money we receive must come from special interest
groups," declared Democrat Jim Wright of Texas. "A seat in the
House of Representatives shouldn't be like a seat on the New
York stock exchange—up for sale to the highest bidder."[36]

The tough rhetoric aside, Congress had no more heart for public financing in 1979 than it had had in 1974 or 1976. Many members played to public worry about the influence of money in politics, but they had little real incentive to change the post-1974 system. The reason was simple: The new system favored incumbents. Most PACs chose to use their money to develop close relationships with existing representatives rather than to expend resources supporting challengers. Self-preservation dictated that members of Congress condemn the system while making sure they could still reap the financial benefits. After months of wrangling, the House and Senate decided to focus their attention on a few limited measures upon which everyone could agree. Democrats and Republicans were united in their belief that the public financing of presidential elections, while generally accepted, had weakened traditional grass roots and party-building activities. With only limited federal funds to spend, both the Democratic and Republican presidential campaigns focused on media advertising, cutting back on purchasing the buttons and bumper stickers that traditionally were used to promote grass roots activity. In the waning days of the 1979 legislative season Congress passed legislation to permit state and local party groups to purchase campaign materials for activities that supported federal candidates. Congressional sponsors believed that this revision would promote party-building activities and increase citizen participation in campaigns.[37]

At the same time that Congress pushed state and local parties to play a more active role in campaigns for national office, the FEC loosened the rules on how parties raised and spent funds. State parties supported a host of candidates for a wide range of offices, from local sheriff to president. State campaign finance laws, where they did exist, were often more permissive than national laws. If a state party organized a voter registration drive that benefited both local and national candidates, would the money raised and spent be governed by federal or state laws? In a controversial

1978 decision the FEC declared that parties had to abide only by state regulations. The result was that political parties could solicit unlimited sums of money from labor and corporate PACs under permissive state guidelines and then redirect the money to help elect federal candidates. This funding quickly became known as soft money because it was not subject to the "hard" limits of federal law. The sole limitation on the source of money was that only American citizens or companies with branches in the United States could contribute.[38]

The new legislation combined with the FEC decision opened another gaping hole in the campaign finance system. Since before 1990 there were no reporting requirements for soft money, it is difficult to know how much the parties spent during the 1980s. The best guess is that the two major parties spent $19.1 million in soft money during the 1980 election cycle, with the Republicans spending $15.1 million and the Democrats $4 million. In 1984 the parties raised and distributed an estimated $21.6 million, with the Republicans again outpacing the Democrats by a margin of $15.6 million to $6 million. But the 1988 Michael Dukakis for president campaign began raising soft money more aggressively, using it to help support its activities in key states. "We have attempted to put ourselves on a level playing field with the Republicans," said the finance chairman of the Dukakis campaign. His opponent, George Bush, followed suit, creating Team 100, consisting of donors of $100,000 or more. By the time the campaign was over, the Democrats had raised an estimated $42 million in soft money compared with the Republicans' $20 million. In just four years the amount of soft money in presidential races almost tripled from $21.6 to $62 million.[39]

The upsurge in soft money produced new calls for reform. In 1990 Common Cause led a fight to close the soft money loophole, charging that it "creates the opportunity for fat cats and special interests to buy influence with the President of the United States." That year the FEC issued new disclosure regulations that placed minor restraints on soft money spending but no restrictions on soft money fund raising. In 1992 congressional Democrats in both the House and the Senate passed an ambitious bill that created voluntary ceilings for spending on congressional races. In exchange for accepting the ceilings, House candidates would receive as much as $200,000 in federal funds for both primary and general elections, and Senate candidates subsidies of up to $1.1 million for television advertising. The bill also placed new restrictions on PAC spending and barred the parties from spending soft money in ways that benefited federal candidates. Once again reformers said the legislation would limit the influence of special interests and restore public confidence in Congress and the election process. But they never had the chance to prove their claim because President Bush vetoed the bill, calling it a taxpayer-financed incumbent protection plan. Adopting the rhetoric of the reformers, Bush said the law would perpetuate "the corrupting influence of special interests" and "would limit political speech protected by the First Amendment."[40]

President Bill Clinton came to office determined to plug the soft money loophole. In his 1992 campaign book he pledged to "end the unlimited soft money contributions." He sounded the reform theme again in his inaugural address: "And so I say to all of you here, let us resolve to reform our politics so that power and privilege no longer shut down the voice of the people. Let us give this capital back to the people to whom it belongs." In May 1993, promising to "change fundamentally the way campaigns are financed," Clinton called for "voluntary caps" on spending for House and Senate races and tighter restrictions on PACs. In return for agreeing to abide by the caps, candidates would receive communications vouchers to pay for broadcast time, vouchers paid for by a new tax on lobbyists. "It's refreshing to have a president who is truly interested in this subject and totally committed to achieving campaign reform this year," declared House Majority Leader Richard Gephardt. Most congressional Democrats did not share

Clinton's enthusiasm for reform, and they convinced him to put the idea on the back burner, saying it would distract attention from his major priority of health care reform. It proved to be a major miscalculation. The health care bill went down to defeat thanks in part to a $14-million advertising blitz by the insurance industry, which used a series of "Harry and Louise" television advertisements to convince voters that health care reform would lead to higher taxes and poor service.[41]

If there was ever a chance that Clinton's proposal would become law, it died in November 1994, when the Republicans took control of the House of Representatives for the first time in fifty years. Private polls showed that the public viewed Clinton as ineffective and liberal, a deadly combination, especially for a candidate elected as a "New Democrat" who had broken with his party's liberal past. He trailed his presumptive Republican opponent, Republican Senate Leader Robert Dole of Kansas, by fifteen points. "You can't imagine how bleak things were inside the Clinton White House in late 1994," recalled adviser George Stephanopoulos. With his poll numbers dipping dangerously low and many pundits predicting that he would be a one-term president, Clinton saw the soft money loophole as a way to save his presidency, and he dropped all talk of reform. Before he could take on Dole, Clinton needed to redefine himself, returning to the successful centrist image that had helped him win election in 1992. The remake would cost money, far more than the $37 million allotted in public financing for the primaries. "If we don't spend $10 million on TV [in 1995], I could lose this thing," Clinton said.[42]

The president turned to the airways to bombard the public with ads that would redefine him and undermine support for his opponent. "One way to be able to control the message would be to buy it," explained Democratic National Committee Chairman Donald L. Fowler. As long as the ads did not specifically tell voters to vote for Clinton, they fell into the amorphous category of "issue ads" and therefore were not charged against the president's spending limit. Though the ads were ostensibly produced by the Democratic party, Clinton took a personal interest in developing them. His private adviser Dick Morris called Clinton "the day-to-day operational director of our TV-ad campaign. . . . He worked over every script, watched each ad, ordered changes in every visual presentation, and decided which ads would run and where. . . . Every ad was his ad." The ads aired nonstop from October until the Democratic convention in August 1996 and were seen by an estimated 125 million Americans three times a week. They were designed to rebuild Clinton's centrist image by showing him tough on crime and by supporting a balanced budget and welfare reform. At the same time the Democratic party aired commercials accusing the Republicans of trying to cut popular social programs. "President Clinton protects Medicare. The Dole-Gingrich budget tried to cut Medicare $270 billion," a narrator intoned while the screen flashed with grainy black-and-white pictures of Dole and House Speaker Newt Gingrich. Clinton, bragged Morris, had "created the first fully advertised presidency in U.S. history."[43]

Not surprisingly, the president's men were obsessed with finding clever ways to raise money to pay for the advertising operation, which cost an estimated $40 million. According to one White House insider, Morris would "sit in these weekly meetings and say, 'We've got to be spending $1 million, $2 million a week. We've got to keep spending, got to find the money, got to find the money.'" The soft money loophole allowed Clinton to circumvent federal contribution caps because donors to the DNC were not limited to the meager one-thousand-dollar-per-election limit applied to campaign donors. Moreover, corporations and labor unions, barred from donating directly to the candidate, could give unlimited soft money to the party.[44]

Taking a direct interest in finding the money, the president showered supporters and fund raisers with presidential perks, such as state dinner invitations, seats aboard Air Force One, tickets to the White House movie theater, and golf outings with him. According to a DNC pamphlet, a $100,000 contribution to the party was worth a private dinner with the president. For a paltry $25,000 an "average" citizen could dine with Al Gore in the vice presidential mansion. According to the *Los Angeles Times,* Clinton "spent far more time in 1996 raising money than any incumbent chief executive in modern history." From January to November the president appeared at 237 fund-raising events, sometimes attending as many as three dinners in one night, and raised a total of $119.2 million in soft money. "A lot of times he would complain," Morris told House investigators, "he would say, 'I haven't slept in three days; every time I turn around they want me to be at a fund-raiser. . . . I cannot think, I can't do anything; every minute of my time is spent at these fund-raisers.' " The money raised from these events was funneled directly into the DNC, which used it to pay for more ads for the Clinton campaign. "For all intents and purposes," noted two *Washington Post* reporters, "the DNC became an extension of the Clinton-Gore campaign, allowing the president to spend an extra $44 million on television ads and effectively obliterating the spending cap."[45]

The Republican nominee Robert Dole complained about the Clinton tactics while mimicking his methods. After suffering through a bruising primary fight against millionaire Steve Forbes, who spent $25 million of his own money on attack ads, Dole locked up the nomination in March but not before spending nearly all his federal money. Fearing that he would be eclipsed by the Clinton advertising blitz, the Republicans spent twenty million dollars of soft money to keep Dole in the public eye. Most of the funds were raised from telecommunications, tobacco, and pharmaceutical companies that hoped their investment would bring relief from federal regulators. The Republican National Committee paid for a sixty-second commercial crafted by Dole's advertising team called "The Story," which devoted fifty-six seconds to Dole's biography and four seconds to the issues he espoused.[46]

In addition to the soft money raised by the parties, more than two dozen organizations spent between $135 million and $150 million on issue advocacy during the election. A report by the Annenberg Public Policy Center found that 90 percent of issue ads named a specific candidate, and the majority were negative ads targeting opponents. Under the aggressive leadership of its new leader, John J. Sweeney, the seventeen-million-member AFL-CIO launched a $35 million advertising and grass roots program to help Democrats regain control of the House. Another liberal group, Citizen Action, spent $7 million blasting the Republicans for cutting education and gutting environmental regulations. The Sierra Club poured $3.5 million into issue ads and spent another $3 million on voter guides. Alarmed by the AFL-CIO's advertising salvo, the U.S. Chamber of Commerce led a belated effort by business groups to retaliate with their own issue ads.[47]

Once again the Supreme Court helped excite the spending free-for-all, ruling in a case involving the Colorado Republican party that political parties had the right to make independent expenditures on behalf of their candidates as long as there was no coordination or communication between the party and the candidate. Critics were puzzled by the decision: How could parties be independent of the candidates they recruited and trained? The verdict allowed political parties to collect and spend as much money as they could to promote their candidates, provided they did not actually suggest voting for them. Nonetheless, both parties exploited the new opening. The "independent" GOP Senate campaign committee raised and spent $10 million over the final three months of the campaign. Democratic donors, thoroughly tapped by President Clinton, were already exhausted and managed to produce only $1.4 million to boost congressional candidates with issue ads.[48]

The 1996 election revealed how the pursuit of cash had frustrated reformers and overwhelmed the nation's fragile campaign finance system. "What was once a loophole in the campaign laws has become a four-lane highway full of Brinks trucks," observed *Newsweek*. In 1996 soft money contributions exceeded $261 million, dwarfing the $60 million federal campaign limit. The Republican party raised $138.2 million; the Democrats hauled in $123.9 million. "In 25 years of following political money, I have seen campaign finance abuses, and I have seen campaign finance abuses," observed Common Cause President Fred Wertheimer. "And I say without hesitation that this election will go down as the worst in modern times, if not in our history." According to the deputy director of the Center for Responsive Politics, a Washington-based nonprofit group, "This is the year of the loophole. There are no limits. There are no rules."[49]

The election shredded what had been left of the campaign finance laws of the 1970s. "Instead of favoring small contributors and just-folks politicians, as post-Watergate reformers intended originally," noted the journalist Jonathan Rauch, the new finance system "favors plutocrats (who can finance their own campaigns), machine politicians (with fund-raising factories) and guerrilla candidates (who need little money). Instead of lightening the burdens of fund raising, the rules have turned politicians into full-time money-grubbers." Edward Kennedy, one of the principal sponsors of the original laws, agreed that "they no longer do the job" because "fund-raisers have carved out loopholes to squeeze and skirt the laws."[50]

The effort to revitalize the local and state political parties by opening up the soft money loophole also backfired on reformers. By 1996 the national parties had co-opted most of the money, leaving state parties and many voters feeling alienated. "The vast majority of the issue advocacy advertising is negative," observed the political scientist Anthony Corrado. "The parties are spending money increasingly not on activities that promote grass roots and greater participation, but on ads which promote cynicism and depress turnout. We've come full circle. A provision of the law that was put in to promote grass-roots activities now stifles it."[51]

An effort designed to restore public faith in the political process had contributed to unprecedented cynicism and suspicion. Fewer than half of all eligible voters chose to cast their ballots in 1996, continuing a long-term trend of low voter turnout. Polls showed the vast majority of Americans believe politicians were corrupted by well-financed special interests. Twenty years after passage of the Campaign Finance Act, New Jersey Senator Bill Bradley declared, "Money is distorting democracy." It "not only determines who wins," he declared, "but often who runs."[52]

FOLLOWING the abuses of the 1996 campaign, the cry for reform reached a fever pitch not heard since Watergate. Common Cause and many other reformers repeated the mantra of 1974: that Americans spent too much money on elections and that only public financing could solve the problem. "The basic problem is that the cost of conducting a campaign for federal office has been bid up to a point that is destructive of the very democratic process it is said to represent," the *Washington Post* editorialized in 1997. "The cost at both the congressional and presidential levels is obscene."[53]

Again depicting the issue as a struggle between the noble "people" and the greedy "special interests," reformers hoped to mold public outrage at the abuses of 1996 into a legislative agenda in support of public financing. In 1997 they rallied around a bipartisan proposal sponsored by Republican Senator John McCain and Wisconsin Democrat Russell Feingold. The original bill outlawed soft money and sharply reduced donations by PACs. In an effort to reduce campaign costs, the bill offered congressional candidates free TV time and discounted postage rates if they accepted spending limits. Participating candidates would be required to raise money in increments of $250 or less, with the majority of funds coming from their home districts. They could exceed their spending limits, however, if a private interest group launched an independent campaign against them. Common Cause hailed the bill as "fair, tough, creative and comprehensive."[54]

But critics continued to hammer away at many of the underlying assumptions of campaign reform. Were campaigns too expensive? The libertarian CATO Institute noted that the parties spent $2.6 billion filling 476 congressional offices in 1996. By contrast, Americans spent $4.5 billion on potato chips and nearly $1 billion on Barbie dolls. In 1994 PACs spent $189 million on congressional races, roughly the same amount of money Kevin Costner spent directing the 1995 movie *Waterworld*. Arguing that there was *not* too much money being spent on politics, critics also charged that it was impossible to separate money from politics without violating First Amendment rights. "The distasteful reality is that politics requires money," noted Robert Samuelson. "To compete, candidates must communicate and to communicate, they need cash. There is no easy way to curb the role of money in politics without curbing free expression." Common Cause argued in favor of spending caps, saying it would level the field and give challengers a fair chance against PAC-financed incumbents. But as many scholars have noted, the result would often be just the opposite: Since challengers need to raise more money than do incumbents, a cap would reinforce the status quo. The same was true of contribution caps on individuals. Though designed to eliminate the influence of "fat cats," they forced candidates to turn to PACs, independent committees, or, in many cases, their own pocketbooks.[55]

Critics also pointed out the limitations of trying to depict the issue as a struggle between "the people" and the "special interests." By the 1990s there were so many political groups representing so many diverse groups that it was hard to figure out who were the "people" and who were the "special interests." It was clear as well that the "people" were not of one mind on the wisdom of campaign finance reform, which had always been a complicated subject that did not affect them directly in the way that health care and education did. While generally disgusted with politics and with politicians, they were uncertain about the proper remedy. A *Washington Post* poll found only 12 percent of Americans favored paying for the system from tax money. "No one in the history of American politics has ever won or lost a campaign on the subject of campaign-finance reform," said Republican Senator Mitch McConnell.[56]

Finally, the failure of past efforts to reform campaign spending convinced many informed people of the futility of trying to limit the flow of money into politics. "There is no way to stop interested people and interested organizations from finding their way around whatever regulations you can devise, unless you're willing to shut off speech and debate," said the political scientist Michael Malbin. "If there's one lesson to be gleaned from the previous round of reforms, it may be that rigid contribution and spending limits, however well intentioned, tend to force money into hidden venues," said the journalist Eliza Newlin Carney. The 1974 reforms were "stupid in retrospect," observed Republican Pete du Point, a former Delaware congressman. "Private-sector lawyers are quicker than government lawyers in finding the loopholes and they always will be."[57]

Nor was the example of the states, which pushed reform more aggressively than Washington, particularly reassuring. During the 1990s many states used the initiative and referendum process to pass new campaign finance laws. By 1996 thirty-five states had passed laws limiting the size of individual contributions. Many states also either prohibited or limited direct contributions from labor unions, corporations, and political action committees. Twenty-two states enacted some form of public financing for statewide candidates. "These initiatives should send a loud and clear message to Members of Congress that there is broad national support for campaign finance reform and that they should act immediately," said Common Cause. The message, however, was not as clear as Common Cause suggested. The state efforts "serve as a warning that the arsenal of regulatory weapons is fairly limited in what can be done in terms of election reform," noted the political scientist Herbert Alexander. States that have limited campaign contributions have discovered that the money flows elsewhere—namely, to PACs and independent groups whose right to spend without limit have been upheld in numerous court challenges. For example, in 1994 voters in Oregon passed Ballot Measure 9, which capped all contributions to state candidates at one hundred dollars in an effort to limit the influence of large special interests and to encourage citizen participation. "By forcing candidates to raise money from average Oregonians instead of professional lobbyists, the new law focuses attention on the concerns of ordinary citizens," said one of the measure's supporters. But it did not turn out that way. Big donors, if barred from giving directly to a campaign or PACs, simply channeled money into independent committees that could both raise and spend money freely. In some state senate races, independent expenditures exceeded the candidates' voluntary limits. "The theory is that if you reduce the power of big players, then you increase the power of small players," observed Malbin, but "our conclusion is that the big players still play."[58]

Any proposal for change must traverse a political, judicial, and ideological minefield. Politicians will not support any changes in the system that take away an advantage they hold or that would give their opponents an edge. "The reality is that most incumbents of both parties—for all that they may whine about the burden of fund-raising—prefer the system under which they were elected to any untested scheme that might replace it," observed journalist David Broder. Republicans, who generally get more support from wealthy people than Democrats, oppose efforts to place limits on political contributions. Democrats, on the other hand, push for low contribution limits but strenuously oppose Republican moves to outlaw soft money contributions from labor unions. Many Republicans favor limiting the amount of money that congressional candidates receive from outside their states or districts. Democrats, who represent poor districts, fear such a prohibition would prevent them from running credible campaigns. House members, who must run every two years and are more dependent on PAC money, are also generally less enthusiastic about comprehensive reform that would prohibit independent expenditures and tighten PAC regulations. Moreover, over all potential proposals for reform hangs the courts' insistence that the right of free political expression not be abridged.[59]

The evolution of campaign finance laws offers a classic case study of why unintended consequences plague American politics. If the post-Watergate Congress had looked into its crystal ball and foreseen the abuses of the 1996 campaign, it would never have passed the 1974 amendments. Reformers had hoped to cleanse the dirty soul of American politics, but as the Supreme Court decision in *Buckley* underscored, any effort to limit campaign spending in a democracy must navigate a maze of competing rights. The Court, taking a more expansive view of individual rights than did Congress, punched a major loophole in the legislation by prohibiting any restrictions of campaign spending. By contrast, the populist language that reformers used to describe the issue was familiar to most Americans, but it made little sense of an issue as complex as money and politics. The result was a whole new universe of campaign financing, a world dominated by the very special interests the new system was supposed to destroy. It is not easy to dispute the journalist Jonathan Rauch's sober conclusion: "Probably no American public policy is a more comprehensive failure than campaign finance reform."[60]

Conclusion

A Few Final Observations

●

ΛLL the laws discussed here were plagued by problems that the sociologist Robert Merton identified more than a half century ago. He classified ignorance, or the failure to obtain sufficient information about possible outcomes, as a major contributor to unintended consequences. But even with adequate information, policy makers may not understand how to weigh it, and the confusion produces unexplained outcomes. Merton also blamed what he called the "Imperious Immediacy of Interest," which occurs when people so desire a particular outcome that they simply ignore the potential for unintended consequences that should be perfectly clear. "Basic Values" can also contribute to unanticipated consequences when "one's fundamental values require that the action be taken" even if it runs counter to common sense. The final villain is "Self-Defeating Predictions," produced when public anticipations of social developments change the course of events by influencing the way people perceive those events.[1]

Certainly a lack of knowledge played a role in the producing of unintended consequences. How could Roosevelt have known that the breakup of the traditional family would transform his modest provision to aid widows with children into the nation's largest and most expensive welfare program? Should Robert Felix and other advocates of community mental health have anticipated that Congress would fail to build the promised community centers? It would have been hard for supporters of immigration reform in 1965 to anticipate the flood of new immigrants from Latin America. Could anyone in 1974 have predicted the explosive growth in PACs or the soaring cost of campaigns? The fact is, legislators are forced to make decisions based on current knowledge and reasonable guesses about the future. Through no fault of their own, that knowledge often turns out to be inadequate, and events move in a different direction from that anticipated.

It is also fair to say that even when they did have the necessary knowledge, reformers often were not sure how to use it. During the 1930s American policy makers had limited experience using federal power to address poverty when they predicted that it would "wither away." By the time Lyndon Johnson's poverty warriors emerged on the scene in the 1960s, however, the nation had had nearly thirty years of evidence showing the persistent and complex nature of the problem. They ignored much of the evidence and launched a war on poverty using many of the same old assumptions. Not only did the administration underestimate the structural roots of poverty, but it raised public expectations that it could never fulfill by calling for total victory.

The war on poverty was the poster child of unintended consequences. Not only was it plagued by faulty assumptions and false expectations, but it also fell victim to the "Imperious Immediacy of Interest." Since the president was so determined to surpass his idol, FDR, and to distinguish himself from his slain predecessor, passing legislation became a goal in itself. As the history of community action reveals, Johnson's administration committed itself to passing a poverty program and only later stumbled on the method for implementing it. The administration then proceeded to push the program through a pliant Congress without defining what it meant by community action. The same rush to pass legislation distorted the intent of the Immigration Act of 1965. The administration wanted to enact a bill that abolished the national origins clause—a worthy goal—but in the legislative brokering that followed, Johnson replaced the emphasis on attracting skilled labor contained in the original Kennedy bill with Feighan's family unification scheme without ever pausing to consider the significance of the shift.

What is most striking about these case studies is how the unanticipated consequences grow out of the peculiarities of American political ideology or what Merton called "Basic Values." The Americans, said Tocqueville in one of his most quoted remarks, "are unanimous upon the general principles that ought to rule human society." Some foreign and native observers have reiterated this point, highlighting key concepts in the American creed: individualism, equality, limited government, economic opportunity, democracy. Not surprisingly, the threads of the American Creed run through the public debates on major pieces of legislation. It is impossible to understand the American approach to welfare, for example, without appreciating the deep undercurrents of individualism and self-help. A corollary faith in the power of local communities to solve pressing social problems infused the war on poverty and the drive for deinstitutionalization. The faith in local democracy convinced John Gardner that the nation's campaign finance system needed to be reformed. A determination to redress social inequality infused Hubert Humphrey's passion for civil rights and Emanuel Celler's determination to abolish the national origins clause.

Legislators invoked the ideals of individualism, self-help, equality, and democracy to build public support for their reforms, but as many scholars have pointed out, similarity in language often disguises deep differences in views. The concepts are so familiar, so much a part of our national lexicon, that few Americans appreciate their complexity or recognize the potential for conflict they create. American political ideology, as the political scientist Robert McCoskey noted, is not "a consistent body of dogmas tending in the same direction, but a conglomerate of ideas which may be and often are logically inconsistent." It is "characteristic of the American mind . . . to hold contradictory ideas simultaneously without bothering to resolve the potential conflict between them." Americans may share a common belief in the doctrine of equality, for example, but as the historian Gordon Wood has noted, the concept always "possessed an inherent ambivalence: on one hand it stressed equality of opportunity which implied social differences and distinctions; on the other hand it emphasized equality of condition which denied these same social differences and distinctions." That inherent tension was built into the Civil Rights Act of 1964 and has played out over the past thirty years in the debate over affirmative action. Conservatives profess a belief in color blindness, arguing that society has an obligation to guarantee every citizen the opportunity to compete as equals. Liberals, on the other hand, contend that equal opportunity necessarily creates or perpetuates inequalities and that only by giving attention to actual results can true equality be achieved.[2]

Appeals to the American Creed may be necessary to build popular support for legislation, but they also allow legislators to avoid confronting difficult questions. Supporters of deinstitutionalization lulled Congress with repeated appeals to the healing power of local communities. In all the public debates and discussions, no one asked Felix or other advocates to define what they meant by mental illness or to provide scientific evidence that community centers were superior to well-managed state hospitals. They did not have to: Everyone "knew" that people were better off in the community. The same problem plagued other initiatives. The Johnson administration promised to eradicate poverty from the land in ten years with a strategy that depended heavily on the concept of community action. Who could argue with an effort that would solve poverty by giving poor people more involvement in local decision making? The discussions about community involvement often clouded debate over more challenging questions: What caused poverty, and how could community action address long-term structural problems of low income

. .

and joblessness? John Gardner invoked familiar populist language of "the people vs. the special interests" to arouse public indignation toward the system of campaign finance. The problems were real, but the rhetoric ignored the ingrained conflict between the public desire to limit campaign spending and an individual right to free speech.

Given the American system of federalism, it was often left to unelected bureaucrats and the judiciary to resolve these conflicting appeals to deeply held American values. The courts played a central role in modifying the original intent of the Civil Rights Act of 1964 and the Federal Election Campaign Finance Act of 1974. In both cases the Supreme Court addressed major questions that Congress had left unresolved. The ambiguity of the Civil Rights Act gave the Equal Employment Opportunity Commission (EEOC) the leeway it needed to develop affirmative action guidelines. Initially the Supreme Court deferred to EEOC rulings, but in recent years it has backtracked in its support. The justices blasted a gaping loophole in campaign finance by arguing that restrictions on contributions violated the First Amendment. The Federal Election Commission (FEC) further redirected the intent of reformers by creating the soft money loophole. The Court's expanded definition of individual rights frustrated the intent of community mental health movement and the war on poverty. In the former, legal rulings made it difficult to commit people with serious mental illness; in the latter, justices forced states to liberalize eligibility requirement for welfare, thus raising costs and expanding welfare rolls.

What should we learn from these examples of unintended consequences in the invention of American social policy? I would not want readers to conclude from these examples that we must abandon our efforts to identify social problems or suspend efforts to use government as a positive force for social change. Awareness that our schemes for national betterment may have lurking within them results we do not like should produce humility, not despair.

The complexities of modern life will always have the capacity to confound the plans of social planners, but the alternative—to be content to drift along at the mercy of events because we fear that whatever we try will have unintended consequences—is far less attractive. Also, to whatever extent undesirable consequences may arise from multitudinous pursuits and diverse views, we must recognize—as James Madison did in the *Federalist Paper No. 10*—that the central task of any republic is somehow to manage factionalism and steer the nation on a wise and proper course through its diverse and competing interests.

No doubt the journey ahead will take us to places we never intended and produce results we never expected. Some of those places and results will be unpleasant and discouraging. On such occasions we must look again at the maps and charts with fresh eyes and try to plot better and wiser courses.

. .

Endnotes

*

Introduction

1. Richard Lattimore, introduction to Aeschylus, *Oresteia,* trans. Richard Lattimore (Chicago: University of Chicago Press, 1953), 14; Edwin Dolin, introduction to *An Anthology of Greek Tragedy,* ed. Albert Cook and Edwin Dolin (Indianapolis: Bobbs-Merrill, 1972), xli; Johann Wolfgang von Goethe, *Faust,* part I, scene iii, line 1,336 *("Ein Teil von jener Kraft, / Die stets das Böse will und stets das Gute schafft");* "Obedient Rebel," *Time* (March 24, 1967), 74; Albert O. Hirschman, "Reactionary Rhetoric," *Atlantic* (May 1989), 63; Adam Smith, *An Inquiry into the Nature and Causes of the Wealth of Nations* (New York: Modern Library, 1937), 423; Alexis de Tocqueville, *The Old Regime and the French Revolution,* trans. Stuart Gilbert (Gloucester, Mass.: Peter Smith, 1978), 176–77.

2. Gladys L. Hobby, *Penicillin: Meeting the Challenge* (New Haven: Yale University Press, 1985), 8; Charles Marwick, "It Takes a Community . . . to Lower the STD Rate," *Journal of the American Medical Association* 278 (July 23/30, 1997), 272; "Ten Leading Nationally Notifiable Infectious Diseases—United States, 1995," *Morbidity and Mortality Weekly Report* 45 (October 18, 1996), 883; Thomas R. Eng and William T. Butler, eds., *The Hidden Epidemic: Confronting Sexually Transmitted Diseases* (Washington, D.C.: National Academy Press, 1997), 34–35; *New York Times,* March 9, 1998.

3. Charles F. Jones, "Science and the Human Condition," *Business Quarterly* 58 (June 22, 1994), 117; Dick Price, "The Toad That Ate Australia," *IEEE Expert* 11 (December 1996), 13; Carol Bishop Hipps, "Kudzu: A Vegetable Menace That Started Out as a Good Idea," *Horticulture* 72 (June–July 1994), 36–39; *New York Times,* April 27, 1997.

4. Jones, "Science and the Human Condition," 117; ibid., 21; Gene I. Rochlin, *Trapped in the Net: The Unanticipated Consequences of Computerization* (Princeton, N.J.: Princeton University Press, 1987); Edward Tenner, *Why Things Bite Back: Technology and the Revenge of Unintended Consequences* (New York: Knopf, 1996).

5. James Gleick, *Chaos: Making a New Science* (New York: Viking, 1987), 8.

6. *Newsday,* March 7, 1989; Charles Handy, *The Age of Paradox* (Boston: Harvard Business School Press, 1994), x; Nohria Nitin and James D. Berkley, "An Action Per-

spective: The Crux of the New Management; Strategy & Organization," *California Management Review* 36 (June 22, 1994), 70–92; J. P. Donlon, "The Paradox Paradigm," *Chief Executive* (January 1995), 32; *Orange County Register,* December 8, 1991; *Los Angeles Times,* October 11, 1987; Tom Peters, *Thriving on Chaos: Handbook for a Management Revolution* (New York: Knopf, 1987), 485.

7. L. R. Jones, "Aaron Wildavsky: A Man and Scholar for All Seasons," *Public Administration Review* 55 (January–February 1995), 3–16; Jeffrey Pressman and Aaron Wildavsky, *Implementation: How Great Expectations in Washington Are Dashed in Oakland* (Berkeley: University of California Press, 1973), 6, 87–124; James Q. Wilson, *Bureaucracy: What Government Agencies Do and Why They Do It* (New York: Basic Books, 1989), 377; Eugene Bardach, *The Implementation Game: What Happens after a Bill Becomes a Law* (Cambridge, Mass.: MIT Press, 1977).

8. Gordon S. Wood, "The Creative Imagination of Bernard Bailyn," in *The Transformation of Early American History: Society, Authority, and Ideology,* ed. James A. Henretta et al. (New York: Knopf, 1991), 46; Gordon Wood, *The Radicalism of the American Revolution* (New York: Knopf, 1992); Joyce Appleby, "The Radical Recreation of the American Republic," *William and Mary Quarterly* 51 (October 1994), 679–83.

9. Robert Michels, *Political Parties: A Sociological Study of the Oligarchical Tendencies of Modern Democracy* (New York: Free Press, 1962); Émile Durkheim, *The Division of Labor in Society* (New York: Free Press, 1993); Robert K. Merton, "The Unanticipated Consequences of Purposive Social Action," *American Sociological Review* 1 (December 1936), 894–904.

10. Charles Murray, *Losing Ground: American Social Policy, 1950–1980* (New York: Basic Books, 1984), 9, 212, 227; Ed Gillespie and Bob Schellhas, eds., *Contract with America: The Bold Plan by Rep. Newt Gingrich, Rep. Dick Armey and the House Republicans to Change the Nation* (New York: Times Books, 1994), 65.

11. J. Anthony Lukas, *Common Ground: A Turbulent Decade in the Lives of Three American Families* (New York: Knopf, 1985); Ronald Formisano, *Boston against Busing: Race, Class, and Ethnicity in the 1960s and 1970s* (Chapel Hill: University of North Carolina Press, 1991); J. Harvie Wilkinson, *From Brown to Bakke: The Supreme Court and School Integration, 1954–1978* (New York: Oxford University Press, 1976).

12. James S. Olson and Randy Roberts, *Where the Domino Fell: America in Vietnam, 1945–1990* (New York: St. Martin's Press, 1991), 282–83; *Washington Post,* January 31, 1980.

13. Joseph Nye, "In Government We Don't Trust," *Foreign Policy* 108 (September 22, 1997), 99; Philip Yancey, "The Folly of Good Intentions," *Christianity Today* 39 (October 23, 1995), 96.

14. Nathan Glazer, "The Limits of Social Policy," *Commentary* 52 (September 1971), 51; Nathan Glazer, *The Limits of Social Policy* (Cambridge, Mass.: Harvard University Press, 1988), 3; David Whitman, "The Law of Welcome Surprises," *U.S. News & World Report* (December 30, 1996), 78; *Washington Post,* April 12, 1995; Charles Murray, *In Pursuit: Of Happiness and Good Government* (New York: Simon and Schuster, 1988), 208. Milton Friedman published the "Invisible Foot" concept in his

Newsweek column, but the idea came from a University of North Texas professor of economics named Dick Armey, today U.S. House majority leader, who mailed it to Friedman. See *Washington Post,* February 21, 1995. For an excellent critique of conservative arguments, see Albert O. Hirschman, "Reactionary Rhetoric," *Atlantic* (May 1989), 63–70. Hirschman stresses that contrary to the conservative stance, unintended consequences are not always undesirable.

15. Robert Post, "Justice for Scalia," *New York Review of Books* (June 11, 1998), 57–62; Antonin Scalia, *A Matter of Interpretation: Federal Courts and the Law* (Princeton, N.J.: Princeton University Press, 1997), 16–18. In his response to Scalia, the legal scholar Ronald Dworkin claimed there existed a "crucial" distinction between what legislators "intended to say in enacting the language they used, and what they intended— or expected or hoped—would be the consequence of their saying it." Other critics have argued that proponents have misrepresented textualism as an alternative to judicial activism. "Scalia's focus on the text often means that it's the Court, and the Court alone, that is going to decide what the right answer is," observed Michael Dorf. See Linda Greenhouse, "Sure Justices Legislate," *New York Times,* July 5, 1988, IV, 6.

16. Michael J. Bennett, *When Dreams Came True: The GI Bill and the Making of Modern America* (Washington, D.C.: Brassey's, 1996); Edward Kiester, Jr., "The G.I. Bill May Be the Best Deal Ever Made by Uncle Sam," *Smithsonian* (November 1994), 128–41.

17. Milton Greenberg, *The GI Bill: The Law that Changed America* (New York: Lickle Publishing, 1997).

18. "The Law of Welcome Surprises," *U.S. News & World Report* (December 30, 1996), 78.

19. *New York Times,* July 26, 1988.

20. Steven F. Lawson, *In Pursuit of Power: Southern Blacks & Electoral Politics, 1965–1982* (New York: Columbia University Press, 1985); Abigail M. Thernstrom, "The Odd Evolution of the Voting Rights Act," *Public Interest* (Spring 1979), 49–76.

21. Ronald Brownstein and Dan Balz, *Storming the Gates: Protest Politics and the Republican Revival* (Boston: Little, Brown, 1996), 357–58.

22. Robert Worth, "Why Deregulation Has Gone Too Far," *Washington Monthly* (July–August, 1998), 10–14.

23. William B. O'Connell, *America's Money Trauma: How Washington Blunders Crippled the U.S. Financial System* (Chicago: Conversation Press, 1992); James R. Barth, *The Great Savings and Loan Debacle* (Washington, D.C.: AEI Press, 1991); *New York Times,* April 10, 1999.

24. John Steele Gordon, "Understanding the S&L Mess," *American Heritage* (February–March 1991), 49–68; Amy Waldman, "Move Over, Charles Keating: Causes of the Savings and Loan Scandal," *Washington Monthly* (May 1995), 26.

25. James C. Scott, *Seeing like a State: How Certain Schemes to Improve the Human Condition Have Failed* (New Haven: Yale University Press, 1998), 1–8.

26. James Morone, *The Democratic Wish: Popular Participation and the Limits of American Government* (New York: Basic Books, 1990), 1; Bernard Bailyn, *The Ideological Origins of*

the American Revolution (Cambridge, Mass.: Harvard University Press, 1967); John D. Donahue, "The Disunited States," *Atlantic* 279 (May 1997), 18.

27. Anthony King, "Ideas, Institutions, and the Policies of Government: A Comparative Analysis, Part I and II," *British Journal of Political Science* 3 (1973), 418–20; Theda Skocpol, "Bringing the State Back In," in *Bringing the State Back In,* ed. Peter Evans, Dietrich Rueschmeyer, and Theda Skocpol (Cambridge, England: Cambridge University Press, 1985), 3–37; Victoria C. Hattam, *Labor Visions and State Power* (Princeton, N.J.: Princeton University Press, 1993); Richard Oestreicher, "Urban Working-Class Political Behavior and Theories of American Electoral Politics, 1870–1940," *Journal of American History* 74 (March 1988), 1261.

28. C. Eugene Steuerle et al., *The Government We Deserve: Responsive Democracy and Changing Expectations* (Washington, D.C.: Urban Institute, 1998), 65–66.

29. Robert J. Samuelson, *The Good Life and Its Discontents: The American Dream in the Age of Entitlement, 1945–1995* (New York: Random House, 1995), 142–43; *Chicago Tribune,* April 9, 1995.

30. Richard E. Cohen, "The Political System Attempts to Cope with Public Loss of Faith in Government," *National Journal* 12 (January 19, 1980), 110; Donahue, "The Disunited States," 18.

31. *Christian Science Monitor,* June 5, 1984; Peter Marris and Martin Rein, *Dilemmas of Social Reform* (Chicago: Aldine Publishing, 1973), 7; Dom Bonafede, "Reform of U.S. System of Government Is on the Minds and Agendas of Many," *National Journal* 17 (June 29, 1985), 1521; Timothy B. Clark, "The President Takes On the 'Iron Triangles,' " *National Journal* 13 (March 28, 1981), 516; Douglass Cater, *Power in Washington* (New York: Random House, 1964); "The Bureaucratic Maw," *Newsweek* (January 26, 1981), 41.

32. Samuelson, *The Good Life and Its Discontents,* 15; John Adams, "Thoughts on Government," in *The Political Writings of John Adams* (New York: Liberal Arts Press, 1954), 86; Michael Kazin, *The Populist Persuasion* (New York: Basic Books, 1995), 2; Samuel P. Huntington, *American Politics: The Promise of Disharmony* (Cambridge, Mass.: Harvard University Press, 1981).

33. Morone, *The Democratic Wish,* 1.

34. *Arizona Republic,* February 1, 1998; *New York Times,* February 1, 1998.

35. "Carter Signs Government-Wide Ethics Bill," *Congressional Quarterly Almanac* (1978), 835–50; Judiciary Committee, U.S. House, 95th Congress, 2d Session, *Special Prosecutor Act of 1978* (June 19, 1975).

36. *New York Times,* February 1, 1998; Henry J. Reske, "The Second Act: Independent Counsel Law Signed," *American Bar Association Journal* 80 (September 1994); *Los Angeles Times,* June 16, 1992.

37. *New York Times,* August 10, 1998.

38. *Newsday,* September 27, 1998; *New York Times,* February 24 and April 14, 1999.

39. "Transcript of President Clinton's Second Inaugural Address to the Nation," *New York Times,* January 21, 1997, A14.

40. Richard Wightman Fox, *Reinhold Niebuhr: A Biography* (New York: Pantheon, 1986);

Benjamin DeMott, "Rediscovering Complexity," *Atlantic* 262 (September 1988), 68; *New York Times,* June 22, 1992.

Chapter 1: The Irony of Reform

1. Congress, House of Representatives, Committee on Ways and Means, *Economic Security Act: Hearings before the Committee on Ways and Means,* 74th Congress, 1st Session (January 30, 1935), 494–99.

2. Lela B. Costin, *Two Sisters for Social Justice: A Biography of Grace and Edith Abbott* (Chicago: University of Illinois Press, 1983), 24, 106, 130–48.

3. Christopher Howard, "Sowing the Seeds of 'Welfare': The Transformation of Mothers Pensions, 1900–1940," *Journal of Policy History* 4 (1992), 188–227; Winifred Bell, *Aid to Dependent Children* (New York: Columbia University Press, 1965), 5–9; Congress, Senate, *Proceedings of the Conference on the Care of Dependent Children,* 60th Congress, 2d Session (January 25–26, 1909), Senate Document 721, 8.

4. Howard, "Sowing the Seeds of 'Welfare,' " 188–227; Bell, *Aid to Dependent Children,* 9–19; Social Security Board, *Social Security in America: The Factual Background of the Social Security Act as Summarized from Staff Reports to the Committee on Economic Security* (Washington, D.C.: U.S. Government Printing Office, 1937), 237–38.

5. Howard, "Sowing the Seeds of 'Welfare,' " 188–227; Paul H. Douglas, *Social Security in the United States: An Analysis and Appraisal of the Federal Social Security Act* (New York: McGraw-Hill, 1936), 185–96; Grace Abbott, *The Child and the State* (Chicago: University of Chicago Press, 1938), 238; Social Security Board, *Social Security in America,* 237–38.

6. Martha E. Davis, *Brutal Need: Lawyers and the Welfare Rights Movement, 1960–1973* (New Haven: Yale University Press, 1993), 7; Linda Gordon, *Pitied but Not Entitled: Single Mothers and the History of Welfare, 1890–1935* (New York: Free Press, 1994), 186; Michael Katz, *In the Shadow of the Poorhouse: A Social History of Welfare in America* (New York: Basic Books, 1996), 220–24; Bell, *Aid to Dependent Children,* 21–27.

7. James H. S. Bossard, "Children in a Depression Decade," *Annals of the American Academy of Political and Social Science* 212 (November 1940), 1–3; Gordon, *Pitied but Not Entitled,* 183–207; James T. Patterson, *America's Struggle against Poverty, 1900–1994* (Cambridge, Mass.: Harvard University Press, 1994), 56–58; Irving Bernstein, *A Caring Society: The New Deal, the Worker, and the Great Depression: A History of the American Worker, 1933–1941* (Boston: Houghton Mifflin, 1985), 17–42.

8. Bernstein, *A Caring Society,* 61–66; Katz, *In the Shadow of the Poorhouse,* 242–45; Alan Brinkley, *Voices of Protest: Huey Long, Father Coughlin, and the Great Depression* (New York: Knopf, 1982); Edward D. Berkowitz, *America's Welfare State: From Roosevelt to Reagan* (Baltimore: Johns Hopkins University Press, 1991), 18–19; Gordon, *Pitied but Not Entitled,* 209–51; William E. Leuchtenberg, *Franklin D. Roosevelt and the New Deal, 1932–1940* (New York: Harper & Row, 1963), 117.

9. Bernstein, *A Caring Society,* 49; Douglas, *Social Security in the United States,* 26–27; Edwin E. Witte, *The Development of the Social Security Act: A Memorandum on the His-*

tory of the Committee on Economic Security and Drafting and Legislative History of the Social Security Act (Madison: University of Wisconsin Press, 1962), 7–75; Berkowitz, *America's Welfare State,* 14–15, 20–21; Joel Handler, "The Transformation of Aid to Families with Dependent Children," *NYU Review of Law and Social Change* 16 (1987), 461; Gilbert Steiner, *Social Insecurity: The Politics of Welfare* (Chicago: Rand McNally, 1966), 19–20.

10. Bernstein, *A Caring Society,* 51–61; Costin, *Two Sisters,* 222; Witte to Abbott, August 17, 1934, Abbott Papers, University of Chicago (UC), Box 54.

11. Social Security Board, *Social Security in America,* 248.

12. Ibid.

13. Witte to Edith Abbott, October 18, 1939, Abbott Papers, UC, Box 54; Social Security Board, *Social Security in America,* 233–50; Bernstein, *A Caring Society,* 58–61; Gordon, *Pitied but Not Entitled,* 266–71.

14. Witte to Edith Abbott, October 18, 1939, Abbott Papers, UC, Box 54; Bernstein, *A Caring Society,* 67–70; Witte, *Development of the Social Security Act,* 164; Gordon, *Pitied but Not Entitled,* 254; *Congressional Record,* 74th Congress, 1st Session, vol. 79, pt. 6 (April 17 to May 4, 1935), 6047, 6063, 5680.

15. Witte, *Development of the Social Security Act,* 163; Abbott, *The Child and the State,* II, 240.

16. Witte, *Development of the Social Security Act,* 162–63; Gordon, *Pitied but Not Entitled,* 272–74.

17. Franklin D. Roosevelt, *The Public Papers and Addresses of Franklin D. Roosevelt,* vol. 5 (New York: Harper & Brothers, 1938–50), 19–21.

18. *San Francisco Chronicle,* January 5, 1997; Gordon, *Pitied but Not Entitled,* 264–65.

19. Leuchtenburg, *Franklin D. Roosevelt and the New Deal,* 130–31; Kenneth Davis, *FDR: The New Deal Years, 1933–37* (New York: Random House, 1986), 459–60.

20. Berkowitz, *America's Welfare State,* 37; *New York Times,* August 15, 1935.

21. *Washington Post,* August 15, 1935; Abraham Epstein, "Our Social Insecurity Act," *Harper's Magazine* 172 (December 1935), 55–66; "How Much Social Security," *New Republic* 83 (July 3, 1935), 209–10.

22. *Washington Post,* August 11, 1935.

23. Berkowitz, *America's Welfare State,* 2.

24. *Washington Post,* August 11, 1935; Berkowitz, *America's Welfare State,* 41.

25. Steven M. Teles, *Whose Welfare?: AFDC and Elite Politics* (Lawrence: University of Kansas Press, 1998), 34–37; Berkowitz, *America's Welfare State,* 47–50.

26. Congress, Senate, Committee on Finance, *Social Security Act Amendments: Hearings before the Committee on Finance,* 76th Congress, 1st Session (1939), 14; John Kenneth Galbraith, *The Affluent Society* (Boston: Houghton Mifflin, 1958), xxiii–xxiv; John Kenneth Galbraith, *A Life in Our Times: Memoirs* (Boston: Houghton Mifflin, 1981), 335–40; Arthur Schlesinger, Jr., "Death Wish of the Democrats," *New Republic* 139 (September 15, 1958), 7–9; "The Future of Liberalism," *Reporter* (May 3, 1956), 8–11; "Where Does the Liberal Go from Here?" *New York Times Magazine,* August 4, 1957, 7–8, 38.

27. Steiner, *Social Insecurity,* 31; Patterson, *America's Struggle against Poverty,* 106.

28. Patterson, *America's Struggle against Poverty,* 68–69, 87–89.

29. Berkowitz, *America's Welfare State,* 103–06; Patterson, *America's Struggle against Poverty,* 107–09; James Sundquist, "Origins of the War on Poverty," in *On Fighting Poverty: Perspectives from Experience,* ed. James Sundquist (New York: Basic Books, 1969), 14–15.

30. Teles, *Whose Welfare?,* 38–39; Steiner, *Social Insecurity,* 41–42; Berkowitz, *America's Welfare State,* 109–10.

31. Congress, House, Committee on Ways and Means, *Public Welfare Amendments of 1962: Hearings before the Committee on Ways and Means,* 87th Congress, 2d Session (1962), 63, 158, 165–74; *New York Times,* July 27, 1962; Steiner, *Social Insecurity,* 36–40; Patterson, *America's Struggle against Poverty,* 130–32; Sundquist, "Origins of the War on Poverty," 15–16.

32. Gilbert Steiner, *The State of Welfare* (Washington, D.C.: Brookings Institution, 1971), 40–47; Berkowitz, *America's Welfare State,* 110–11; Patterson, *America's Struggle against Poverty,* 132–33.

33. Heller to Sorensen, December 20, 1963, Administrative History of the Council of Economic Advisers, Lyndon B. Johnson Library (LBJL), Box 3; Richard A. Cloward and Lloyd Ohlin, *Delinquency and Opportunity: A Theory of Delinquent Gangs* (Glencoe, Ill.: Free Press, 1960), 91–96, 211; Sundquist, "Origins of the War on Poverty," 11; Allen J. Matusow, *The Unraveling of America: A History of Liberalism in the 1960's* (New York: Harper & Row, 1984), 108–22; Patterson, *America's Struggle against Poverty,* 134–38.

34. Matusow, *The Unraveling of America,* 121–22.

35. Nicholas Lemann, "The Unfinished War," *Atlantic* 262 (December 1988), 37–56; Matusow, *The Unraveling of America,* 123–24; James Sundquist, *Politics and Policy: The Eisenhower, Kennedy, and Johnson Years* (Washington, D.C.: Brookings Institution, 1968), 141–42.

36. Matusow, *The Unraveling of America,* 123.

37. Lyndon B. Johnson, "Annual Message to the Congress on the State of the Union," January 8, 1964, *Public Papers of the Presidents: Lyndon B. Johnson,* vol. 1 (Washington, D.C.: U.S. Government Printing Office, 1965), 114; U.S. President, *Economic Report of the President: Transmitted to the Congress, January 1964, Together with the Annual Report of the Council of Economic Advisers* (Washington, D.C.: U.S. Government Printing Office, 1964), 55, 77.

38. Michael L. Gillette, *Launching the War on Poverty: An Oral History* (New York: Twayne, 1996), 66; Lemann, "The Unfinished War," 37–56; Matusow, *The Unraveling of America,* 124–25; Patterson, *America's Struggle against Poverty,* 138–41.

39. Daniel Moynihan, "Professors and the Poor," in *On Understanding Poverty,* ed. Daniel Moynihan (New York: Basic Books, 1968), 12–13; Patterson, *America's Struggle against Poverty,* 14–15; Lemann, "The Unfinished War," 37–56; Sundquist, "Origins of the War on Poverty," 26–27; "President's 'War on Poverty' Approved," *Congressional Quarterly Almanac* 20 (1964), 213–15.

40. Sundquist, "Origins of the War on Poverty," 3, 29; *Congressional Record,* 88th Congress, 2d Session, vol. 110, pt. 14 (August 6, 1964), 18315.

41. Congress, House, *Minority Views, Economic Opportunity Act of 1964,* 88th Congress, 2d Session (1964), 74; *Congressional Record,* 88th Congress, 2d Session, vol. 110, pt. 14 (August 5, 1964), 18199; "President's 'War on Poverty' Approved," 208, 215–29; *New York Times,* February 16, 1964.

42. "President's 'War on Poverty' Approved," 208, 215–29.

43. Ibid.; Frances Fox Piven and Richard A. Cloward, *Regulating the Poor: The Functions of Public Welfare* (New York: Pantheon, 1971), 271; Sundquist, *Politics and Policy,* 147–49; John W. Carley to Yarmolinsky and McCarthy, July 30, 1964, Moyers Papers, LBJL, Box 39.

44. Sundquist, *Politics and Policy,* 149–50; *Washington Post,* August 10, 1964; *New York Times,* August 9, 1964; Matusow, *The Unraveling of America,* 126.

45. *Washington Post,* August 5, 1964; *New York Times,* August 7, 1964.

46. *New York Times,* January 3, 1969; Steiner, *Social Insecurity,* 33; Patterson, *America's Struggle against Poverty,* 171.

47. Piven and Cloward, *Regulating the Poor,* 289.

48. Lawrence Bailis, *Bread or Justice: Grassroots Organizing in the Welfare Rights Movement* (Lexington, Mass.: Lexington Books, 1974); Susan Handley Hertz, *The Welfare Mothers Movement: A Decade of Change for Poor Women* (Washington, D.C.: University Press of America, 1981), 32–37; Richard Cloward and Frances Fox Piven, "A Strategy to End Poverty," *Nation* 202 (May 2, 1966) 510–17.

49. "A Nation Aroused," OEO 1st Annual Report, 1965, McPherson Papers, LBJL, Box 4; Davis, *Brutal Need,* 22–69; Piven and Cloward, *Regulating the Poor,* 306; Teles, *Whose Welfare?,* 105–07; Earl Johnson, Jr., *Justice and Reform: The Formative Years of the American Legal Services Program* (New Brunswick, N.J.: Transaction Books, 1978), 178–80.

50. Davis, *Brutal Need,* 81–118; Pamela Coyle, "Rights or Responsibilities?," *American Bar Association Journal* 82 (April 1995); R. Shep Melnick, "Interpreting Entitlements: The Politics of Statutory Construction," *Brookings Review* 12 (Winter 1994), 40.

51. Steiner, *Social Insecurity,* 90.

52. Melnick, "Interpreting Entitlements," 40; Matusow, *The Unraveling of America,* 269–70.

53. "The Problem of Poverty in America," Economic Report of the President, January 1964, Administrative History of OEO, LBJL, Box 2; Shriver, "Testimony before the House Education and Labor Committee," March 17, 1964, WHCF, FG, LBJL, Box 124; Sundquist, *Politics and Policy,* 154; Patterson, *America's Struggle against Poverty,* 149–54.

54. "The Tide of Progress," OEO 3d Annual Report, 1967, WHCF, FG, LBJL, Box 126; Sanford Kravitz, "The Community Action Program—Past, Present, and its Future?" in *On Fighting Poverty,* ed. Sundquist, 60.

55. Patterson, *America's Struggle against Poverty,* 152, 171–72.

56. Nancy Woloch, *Women and the American Experience* (New York: Knopf, 1984), 500–05; Teles, *Whose Welfare?*, 55–59.

57. Connie de Boer, "The Polls: Women at Work," *Public Opinion Quarterly* 41 (Summer 1977), 272; Hazel Erskine, "The Polls: Women's Role," *Public Opinion Quarterly* 35 (Summer 1971), 275–90; Teles, *Whose Welfare?*, 56–57; *San Francisco Chronicle*, January 5, 1997.

58. Nicholas Lemann, *The Promised Land: The Great Black Migration and How It Changed America* (New York: Knopf, 1991), 70; Piven and Cloward, *Regulating the Poor*, 218.

59. Steiner, *Social Insecurity*, 32; Woloch, *Women and the American Experience*, 564–66.

60. Christopher Jencks, "The Hidden Paradox of Welfare Reform," *American Prospect* 32 (May–June 1997), 33.

61. Thomas Byrne Edsall and Mary D. Edsall, *Chain Reaction: The Impact of Race, Rights, and Taxes on American Politics* (New York: W. W. Norton, 1991), 99–115; Patterson, *America's Struggle against Poverty*, 172; "Welfare: Trying to End the Nightmare," *Time* (February 8, 1971), 14–23.

62. Steiner, *The State of Welfare*, 75; Patterson, *America's Struggle against Poverty*, 192–93.

63. Paterson, *America's Struggle against Poverty*, 194–98; Teles, *Whose Welfare?*, 89–94.

64. Julie Kosterlitz and W. John Moore, "Saving the Welfare State," *National Journal* (May 14, 1988), 1276; John L. Palmer, "Social Policy: Challenging the Welfare State," in *The Reagan Record: An Assessment of America's Changing Domestic Priorities*, ed. John Palmer and Isabel Sawhill (Cambridge, Mass.: Ballinger Publishing Co., 1984).

65. Thomas J. Duesterberg, "Reforming the Welfare State," *Society* (September 1, 1998), 44; Michael Reese, "Life below the Poverty Line," *Newsweek* (April 5, 1982), 20; Lemann, "The Unfinished War," 37–56; Kosterlitz and Moore, "Saving the Welfare State," 1276; Katz, *In the Shadow of the Poorhouse*, 295–99.

66. Charles Murray, *Losing Ground: American Social Policy, 1950–1980* (New York: Basic Books, 1984), 9, 212, 227; Sidney Blumenthal, *The Rise of the Counter-Establishment: From Conservative Ideology to Political Power* (New York: Times Books, 1986); William Berman, *America's Right Turn: From Nixon to Clinton* (Baltimore: Johns Hopkins University Press, 1998); Patterson, *America's Struggle against Poverty*, 213.

67. Kosterlitz and Moore, "Saving the Welfare State"; Tom Bethell, "They Had a Dream; The Challenge of Welfare Reform," *National Review* (August 23, 1993), 31; Patterson, *America's Struggle against Poverty*, 231–33; Katz, *In the Shadow of the Poorhouse*, 305–09.

68. Michael Tanner, "Ending Welfare as We Know It," *USA Today Magazine*, March 1995, 16; Bethell, "They Had a Dream:" The Challenge of Welfare Reform," 31; Patterson, *America's Struggle against Poverty*, 233–36.

69. Robert Kuttner, "The Declining Middle," *Atlantic* (July 1983); James Fallows, "America's Changing Economic Landscape," *Atlantic* (March 1985), 47; Thomas Edsall, "The Return of Inequality," *Atlantic* (June 1988), 86; Bruce Steinberg, "The Mass Market Is Splitting Apart," *Fortune* (November 28, 1983).

70. Tanner, "Ending Welfare as We Know It"; David Whitman, "War on Welfare De-

pendency," *U.S. News & World Report* (April 20, 1992), 34; Thomas Sancton, "How to Get America Off the Dole," *Time* (May 25, 1992), 44.

71. Katz, *In the Shadow of the Poorhouse,* 310–12; Duesterberg, "Reforming the Welfare State," 44; *Los Angeles Times,* April 2, 1992.

72. Jeffrey Katz, "A Welcome but Unwieldy Idea? Putting an End to Welfare," *Congressional Quarterly* 51 (February 27, 1993), 461; *New York Times,* April 22, 1994; Julie Kosterlitz, "Reexamining Welfare," *National Journal* 49 (December 6, 1986), 2926; Kent Weaver, "Old Traps, New Twists: Why Welfare Is So Hard to Reform in 1994," *Brookings Review* 12 (Summer 1994), 18; Mary Jo Bane and David T. Ellwood, *Welfare Realities: From Rhetoric to Reform* (Cambridge, Mass.: Harvard University Press, 1994); Lawrence M. Mead, "The Politics of Poverty: Toward a New Debate," *Current* 358 (December 1993), 21.

73. Steven M. Gillon, *The Democrats' Dilemma: Walter F. Mondale and the Liberal Legacy* (New York: Columbia University Press, 1992), ix–xi; Jeffrey Katz, "Clinton Plans Major Shift in Lives of Poor People," *Congressional Quarterly* 52 (January 22, 1994), 117; *Los Angeles Times,* June 20, 1994.

74. Dan Goodgame, "Right Makes Might," *Time* (November 21, 1994), 52; *Houston Chronicle,* August 25, 1996; *Los Angeles Times,* February 11, 1996. For the best books on Clinton and the Republican Congress, see Elizabeth Drew, *Showdown: The Struggle between the Gingrich Congress and the Clinton White House* (New York: Simon & Schuster, 1996); Dan Balz and Ronald Brownstein, *Storming the Gates: Protest Politics and the Republican Revival* (Boston: Little, Brown, 1996).

75. *Los Angeles Times,* February 11, 1996; *New York Times,* August 4, 1996.

76. Katz, *In the Shadow of the Poorhouse,* 328–30; Jencks, "The Hidden Paradox of Welfare Reform," 33; Tanner, "Ending Welfare as We Know It," 16.

77. Katz, *In the Shadow of the Poorhouse,* 330–31; *New York Times,* August 9, 1996.

78. *Los Angeles Times,* June 20, 1994.

Chapter 2: The Politics of Deinstitutionalization

1. Congress, Senate, Committee on Labor and Public Welfare. Subcommittee on Mental Health and Retardation, 88th Congress, 1st Session (March 5–7, 1963), 191.

2. Robert Felix Oral History, Columbia University Oral History Project (CUOHP), 23, 37.

3. The Felix Papers at the National Library of Medicine (NLM) contain many of the original speech text in which Felix articulated his ideas about community mental health. Especially useful are: "Mental Public Health: A Blueprint," April 21, 1945, NLM, Box 1; "Factors in the Development of a Federal Mental Health Program," May 23, 1946, NLM, Box 1; "The Healing Community," May 19, 1959, NLM, Box 2; "Recent Developments in Community Mental Health Programs," May 21, 1962, NLM, Box 3; and "Implementing the Proposals Contained in the President's Special Message on Mental Illness," February 8, 1963, NLM, Box 3. For his published

writings on the subject, see Felix, "Mental Disorders as a Public Health Problem," *American Journal of Psychiatry* 106 (December 1949), 401–05; Felix and Morton Kramer, "Extent of the Problem of Mental Disorders," *Annals of the Academy of Political and Social Science* 286 (March 1953), 14; *New York Times,* July 4, 1951; Felix, "A Model for Comprehensive Mental Health Centers," *American Journal of Public Health* 54 (December 1964), 1964–69; Felix, "Community Mental Health: A Federal Perspective," *American Journal of Psychiatry* 121 (November 1964), 428–32; Congress, House, Committee on Interstate and Foreign Commerce, Subcommittee on Health and Science, *Hearings on the Mental Health Study Act of 1955,* 84th Congress, 1st Session (March 8–11, 1955), 10.

4. Elizabeth Brenner Drew, "The Health Syndicate: Washington's Noble Conspirators," *Atlantic Monthly* (December 1967), 75–82; Henry A. Foley and Steven S. Sharfstein, *Madness and Government: Who Cares for the Mentally Ill?* (Washington, D.C.: American Psychiatric Press, 1983), 20–25.

5. For the best analysis of the origins, development, and consequences of the community mental health movement, see Gerald N. Grob, *From Asylum to Community: Mental Health Policy in Modern America* (Princeton, N.J.: Princeton University Press, 1991) and two books by the psychiatrist E. Fuller Torrey: *Nowhere to Go: The Tragic Odyssey of the Homeless Mentally Ill* (New York: Harper & Row, 1988) and *Out of the Shadows: Confronting America's Mental Illness Crisis* (New York: John Wiley, 1997). David F. Musto offers valuable insight in "Whatever Happened to 'Community Mental Health?," *Public Interest* 39 (Spring 1975), 53–79. Also useful are Phil Brown, *The Transfer of Care: Psychiatric Deinstitutionalization and Its Aftermath* (London: Routledge, 1985); Jack R. Ewalt and Patricia L. Ewalt, "History of the Community Psychiatry Movement," *American Journal of Psychiatry* 126 (July 1969), 43–52; and John J. Stretch, "Community Mental Health: The Evolution of a Concept in Social Policy," *Community Mental Health Journal* 3 (Spring 1967), 5–12.

6. Grob, *From Asylum to Community,* 70–92; A. Q. Maisel, "Bedlam 1946: Most U.S. Mental Hospitals Are a Shame and a Disgrace," *Life* (May 6, 1946), 102–18; M. J. Ward, *The Snake Pit* (New York: Random House, 1946); Albert Deutsch, *The Shame of the States* (New York: Harcourt Brace, 1948), 28.

7. Judith P. Swazey, *Chlorpromazine in Psychiatry: A Study of Therapeutic Innovation* (Cambridge, Mass.: MIT Press, 1974); "Pills for the Mind: New Era in Psychiatry," *Time* (March 7, 1955), 63.

8. Council of State Governments, *The Mental Health Programs of the Forty-Eight States* (Chicago: Council of State Governments, 1950), 4–13; *New York Times,* February 9 and February 21, 1954.

9. Gerald Grob, *The Mad among Us: A History of the Care of America's Mentally Ill* (Cambridge, Mass.: Harvard University Press, 1994), 211; Robert Felix Oral History, CUOHP, 46, 55; Felix, "Mental Disorders as a Public Health Problem," 405.

10. Joint Commission on Mental Illness and Health, *Action for Mental Health: Digest of Final Report of Joint Commission on Mental Illness and Health,* John F. Kennedy Library (JFKL), Agency Files—HEW, Box 39; Henry A. Foley, *Community Mental Health Leg-*

islation: The Formative Process (Lexington, Mass.: Lexington Books, 1975), 15–28; Grob, *From Asylum to Community,* 187–208; Torrey, *Nowhere to Go,* 90–96; Stretch, "Community Mental Health: The Evolution of a Concept in Social Policy," 5–12.

11. Kennedy to Ribicoff, December 1, 1961, Agencies File—HEW, JFKL, Box 39; Foley, *Community Mental Health Legislation,* 33–41; Grob, *From Asylum to Community,* 221–22.

12. Secretary of Health, Education, and Welfare to Kennedy, November 30, 1962, Myer Feldman Papers, JFKL, Box 12; Foley, *Community Mental Health Legislation,* 42–52; Grob, *From Asylum to Community,* 222–27.

13. "Special Message on Mental Illness and Mental Retardation," February 5, 1963, President's Office Files, Legislative Files, JFKL, Box 52; *New York Times,* February 8, 1963.

14. Congress, House, Committee on Interstate and Foreign Commerce. Subcommittee on Mental Health, 88th Congress, 1st Session (March 26, 27, and 28, 1963), 42–49, 92–102, 326–42; Congress. Senate, Committee on Labor and Public Welfare. Subcommittee on Health, 88th Congress, 1st Session (March 5, 6, and 7, 1963), 15–23, 41–45; "Congress Enacts New Mental Health Programs," *Congressional Quarterly Almanac* (1963), 222–28; Foley and Sharfstein, *Madness and Government,* 54–63.

15. Robert K. Merton, "The Unanticipated Consequences of Purposive Social Action," *American Sociological Review* 1 (December 1936), 894–904; Congress, House, Committee on Interstate and Foreign Commerce, Subcommittee on Mental Health (Supplemental), 88th Congress, 1st Session (July 10 and 11, 1963), 19.

16. Foley and Sharfstein, *Madness and Government,* 63–79; Grob, *From Asylum to Community,* 227–34; *New York Times,* March 27, May 28, and August 15, 1963. Congress added the staffing grants in 1965, when President Johnson signed the Community Mental Health Centers Act Amendments, which authorized $224,174,000 for initial staffing over a seven-year period.

17. "Congress Enacts New Mental Health Programs," *Congressional Quarterly Almanac* (1963), 222–28; Foley, *Community Mental Health Legislation,* 83.

18. *New York Times,* March 26, 1962; Felix, "A Model for Comprehensive Mental Health Centers," 1966; Felix, "Implementing the Proposals Contained in the President's Special Message on Mental Illness," February 8, 1963, NLM, Box 3.

19. Torrey, *Out of the Shadows,* 8–10; William DeRisi and William A. Vega, "The Impact of Deinstitutionalization on California's State Hospital Population," *Hospital and Community Psychiatry* 34 (February 1983), 140–45.

20. It is important to note that most of the patients in the survey had been discharged into "well-staffed structured community residential treatment settings such as group homes or intensely supervised apartments." Torrey, *Out of the Shadows,* 85.

21. Ibid., 4–5; W. Brewer Grant, "The Patients Nobody Wants," *Mental Hygiene* 54 (January 1970), 162–65.

22. Between 1965 and 1973 Congress authorized $600 million for new centers but spent only $245.5 million on construction. The Johnson administration spent $195

million of the $260 million appropriated by Congress, or roughly 75 percent of funds. Under Nixon, only $50.5 million of the $340 million was spent, representing only 15 percent of budgeted funds. See Brown, *The Transfer of Care,* 52; *Buffalo News,* May 16, 1994.

23. Foley and Sharfstein, *Madness and Government,* 134–37; *Los Angeles Times,* February 4, 1991.

24. *Buffalo News,* May 16, 1994; *New York Times,* May 22, 1989.

25. Foley, *Community Mental Health Legislation,* 89–98; Rael Jean Isaac and Virginia C. Armat, *Madness in the Streets: How Psychiatry and the Law Abandoned the Mentally Ill* (New York: Free Press, 1990), 81.

26. Ernest M. Gruenberg and Janet Archer, "Abandonment of Responsibility for the Seriously Mentally Ill," *Milbank Memorial Fund Quarterly* 57/4 (1979), 485–506; Uri Aviram, "Community Care of the Seriously Mentally Ill: Continuing Problems and Current Issues," *Community Mental Health Journal* 26 (February 1990), 69–87; David L. Cutler, "Clinical Care Update: The Chronically Mentally Ill," *Community Mental Health Journal* 21 (Spring 1985), 3–13.

27. Torrey, *Nowhere to Go,* 150–56. Without the expected shift in resources, state and local funding for CMHCs actually fell from 45.4 percent to 37.9 percent between 1969 and 1975. David A. Dowell and James A. Ciarlo, "Overview of the Community Mental Health Centers Program from an Evaluation Perspective," *Community Mental Health Journal* 19 (Summer 1983), 98–99.

28. Torrey, *Nowhere to Go,* 144–50; Henry Santiestevan, *Deinstitutionalization: Out of their Beds and into the Streets* (Washington, D.C.: American Federation of State, County and Municipal Employees, 1975), 10; Richard Woy, Daniel B. Wasserman, and Risa Weiner-Pomerantz, "Community Mental Health Centers: Movement away from the Model?" *Community Mental Health Journal* 17 (Winter 1981), 265–76. Adding to the problem was the fact that most psychiatrists, many trained with public funds, chose more lucrative private practice, producing a severe shortage of trained personnel to staff the centers. Dr. John A. Talbott noted the irony of the situation when he commented that psychiatry is "one of the few specialties where the most skilled practitioners take care of the least impaired patients." See *New York Times,* March 16, 1986.

29. Andrew Bates, "Mental Health Spas: How Money Intended for Homeless Psychotics Went to Suburban Neurotics," *Washington Monthly* (December 1990), 26.

30. Comptroller General of the United States, *Returning the Mentally Disabled to the Community: Government Needs to Do More* (Washington, D.C.: General Accounting Office, 1977), 10–16; Grob, *From Asylum to Community,* 267–70.

31. Comptroller General, *Returning the Mentally Disabled to the Community,* 10–16; Torrey, *Out of the Shadows,* 92–94; James H. Swan, "The Substitution of Nursing Home for Inpatient Psychiatric Care," *Community Mental Health Journal* 23 (Spring 1987), 3–18; George M. Anderson, "Ex-Mental Patients and the New Snake Pits," *America* 135 (September 4, 1976), 90–94; Howard H. Goldman, Neal H. Adams, and Carl A. Taube, "Deinstitutionalization: The Data Demythologized," *Hospital and Commu-*

nity Psychiatry 34 (February 1983), 129–34; William R. Shadish, Jr., Arthur J. Lurigio, and Dan A. Lewis, "After Deinstitutionalization: The Present and Future of Mental Health Long-Term Care Policy," *Journal of Social Issues* 45/3 (1989), 3; Brown, *The Transfer of Care,* 93–104.

32. Comptroller General, *Returning the Mentally Disabled to the Community,* 13; Mary Adelaide Mendelson, *Tender Loving Greed: How the Incredibly Lucrative Nursing Home "Industry" Is Exploiting America's Old People and Defrauding Us All* (New York: Vintage, 1975). See also Brown, *The Transfer of Care,* 104–09.

33. In 1985 it cost New York State $41,651 a year to keep a patient in the state hospital. Once he or she was discharged, the federal government picked up the tab. Paul Lerman, *Deinstitutionalization and the Welfare State* (New Brunswick, N.U.: Rutgers University Press, 1982), 94; Torrey, *Out of the Shadows,* 95–96.

34. Comptroller General, *Returning the Mentally Disabled to the Community,* 16–19; Peter Keenig, "The Problem that Can't Be Tranquilized," *New York Times Magazine,* May 21, 1978, 14; Torrey, *Out of the Shadows,* 61–66.

35. Comptroller General, *Returning the Mentally Disabled to the Community,* 16–19; *New York Times,* March 19, 1976, and November 19, 1979; Joan Hatch Lennox, *Communities of the Alone: Working with Single Room Occupants in the City* (New York: Association Press, 1971).

36. *New York Times,* February 13, 1972 and March 19 and May 27, 1978; Kenneth Minkoff, "A Map of Chronic Mental Patients," in *The Chronic Mental Patient,* ed. John A. Talbott (Washington, D.C.: The American Psychiatric Association, 1978), 18–19; John A. Talbott, "Current Clichés and Platitudes in Vogue in Psychiatric Vocabularies," *Hospital and Community Psychiatry* 26 (1975), 530; Robert Stevens and Rosemary Stevens, *Welfare Medicine in America: A Case Study of Medicaid* (New York: Free Press, 1974). The Public Health Service estimated that of the approximately 1.7 million chronic patients in 1977, about 1.15 million resided in nursing homes or boarding homes, 250,000 were in mental hospitals, 150,000 to 170,000 lived with families. The rest were homeless, living in halfway houses, or in jail. See Shadish et al., "After Deinstitutionalization," 3.

37. Walter Goodman, "The Constitution v. the Snakepit," *New York Times Magazine,* March 17, 1974, 21; W. Robert Curtis, "The Deinstitutionalization Story," *Public Interest* 85 (Fall 1986), 34–49; Torrey, *Nowhere to Go,* 156–60; Isaac and Armat, *Madness in the Streets,* 128–41.

38. Torrey, *Nowhere to Go,* 157; Torrey, *Out of the Shadows,* 141–54.

39. *New York Times,* November 13, 1987.

40. *New York Times,* July 30, 1972; Steven P. Segal and Jim Baumohl, "The New Chronic Patient: The Creation of an Undeserved Population," in *Reaching the Underserved: Mental Health Needs of Neglected Populations,* ed. Lonnie R. Snowden (Beverly Hills, Calif.: Sage Publications, 1982), 111.

41. Comptroller General, *Returning the Mentally Disabled to the Community,* 21; Richard Lamb, "What Did We Really Expect from Deinstitutionalization?," *Hospital and Community Psychiatry* 32 (February 1981), 105–09; "The Revolving Door of Re-

cidivism," *Psychology Today* (September 1974), 32, 138; Matt Clark, "The New Snake Pits," *Newsweek* (May 15, 1978), 93–94.

42. Ellen L. Bassuk and Samuel Gerson, "Deinstitutionalization and Mental Health Services," *Scientific American* 238 (February 1978), 50.

43. Torrey, *Out of the Shadows,* 25–42; John R. Belcher, "Are Jails Replacing the Mental Health System for the Homeless Mentally Ill?," *Community Mental Health Journal* 24 (Fall 1988), 185–95; Richard Warner, "Deinstitutionalization: How Did We Get Where We Are?," *Journal of Social Issues* 45/3 (1989), 17–30. This entire 186-page issue of the *Journal of Social Issues* was devoted to the topic "After Deinstitutionalization."

44. "The Homeless: Out in the Cold," *Newsweek* (December 16, 1985), 22–23; Nancy Gibbs, "Answers at Last," *Time* (December 17, 1990), 44; Elizabeth Ehrlich, "Homelessness: The Policy Failure Haunting America," *Business Week* (April 25, 1988), 132–38.

45. Christopher Jencks, *The Homeless* (Cambridge, Mass.: Harvard University Press, 1994), 16–17; Ellen L. Bassuk, "The Homeless Problem," *Scientific American* 251 (July 1984), 40–45; Stephen M. Goldfinger, "Introduction: Perspectives on the Homeless Mentally Ill," *Community Mental Health Journal* 26 (October 1990), 387–90; *Washington Post,* November 9, 1991; H. Richard Lamb, "Deinstitutionalization and the Homeless Mentally Ill," *Hospital and Community Psychiatry* 35 (September 1984), 903.

46. Keenig, "The Problem that Can't Be Tranquilized," 14; J. C. Bonovitz and J. S. Bonovitz, "Diversion of the Mentally Ill into the Criminal Justice System: The Police Intervention Perspective," *American Journal of Psychiatry* (1981), 973–76.

47. "Emptying the Mental Wards: New Treatment Stirs a Controversy," *U.S. News & World Report* (February 24, 1975), 71; Charles Krauthammer, "How to Save the Homeless Mentally Ill," *New Republic* (February 8, 1988), 24.

48. *New York Times,* October 30, 1984, and February 13, 1991; A. F. Panzetta, "Whatever Happened to Community Mental Health: Portents for Corporate Medicine," *Hospital and Community Psychiatry* 36 (1985), 1174–79.

49. Felix, *Mental Illness: Progress and Prospects,* 68; Grob, *From Asylum to Community,* 234–35.

50. Grob, *From Asylum to Community,* 234–35.

51. Felix, "A Model for Comprehensive Mental Health Centers," 1964; *New York Times,* March 19, 1978; Saul Feldman, "Out of the Hospital, onto the Streets: The Overselling of Benevolence," *Hastings Center Report* 13 (June 1983), 6; H. G. Whittington, "The Third Psychiatric Revolution—Really?," *Community Mental Health Journal* 1 (Spring 1965), 73–80.

52. Isaac and Armat, *Madness in the Streets,* 67; Leona L. Bachrach, "Deinstitutionalization of Mental Health Services in Rural Areas," *Hospital and Community Psychiatry* 28 (September 1977), 669–70; *New York Times,* March 19, 1978.

53. Isaac and Armat, *Madness in the Streets,* 165; Carlo A. Weber, "Old Wine, New Skins: Community Mental Health," *America* 129 (November 10, 1973), 353–55;

Torrey, *Nowhere to Go,* 42; David Mechanic, *Mental Health and Social Policy* (Englewood Cliffs, N.J.: Prentice Hall, 1989), 33–34; Grob, *From Asylum to Community,* 243; William Gaylin, "What's Normal?," *New York Times Magazine,* April 1, 1973, 14; Melvin Sabshin, "The Anti-Community Mental Health 'Movement,' " *American Journal of Psychiatry* 125 (February 1969), 1005–12; Franklyn N. Arnhoff, "Social Consequences of Policy toward Mental Illness," *Science* 188 (June 27, 1975), 1277–81.

54. Mike Gorman, "Community Mental Health: The Search for Identity," *Community Mental Health Journal* 6 (October 1970), 349; James Ridgeway, "Treating Mental Illness," *New Republic* (June 10, 1967), 13–15; Donald G. Langeley, "The Community Mental Health Center: Does It Treat Patients?," *Hospital and Community Psychiatry* 31 (December 1980), 815–19; Torrey, *Nowhere to Go,* 128–37; Curtis, "The Deinstitutionalization Story," 34–49.

55. *New York Times,* March 19, 1978; Torrey, *Out of the Shadows,* 142–43; Isaac and Armat, *Madness in the Streets,* 109–24; Walter Goodman, "The Constitution v. the Snakepit," *New York Times Magazine,* March 17, 1974, 21; Charles Krauthammer, "When Liberty Really Means Neglect," *Time* (December 2, 1985), 103.

56. United States, the President's Commission on Mental Health, *Report of the Task Panel on Deinstitutionalization, Rehabilitation, and Long-Term Care* (Washington, D.C.: U.S. Government Printing Office, 1978), 362; Comptroller General, *Returning the Mentally Disabled to the Community,* 5.

57. Jonathan F. Borus, "Deinstitutionalization of the Chronically Mentally Ill," *New England Journal of Medicine* 305 (August 6, 1981), 341.

58. Leona L. Bachrach, "Deinstitutionalization and the Future: The Past as Prologue," in *Psychiatry Takes to the Streets: Outreach and Crisis Intervention for the Mentally Ill,* ed. Neal L. Cohen (New York: Guilford Press, 1990), 275; *Los Angeles Times,* June 19, 1994; *Buffalo News,* May 16, 1994; *New York Times,* May 22, 1989.

Chapter 3: The Strange Career of Affirmative Action

1. *New York Times,* March 31, 1964; Robert Mann, *The Walls of Jericho: Lyndon Johnson, Hubert Humphrey, Richard Russell, and the Struggle for Civil Rights* (New York: Harcourt Brace, 1996), 406–07.

2. Carl Solberg, *Hubert Humphrey: A Biography* (New York: W. W. Norton, 1984), 11–20.

3. Carl M. Brauer, *John F. Kennedy and the Second Reconstruction* (New York: Columbia University Press, 1986), 259–78; Harvard Sitkoff, *The Struggle for Black Equality, 1954–1980* (New York: Hill & Wang, 1981), 129–51; John F. Kennedy, "Radio and Television Report to the American People on Civil Rights," June 11, 1963, *Public Papers of the Presidents: John F. Kennedy, 1963* (Washington, D. C.: U.S. Government Printing Office, 1964), 468–71.

4. Mann, *The Walls of Jericho,* 373; Charles and Barbara Whalen, *The Longest Debate* (Cabin John, Md.: Seven Locks Press, 1985), 29–70; Hugh Davis Graham, "The

Origins of Affirmative Action: Civil Rights and the Regulatory State," *Annals of the American Academy of Political and Social Sciences* 523 (September 1992), 53; Paul Craig Roberts and Lawrence M. Stratton, *The New Color Line: How Quotas and Privilege Destroy Democracy* (Washington, D. C.: Regnery Publishing, 1995), 68.

5. Mann, *The Walls of Jericho,* 380–84.

6. For Smith's remarks, see *Congressional Record,* 88th Congress, 2d Session (February 7, 1964), vol. 100, pt. 2, 2462–2513. Smith never intended his ploy to lay the legal foundation for the modern feminist movement, making his amendment an interesting case study of unintended consequences. I have chosen not to focus on the amendment because of the difficulty of discerning intent. Smith later admitted that he had offered the amendment "as a joke," and Congress adopted it after hasty debate in the House under the "five minute" rule. The entire debate covered only nine pages of the *Congressional Record.* "The sex amendment," noted one observer, "can best be described as an orphan, since neither the proponents nor the opponents of Title VII seem to have felt any responsibility for its presence in the bill. It is somewhat misleading, therefore, to speak of an intent of Congress with respect to its application. . . ." See Richard K. Berg, "Equal Employment Opportunity under the Civil Rights Act of 1964," *Brooklyn Law Review* 31 (1965), 79. Furthermore, the EEOC claimed that it initially moved cautiously on the issue of sex discrimination "in view of the paucity of relevant legislative history revealing the intent of Congress in this area." Equal Employment Opportunity Commission (EEOC), Administrative History (1968), White House Special Files, (LBJL), Box 1, 238. In a famous 1986 Supreme Court case defining sexual harassment, Justice William Rehnquist observed that "we are left with little legislative history to guide us." He went on, however, to state "without question" that "when a supervisor sexually harasses a subordinate because of the subordinate's sex, that supervisor 'discriminates' on the basis of sex." See *Meritor Savings Bank v. Mechelle Vinson et al.* 477 US 57 (1986).

7. *Revolution in Civil Rights,* 4th ed. (Washington, D. C.: Congressional Quarterly Service, 1968), 54.

8. Taylor Branch, *Pillar of Fire: America In the King Years, 1963–65* (New York: Simon and Schuster, 1998), 300; Mann, *The Walls of Jericho,* 399–401; "The Filibuster Begins," *Newsweek* (March 23, 1964), 27; *Washington Post,* March 10, 1964; *New York Times,* March 10, 1964.

9. Mann, *The Walls of Jericho,* 395–99.

10. *New York Times,* January 16, 1964; *Washington Post,* March 21, 1964.

11. *New York Times,* November 22, 1964. For reversal, see *New York Times,* March 25, 1966.

12. "Statement of the President upon Signing Order Establishing the President's Committee on Equal Employment Opportunity," *Public Papers of the Presidents 1961* (Washington, D.C.: U.S. Government Printing Office, 1961), 150.

13. Hugh Davis Graham, *The Civil Rights Era: Origins and Development of National Policy, 1960–1972* (New York: Oxford University Press, 1990), 110–13; A. H. Raskin, "Civil Rights: The Law and the Unions," *Reporter* (September 10, 1964), 24.

14. *New York Times,* May 8, 1964; "Coming Soon: New Rules for Hiring, Firing, Promoting," *U.S. News & World Report* (May 24, 1965), 86.

15. *Congressional Record,* 88th Congress, 2d Session (March 30, 1964), vol. 110, pt. 5, 6549.

16. Ibid., vol. 110, pt. 6 (April 9, 1964), 7420.

17. Ibid. (April 8, 1964), vol. 110, pt. 6, 7213, 7218, 7246; (April 9, 1964), 7375, 7380.

18. Ibid. (April 8, 1964), 7213.

19. Mann, *The Walls of Jericho,* 395, 409–10; Graham, *The Civil Rights Era,* 145–49.

20. *New York Times,* May 14, 1964; Mann, *The Walls of Jericho,* 417–19.

21. Public Law 88-352, July 2, 1964, reprinted in Paul M. Downing, *The Civil Rights Act of 1964: Legislative History; Pro and Con Arguments; Text* (Washington, D. C.: Library of Congress Legislative Reference Service, 1965), LRS-64.

22. Ibid., LRS-62.

23. *Congressional Record,* 88th Congress, 2d Session (June 4, 1964), vol. 110, pt. 10, 12723–24; *New York Times,* May 14, 1964.

24. *Washington Post,* June 11, 1964; "The Historic Vote: 71 to 29," *Newsweek* (June 22, 1964), 25; *New York Times,* June 11, 1964.

25. Allen J. Matusow, *The Unraveling of America: A History of Liberalism in the 1960s* (New York: Harper and Row, 1984), 95; ". . . Shall Now Also Be Equal," *Newsweek* (July 13, 1964), 17.

26. Francis J. Vaas, "Title VII: Legislative History," *Boston College Industrial and Commercial Law Review* 7 (1965–66), 444.

27. EEOC, Administrative History, 56.

28. *New York Times,* May 3, 1965; "Putting Teeth in the Hiring Process," *Business Week* (May 29, 1965), 32.

29. Blumrosen has written extensively about his experiences on the EEOC. See Alfred W. Blumrosen, "Antidiscrimination Laws in Action in New Jersey: A Law-Sociology Study," *Rutgers Law Review* 19 (Winter 1965), 187; "Administrative Creativity: The First Year of the Equal Employment Opportunity Commission," *George Washington Law Review* 38 (May 1970), 695–752; "The Duty of Fair Recruitment under the Civil Rights Act of 1964," *Rutgers Law Review* 22 (Spring 1968), 465–536; *Black Employment and the Law* (New Brunswick, N. J.: Rutgers University Press, 1971); *Modern Law: The Law Transmission System and Equal Employment Opportunity* (Madison: University of Wisconsin Press, 1993).

30. Blumrosen, "Administrative Creativity," 701–03; *Modern Law,* 64–67.

31. *New York Times,* May 11, June 2, and June 3, 1965; May 8, 1966; May 12, May 13, August 26, August 31, September 22, and November 9, 1966; June 28 and August 5, 1967.

32. Graham, "The Origins of Affirmative Action," 55; *Wall Street Journal,* April 12, 1967; Richard Nathan, *Jobs and Civil Rights: The Role of the Federal Government in Promoting Equal Opportunity in Employment and Training,* Clearinghouse publication no. 16 (Washington, D.C.: U.S. Government Printing Office, 1969).

33. "Slough of Equality," *Nation* (February 13, 1967), 197; *Wall Street Journal,* May 28, 1965; Graham, *The Civil Rights Era,* 190.

34. EEOC, Administrative History, 116.

35. Blumrosen, *Modern Law,* 73–77.

36. Graham, *The Civil Rights Era,* 249; Samuel C. Jackson, "EEOC v. Discrimination, Inc.," *Crisis* (January 1968), 16–17.

37. Blumrosen, *Modern Law,* 75; EEOC, Administrative History, 248–49.

38. Bayard Rustin, "From Protest to Politics: The Future of the Civil Rights Movement," *Commentary* 39 (February 1965), 25–27; Daniel Patrick Moynihan, "The Negro Family: The Case for National Action," in *The Moynihan Report and the Politics of Controversy,* ed. Lee Rainwater and William L. Yancey (Cambridge, Mass.: M.I.T. Press, 1967), 41–124; Nicholas Lemann, "Slumlord; Pat Moynihan Has Done Some Great Things—but Betraying the Poverty Warriors Isn't One of Them," *Washington Monthly* (May 1991), 39.

39. Lyndon B. Johnson, "To Fulfill These Rights," in *The Affirmative Action Debate,* ed. George E. Curry (Reading, Mass.: Addison-Wesley, 1996), 16–24; *New York Times,* June 5, 1964.

40. *Report of the National Advisory Commission on Civil Disorders* (New York: E. P. Dutton, 1968), 115, 116, 164; Joe R. Feagin, *Ghetto Revolts: The Politics of Violence in American Cities* (New York: Macmillan, 1973), 101–05; Robert M. Fogelson, *Violence as Protest: A Study of Riots and Ghettoes* (Garden City, N.Y.: Doubleday, 1971), 1–5.

41. *New York Times,* July 22, 1979; *Time* (August 11, 1967); John David Skrentny, *The Ironies of Affirmative Action: Politics, Culture, and Justice in America* (Chicago: University of Chicago Press, 1996), 76–87.

42. Institute of Labor and Industrial Relations, "A Study of Patterns of Discrimination in Employment for the Equal Employment Opportunity Commission" (September 1966), in *EEOC Administrative History,* vol. 2, 1; Nathan, *Jobs and Civil Rights,* 46.

43. Blumrosen, "Administrative Creativity," 713–23.

44. Blumrosen, *Black Employment and the Law,* 67–69; "Administrative Creativity," 713–23. EEOC, Administrative History, 67, 137; Skrentny, *The Ironies of Affirmative Action,* 127–28.

45. EEOC, Administrative History, 129–30; Graham, *The Civil Rights Era,* 199.

46. Graham, *The Civil Rights Era,* 241–44.

47. "Opening the Record on Jobs for Negroes," *Business Week* (August 12, 1967), 128–30; EEOC, Administrative History, 155.

48. Graham, *The Civil Rights Era,* 278–84.

49. "Congress & Minority Employment Policy," *Congressional Digest* 49 (March, 1970), 82; William B. Gould, *Black Workers in White Unions: Job Discrimination in the United States* (Ithaca: Cornell University Press, 1977), 172–88.

50. House Committee on Appropriations, Hearings, 90th Congress, 2d Session (1968), 896–97; Herman Belz, *Equality Transformed: A Quarter-Century of Affirmative Action* (New Brunswick, N.J.: Transaction Publishers, 1991), 31; Graham, *The Civil Rights Era,* 282–90.

51. *Los Angeles Times,* November 4, 1991; Nathan, *Jobs and Civil Rights,* 110–11; Belz, *Equality Transformed,* 31–34; Graham, *The Civil Rights Era,* 290–97.
52. *Washington Post,* June 13, 1995.
53. "Congress & Minority Employment Policy," *Congressional Digest* 49 (March 1970), 82; Arthur A. Fletcher, "A Personal Footnote in History," in *The Affirmative Action Debate,* ed. Curry, 25–30.
54. William Safire, *Before the Fall: An Inside of the Pre-Watergate White House* (Garden City, N.Y.: Doubleday, 1975), 585; Tom Wicker, *One of Us: Richard Nixon and the American Dream* (New York: Random House, 1995), 523; Herbert S. Parmet, *Richard Nixon and His America* (Boston: Little, Brown, 1990), 600.
55. *New York Times,* September 24, 1969; Graham, *The Civil Rights Era,* 326–29.
56. *Washington Post,* December 22, 1978; Graham, *The Civil Rights Era,* 331–34.
57. *New York Times,* September 24, 1969; "Congress & Minority Employment Policy," *Congressional Digest* 49 (March 1970), 76, 78, 80, 82.
58. Belz, *Equality Transformed,* 37.
59. Roberts and Stratton, *The New Color Line,* 102–04; Andrew Kull, *The Color-Blind Constitution* (Cambridge, Mass.: Harvard University Press, 1992), 183.
60. Safire, *Before the Fall,* 571, 585.
61. Alexis de Tocqueville, *Democracy in America,* trans. H. Reeve (New York: Oxford University Press, 1947), vol. 1, ch. 16, 177; William F. Swindler, *The Constitution and Chief Justice Marshall* (New York: Dodd, Mead, 1978), 141.
62. *Los Angeles Times,* November 3, 1991; *Atlanta Journal and Constitution,* July 1, 1991.
63. *Griggs v. Duke Power Company,* 401 U.S. 430–31 (1971); *New York Times,* March 9, 1971; *Washington Post,* March 9, 1971.
64. Alfred W. Blumrosen, "Strangers in Paradise: *Griggs v. Duke Power Co.* and the Concept of Employment Discrimination," *Michigan Law Review* 71 (November 1972), 59–109.
65. Paul D. Moreno, *From Direct Action to Affirmative Action: Fair Employment Law and Policy in America, 1933–1972* (Baton Rouge: Louisiana State University Press, 1997), 280.
66. "Impact of Bakke Decision," *U.S. News & World Report* (July 10, 1978), 14; "Bakke-lash," *Economist* (July 1, 1978), 31; James W. Singer, "Reverse Discrimination— Will Bakke Decide the Issue," *National Journal* 9 (September 17, 1977), 1436; J. Harvie Wilkinson, *From Brown to Bakke: The Supreme Court and School Integration* (New York: Oxford University Press, 1979), 253–306.
67. "The Landmark Bakke Ruling," *Newsweek* (July 10, 1978), 19; *Washington Post,* June 29, 1978.
68. *New York Times,* June 29 and July 2, 1978.
69. *Washington Post,* June 28, 1979; *New York Times,* December 12, 1978, and June 28, 1979; *Los Angeles Times,* November 4, 1991.
70. *United Steelworkers of America, AFL-CIO-CLC v. Weber, et al.,* 443 U.S. 193–201, 202, 205–06 (1979).
71. Ibid., 216, 219–22, 254–55.

72. Michael Schaller, *Reckoning with Reagan: America and Its President in the 1980s* (New York: Oxford University Press, 1992), 79–83; David M. O'Brien, "The Reagan Judges: His Most Enduring Legacy?," in *The Reagan Legacy,* ed. Charles O. Jones (Chatham, N.J.: Chatham House Publishers, 1988), 60–101.

73. *Los Angeles Times,* June 13, and 18, 1995; *New York Times,* June 13 and 18, 1995; Jane Mayer and Jill Abramson, *Strange Justice: The Selling of Clarence Thomas* (Boston: Houghton Mifflin, 1994).

74. Arch Puddington, "What to Do about Affirmative Action," *Commentary* 99 (June 1995), 21; *Washington Post,* May 25, 1990.

75. Puddington, "What to Do about Affirmative Action"; Kull, *The Color-Blind Constitution,* 1–3; Charles T. Canady, "The Meaning of American Equality," in *The Affirmative Action Debate,* ed. Curry, 277–87.

76. Gunnar Myrdal, *An American Dilemma: The Negro Problem and Modern Democracy* (New York: Pantheon Books, 1962), vols. 1 and 2; David W. Southern, *Gunnar Myrdal and Black-White Relations* (Baton Rouge: Louisiana State University Press, 1987), 49–70; Jesse Jackson, "Race-Baiting and the 1996 Presidential Campaign," in *The Affirmative Action Debate,* ed. Curry, 288–98; *Regents of University of California v. Bakke,* 438 U.S. 265, 407 (1978) (Blackmun, J., concurring in part).

77. *Los Angeles Times,* November 5, 1991.

78. *Washington Post,* January 19, 1986; *New York Times,* January 12, 1989. For a full analysis of public attitudes on race relations, see Seymour Martin Lipset, *American Exceptionalism: A Double-Edged Sword* (New York: W. W. Norton, 1996), 113–50; Andrew Hacker, *Two Nations: Black and White, Separate, Hostile, Unequal* (New York: Charles Scribner's, 1992).

79. Linda Faye Williams, "Tracing the Politics of Affirmative Action," in *The Affirmative Action Debate,* ed. Curry, 241–57; *Washington Post,* July 23, 1990; Lipset, *American Exceptionalism,* 139–40; Lipset, "Whites, Blacks, and the Debate over Affirmative Action," *New Democrat* (May–June 1995), 9; *Washington Post,* July 31, 1988.

80. *Los Angeles Times,* September 4, 1996.

81. Robert S. Boynton, "The New Intellectuals," *Atlantic* (March 1995), 53–68; Shelby Steele, "The Race Not Run," *New Republic* (October 7, 1996), 23; Shelby Steele, *The Content of Our Character: A New Vision of Race in America* (New York: Harper Perennial, 1991), 113; Stephen Carter, *Reflections of an Affirmative Action Baby* (New York: Basic Books, 1991); Jeff Howard and Ray Hammond, "Rumors of Inferiority," in *Racial Preference and Racial Justice,* ed. Russell Nieli (Washington, D. C.: Ethics and Public Policy Center, 1991), 367–82; *Washington Post,* May 18, 1990; Robert L. Woodson, Sr., "Personal Responsibility," in *The Affirmative Action Debate,* ed. Curry, 111–20; *New York Times,* March 24, 1989; William Julius Wilson, *The Truly Disadvantaged* (Chicago: University of Chicago Press, 1987). For a critical perspective on black neoconservatives, see Adolph Reed, Jr, "The Descent of Black Conservatism," *Progressive* 61 (October 1997), 18.

82. Barbara Bergmann, *In Defense of Affirmative Action* (New York: Basic Books, 1996); M. V. Badgett and Heidi Hartmann, "The Effectiveness of Equal Opportunity Em-

ployment Policies," in *Economic Perspectives on Affirmative Action,* ed. Margaret Simms (Washington, D.C.: Joint Center for Political and Economic Studies, 1995); Heidi Hartmann, "Who Has Benefited from Affirmative Action in Employment?," in *The Affirmative Action Debate,* ed. Curry, 77–95; *Atlanta Journal and Constitution,* November 2, 1997; *Los Angeles Times,* September 10, 1995.

83. *New York Times,* April 5, 1998.

84. Nathan Glazer, "In Defense of Preference," *New Republic* (April 6, 1998), 20; *New York Times,* April 5, 1998. *Commentary* devoted its March 1998 issue to neoconservatives who reconsidered their position on affirmative action.

85. *New York Times,* April 5, 1998.

Chapter 4: Still the Golden Door?

1. *Congressional Record,* 89th Congress, 1st Session (August 24, 1965), vol. 111, pt. 16, 21579.

2. Robert A. Divine, *American Immigration Policy, 1924–1952* (New Haven: Yale University Press, 1957), 26–51; Elliott Robert Barkan, *And Still They Come: Immigrants and American Society 1920s to the 1990s* (Wheeling, Ill.: Harlan Davidson, 1996), 9–14.

3. *Congressional Record,* 89th Congress, 1st Session (August 25, 1965), vol. 111, pt. 16, 21755; David M. Reimers, *Still the Golden Door: The Third World Comes to America* (New York: Columbia University Press, 1992), 61–91; "Lifting the Quota," *Time* (August 13, 1965), 17A.

4. Divine, *American Immigration Policy, 1924–1952,* 164–91; United States President, *Public Papers of the Presidents of the United States* (Washington, D.C.: U.S. Government Printing Office, 1966), Harry S. Truman, 1952, 443.

5. Abba Schwartz, *The Open Society* (New York: William Morrow, 1968), 99–112; Reimers, *Still the Golden Door,* 62–63; David M. Reimers, "An Unintended Reform: The 1965 Immigration Act and Third World Immigration to the United States," *Journal of American Ethnic History* 2 (Fall 1983), 9–28; William S. Stern, "H.R. 2580: The Immigration and Nationality Amendments of 1965—A Case Study" (Ph.D. diss., New York University, 1974), 26–54; Stephen Thomas Wagner, "The Lingering Death of the National Origins Quota System: A Political History of the United States Immigration Policy, 1952–1965" (Ph.D. diss., Harvard University, 1986), 359–76; "Congress and U.S. Immigration Policy," *Congressional Digest* 44 (May 1965), 131–60; "National Quotas for Immigration to End," *Congressional Quarterly Almanac* 21 (1965), 459–82.

6. Schwartz, *The Open Society,* 22–34, 112–16.

7. *New York Times,* July 24, 1963; *Washington Post,* July 24, 1963.

8. "Proposed Immigration Legislation," 89th Congress, *Blue Book,* January 1965, Ex-Im, WHCF, Box 1, Lyndon Baines Johnson Library (LBJL); *New York Times,* August 14, 1964.

9. *Congressional Record,* 89th Congress, 1st Session (August 25, 1965), vol. 111, pt. 16, 21812; Congress. House. Committee on the Judiciary. Subcommittee No. 1, *Immigration. Part 2,* 88th Congress, 2d Session (July 2, 22, 23, 27, 29 and August 3, 1964), 388–89, 418; Congress. Senate. Committee on the Judiciary. Subcommittee on Immigration and Naturalization, *Immigration. Part One,* 89th Congress, 1st Session (February 10, 24, and 25 and March 1, 3–5, 11, 1965), 2. Here is how the administration did the math. Changes in a number of provisions—making parents nonquota, abolishing the Asian-Pacific Triangle, giving both Jamaica and Trinidad and Tobago nonquota status, and increasing the minimum per country from 100 to 200—added approximately 25,700 new positions. The bill also permitted use of the approximately 55,000 quota positions that went unused each year, making for an overall increase of slightly less than 81,000. The administration subtracted from that number the 21,000 immigrants who entered each year under "special legislation passed to relieve pressures created by the existing system," and that left "approximately 60,000 as the estimated annual net increase in the volume of immigration under the provisions of the Administration bill." The administration was quick to point out, however, "that of this approximately 60,000 increase, some 55,000 are already authorized under the provisions of existing law; consequently the increase per year would be only about 5,000 more immigrants than those presently authorized." See "Proposed Immigration Legislation."

10. Reimers, *Still the Golden Door,* 72–74; "Proposed Immigration Legislation"; "Common Misapprehensions About the Administration's 1965 Immigration Bill, H.R. 2580," Legislative Background—Immigration Law, Box 1, LBJL; Congress, Senate, *Immigration,* (1965).

11. Norbert Schlei to Johnson, May 7, 1965, Ex Le/IM, WHCF, Box 73, LBJL; *New York Times,* August 25, 1965; Reimers, *Still the Golden Door,* 69–70; "An Obscure Congressman to Keep an Eye On," *Life* (June 4, 1965), 34.

12. Paul Duke and Stanley Meisler, "Immigration: Quotas vs. Quality," *Reporter* (January 14, 1965), 30; *Washington Evening Star,* June 8, 1965; "National Quotas for Immigration to End," 463; Wagner, "The Lingering Death of the National Origins Quota System," 391–92.

13. *New York Times,* April 11, 1964; *Washington Post,* May 18, 1964; *Northern Virginia Sun,* May 17, 1965; *Washington Evening Star,* June 23, 1964; *Wall Street Journal,* October 4, 1965; Schwartz, *The Open Society,* 121–22.

14. *Baltimore Sun,* February 4 and 5, 1965; *Cleveland Plain Dealer,* February 23, 1965.

15. Schlei to Johnson, May 7, 1965, Ex Le/IM, WHCF, Box 73, LBJL.

16. Jack Valenti to Johnson, May 14, 1965, Name File, Feighan, Box 46, LBJL; Perry Barber to Valenti, July 8, 1965, Legislative Files—Immigration, Box 1, LBJL; Schlei to Johnson, May 7, 1965, Legislative Files—Immigration, Box 1, LBJL; Valenti to Johnson, May 8, 1965, Legislative Background—Immigration, Box 1, LBJL.

17. Schlei, "Possible Amendments to the Administration's Immigration Bill, H.R. 2580," June 4, 1965, Legislative Background—Immigration, Box 1, LBJL; Schlei to

Valenti, "Administration's Immigration Bill (H.R. 2580) as Reported by the House Judiciary Committee," August 3, 1965, Executive Office File, Legislation—Immigration, Box 73, LBJL.

18. "National Quotas for Immigration to End," 461–62; Reimers, *Still the Golden Door,* 70–71; Reimers, "An Unintended Reform," 18–19.

19. Deane and David Heller, "Our New Immigration Law," *American Legion Magazine* 80 (February 1966), 6–9, 39–41; *Congressional Record,* 89th Congress, 1st Session (August 25, 1965), col. 111, pt. 16, 21812; Congress, Senate, *Immigration* (1965), 2; *Wall Street Journal,* October 4, 1965.

20. Reimers, *Still the Golden Door,* 75–80; *Washington Evening Star,* June 23, 1964.

21. *New York Times,* July 13 and August 28, 1965; "National Quotas for Immigration to End," 472.

22. Reimers, *Still the Golden Door,* 80–81.

23. "National Quotas for Immigration to End," 462; *New York Times,* October 4, 1965.

24. Reimers, "An Unintended Reform," 19–21; *New York Times,* May 29, 1966, March 18, 1968, and August 31, 1970; "The New Americans—Where They're Coming From," *U.S. News & World Report* (June 14, 1971), 12–14; "The New Immigration," *Editorial Research Reports* (December 13, 1974), 927–33; Thomas Muller, *Immigrants and the American City* (New York: New York University Press, 1993), 260.

25. From 1880 to 1890, and again from 1900 to 1910, the average annual flow of immigrants was equal to more than 1 percent of the American population. From 1970 to 1979 it was one-fifth of 1 percent. The foreign-born made up 4.7 percent of the population in 1970; they made up 8.8 percent in 1940 and 14.8 percent in 1910.

26. Bernt Bratsberg, "Legal versus Illegal U.S. Immigration and Source Country Characteristics," *Southern Economic Journal* 61 (January 1995), 715–27; James P. Smith and Barry Edmonston, eds., *The New Americans: Economic, Demographic, and Fiscal Effects of Immigration* (Washington, D.C.: National Academy Press, 1997), 3.

27. Theodore White, *America in Search of Itself: The Making of the President, 1956–1980* (New York: Harper & Row, 1982), 363; *Cleveland Plain Dealer,* July 27, 1965; Betty Boyd Caroli, "Recent Immigration to the United States," *Trends in History* 2 (Summer 1982), 49–69.

28. Scott McConnell, "The New Battle over Immigration," *Fortune* (May 9, 1988), 89–102.

29. Smith and Edmonston, *The New Americans,* 41; McConnell, "The New Battle over Immigration," 89–102; Roger Daniels, *Coming to America: A History of Immigration and Ethnicity in American Life* (New York: HarperCollins, 1990), 341–43.

30. At first the Immigration and Naturalization Service (INS) counted the refugees against the Western Hemisphere quota, but in 1976 Congress declared the refugees exempt. The courts went even further. In 1978 Illinois District Judge John Grady held that 144,999 places charged against the ceiling for Cubans between 1968 and 1976 be made available retroactively to others in the Western Hemisphere. See

Daniels, *Coming to America*, 344–49; "The Cuban Tide Is a Flood," *Newsweek* (May 19, 1980), 28; Reimers, "An Unintended Reform," 20–22.

31. Charles B. Keely, "Immigration Composition and Population Policy," *Science* 185 (August 16, 1974), 591–93; *New York Times*, May 21, 1966.

32. *New York Times*, November 15, 1966; Willard Wirtz to John Roche, June 5, 1967, Legislative Files—Immigration, Box 1, LBJL; Wirtz to Harry McPherson, March 20, 1968, Legislative Files—Immigration, Box 1, LBJL.

33. "More Asians Pour into U.S. Melting Pot," *U.S. News & World Report* (October 13, 1975), 70–71; Reimers, *Still the Golden Door*, 92–99.

34. Setsuko Matsunga Nishi, "The New Wave of Asian Americans," *New York Affairs* 5 (Spring 1979), 82–96; Monica Boyd, "The Changing Nature of Central and South eastern Asian Immigration to the United States: 1961–72," *International Migration Review* 8 (Winter 1974), 507–19; *New York Times*, November 14, 1977; "The New Immigrants," 929.

35. Thomas D. Dublin, "Foreign Physicians: Their Impact on U.S. Health Care," *Science* 185 (August 1974), 407–14; Stephen S. Mick, "The Foreign Medical Graduate," *Scientific American* 232 (February 1975), 14–20; Charles B. Keely, "Philippine Migration: Internal Movements and Emigration to the United States," *International Migration Review* 7 (Summer 1973), 177–87; Reimers, *Still the Golden Door*, 100–02.

36. Nishi, "The New Wave of Asian Americans," 82–96; Boyd, "The Changing Nature of Central and Southeastern Asian Immigration," 507–19; Roger Daniels, *Coming to America*, 355; McConnell, "The New Battle over Immigration," 89–102.

37. Nishi, "The New Wave of Asian Americans," 82–96; Daniels, *Coming to America*, 350–70; *New York Times*, June 28, 1967; "Now a Growing Surge of Immigrants from Asia," *U.S. News & World Report* (November 26, 1973), 94–95.

38. Printed in "The New Immigrants," 928.

39. Wayne A. Cornelius, "Mexican Migration to the United States: An Introduction," in *Mexican Migration to the United States: Origins, Consequences, and Policy Options*, ed. Cornelius and Jorge A. Bustamante (San Diego: Center for U.S.-Mexican Studies, 1989), 1–24; Daniels, *Coming to America*, 371–84; Reimers, *Still the Golden Door*, 123–32; Elliott Abrams and Franklin S. Abrams, "Immigration Policy—Who Gets In and Why?," *Public Interest* 38 (Winter 1975), 12–16.

40. Charles B. Keely, "Illegal Migration," *Scientific American* 246 (March 1982), 41–47; Abrams and Abrams, "Immigration Policy—Who Gets In and Why?," 21–24; *New York Times*, December 29, 1974.

41. *New York Times*, December 29, 1974.

42. Cornelius, "The U.S. Demand for Mexican Labor," 25–48; Georges Vernez and David Ronfeldt, "The Current Situation in Mexican Immigration," *Science* 251 (March 8, 1991), 1189; Keely, "Illegal Migration," 41–48; Leslie Aldridge Westoff, "Should We Pull Up the Gangplank?," *New York Times Magazine*, September 16, 1973, 82.

43. Philip Martin, "Mexican-U.S. Migration: Policies and Economic Impacts," *Chal-*

lenge 38 (March 1995), 56; Keely, "Illegal Migration," 41–48; "Illegal Aliens: Invasion out of Control," *U.S. News & World Report* (January 29, 1979), 38–42.

44. George Borjas, "Tired, Poor, on Welfare," *National Review* (December 13, 1993), 40; Vernez and Ronfeldt, "The Current Situation in Mexican Immigration," 1189.

45. John B. Judas, "Bipartisan Law v. Good Law," *New Republic* (December 23, 1996), 23; *Dallas Morning News,* October 27, 1996; *Washington Post,* October 1, 1996; Daniels, *Coming to America,* 397.

46. Judas, "Bipartisan Law v. Good Law," 23; McConnell, "The New Battle over Immigration," 89–102; Reimers, *Still the Golden Door,* 246–52; Smith and Edmonston, *The New Americans,* 28–30.

47. *Washington Post,* December 4, 1994; Stewart Powell, "Illegal Aliens: Invasion out of Control?," *U.S. News & World Report* (January 29, 1979), 38; "At America's Door," *Economist* (July 24, 1993), 11–12; "So, Does America Want Them or Not?," *Economist* (July 19, 1997), 25–27.

48. *Orlando Sentinel Tribune,* May 10, 1998; *Arizona Republic,* February 23, 1977; Christopher John Farley, "The Art of Diversity," *Time* (December 13, 1993), 20.

49. Muller, *Immigrants and the American City,* 111–18; *New York Times,* July 19, 1998.

50. Smith and Edmonston, *The New Americans,* 58–62; *Los Angeles Times,* November 14, 1993. Muller, *Immigrants and the City,* 169–70; *Washington Post,* February 22, 1998. On the larger trend of racial segregation, see Douglas S. Massey and Nancy A. Denton, *American Apartheid: Segregation and the Making of the Underclass* (Cambridge, Mass.: Harvard University Press, 1993).

51. Smith and Edmonston, *The New Americans,* 196–203; George Borjas, "Know the Flow: Economics of Immigration," *National Review* (April 17, 1995), 44; *Boston Globe,* October 13, 1991; *Washington Post,* February 22, 1998.

52. Julian Simon, *The Economic Consequences of Immigration* (New York: Blackwell / Cato Institute, 1989); Vernon M. Briggs, Jr., and Stephen Moore, *U.S. Immigration Policy and the American Economy* (Washington, D.C.: American University Press, 1994); Dick Kirschten, "Come In! Keep Out!," *National Journal* (May 19, 1998), 1206; Nicolaus Mills, *Arguing Immigration: The Debate over the Changing Face of America* (New York: Touchstone, 1994).

53. Borjas, "Know the Flow: Economics of Immigration," 44; *Boston Globe,* October 13, 1991; *Los Angeles Times,* November 21, 1993; Smith and Edmonston, *The New Americans,* 4–12; Berna Miller, "Educating the 'Other' Children," *American Demographics* 19 (October 1997), 49.

54. *Los Angeles Times,* November 14, 1993; Gregory Rodriguez, "The Browning of California," *New Republic* (September 2, 1996), 18–19.

55. Peter Brimelow, *Alien Nation* (New York: Random House, 1995); Richard Lamm and Gary Imhoff, *The Immigration Time-Bomb: The Fragmenting of America* (New York: Dutton, 1985), 76–98; Arthur M. Schlesinger, Jr., *The Disuniting of America: Reflections on a Multicultural Society* (New York: W. W. Norton, 1992), 15–18.

56. Peter H. Schuck, "The New Immigration and the Old Civil Rights," *American Prospect* 19 (Fall 1993), 102; *San Diego Union-Tribune,* February 11, 1986; *New York Times,* Feb-

ruary 22, 1987 and December 7, 1986; "The Difficulty of Digesting a Foreign Body," *Economist* (June 16, 1984), 29.

57. *New York Times,* April 17, 1994; Smith and Edmonston, *The New Americans,* 365–94; Tom Morgenthau, "America: Still a Melting Pot," *Newsweek* (August 9, 1993), 16.

58. *New York Times,* July 19, 1998.

59. Muller, *Immigrants and the City,* 250–62; *New York Times,* August 8, 1979; *Wall Street Journal,* September 25, 1980; Jack Miles, "Blacks vs. Browns: African Americans and Latinos," *Atlantic* 270 (October 1992), 41.

60. Muller, *Immigrants and the American City,* 260; Miles, "Blacks vs. Browns: African Americans and Latinos," 51.

61. *Wall Street Journal,* May 22, 1980; *Washington Post,* May 14, 1990.

62. Schuck, "The New Immigration and the Old Civil Rights," 102; Jim Sleeper, "The End of the Rainbow: America's Changing Urban Politics," *New Republic* (November 1, 1993), 20; Peter Beinart, "New Bedfellows," *New Republic* (August 18, 1997), 22.

63. Michael Barone, "The New America," *U.S. News & World Report* (July 10, 1995), 18; Muller, *Immigrants and the American City,* 254.

64. *Boston Globe,* October 13, 1991.

65. Daniels, *Coming to America,* 338.

Chapter 5: The Politics of Campaign Finance Reform

1. Paul R. Wieck, "The John Gardner Brigade," *New Republic* 168 (June 2, 1973), 21–23; Elizabeth Drew, "A Reporter at Large: Conversation with a Citizen," *New Yorker* (July 23, 1973), 35–55; Tom Bethell, "Taking a Hard Look at Common Cause," *New York Times Magazine,* August 24, 1980, 34; Congress, House, Committee on House Administration, Subcommittee on Elections, *Hearings on Federal Election Reform,* 93d Congress, 1st Session (November 29, 1973), 385.

2. Herbert E. Alexander, *Financing Politics: Money, Elections, and Political Reform* (Washington, D.C.: Congressional Quarterly, 1984), 5; Mary W. Cohn, ed., *Congressional Campaign Finances: History, Facts, and Controversy* (Washington, D.C.: Congressional Quarterly, 1992), 29–38; David Adamany and George Agree, "Election Campaign Financing: The 1974 Reforms," *Political Science Quarterly* 90 (Summer 1975), 201–05.

3. Joseph P. Albright, "The Price of Purity," *New York Times Magazine,* September 1, 1974, 12, 32, 35.

4. Alexander, *Financing Politics,* 35–37; Adamany and Agree, "Election Campaign Financing," 201–05; Albright, "The Price of Purity," 12, 32, 35.

5. Congress, Senate, Select Committee on Presidential Campaign Activities, *Final Report,* 93d Congress, 2d Session (1974), 446–71, 492–93; Fred Wertheimer and Randy Huwa, "Campaign Finance Reforms: Past Accomplishments, Future Challenges," *New York University Review of Law and Social Change* 10 (1980–81); Adamany and Agree, "Election Campaign Financing," 205–08.

6. Congress, Senate, Committee on Government Operations, *Hearings on a Survey of*

Public Attitudes, 93d Congress, 1st Session (1973), 6–8; *Washington Post,* September 19, 1974; "Campaign Money: Prospects for Reform," *Time* (April 22, 1974), 28–31; *Washington Post,* September 19, 1974; "Congress Wrestles with Campaign Financing," *Business Week* (September 15, 1973), 170.

7. "Campaign Financing: Growing Pressure to Go Public," *Congressional Quarterly Weekly Report* (March 30, 1974), 797.

8. Congress, Senate, Committee on Rules and Administration, *Federal Election Campaign Act Amendments of 1974,* 93d Congress, 2d Session (February 21, 1974), 11–19; For debate on the Senate floor, see the *Congressional Record,* 93d Congress, 2d Session (March 26–April 11), vol. 120, pt. 7, 8444–60; For a summary of the Senate bill, see "Congress Clears Campaign Financing Reform," *Congressional Quarterly Almanac* 30 (1974), 5–15.

9. "Public Financing of Campaigns Survives Senate Votes," *Congressional Quarterly* (March 30, 1974), 855–56; "Senate Passes Campaign Reform Bill with Public Funding," *Congressional Quarterly Weekly Review* (April 13, 1974), 927–31; *New York Times,* October 11 and 28, 1974.

10. *Washington Post,* March 26, 1974; *New York Times,* March 27, 1974. For Broder's opinion, see *Washington Post,* August 28, February 1, and October 6, 1974; Walter Pincus, "Campaign Kitties," *New Republic* 170 (March 16, 1974), 17.

11. *New York Times,* April 10, 1974; "Congress Clears Campaign Financing Reform," *Congressional Quarterly Weekly Report* (October 12, 1974), 2865–70.

12. *Los Angeles Times,* February 12, 1989; *New York Times,* February 28, 1974; "Congress Clears Campaign Financing Reform," *Congressional Quarterly Almanac* (1974), 611–33; *Washington Post,* June 29, 1974; *New York Times,* June 2, 1974. In 1976 Hays was forced to resign from Congress when the press revealed that he was having an affair with a young clerk in his office, Elizabeth Ray. "I can't type. I can't file. I can't even answer the phone," she confessed.

13. *New York Times,* July 2, 1974; Congress, House, Committee on Administration, *Federal Election Campaign Act Amendments of 1974,* 93d Congress, 2d Session (July 30, 1974); *Congressional Record,* 93d Congress, 2d Session (August 7 and 8, 1974), vol. 120, pt. 20; "Speedy Conference on Campaign Reform Seen," *Congressional Quarterly Weekly Report* (August 17, 1974), 2233–38; "Congress Clears Campaign Financing Reform," 18–22.

14. Congress, House, Committee on House Administration, Conference Report, *Federal Election Campaign Act Amendments of 1974,* 93d Congress, 2d Session (October 7, 1974); "Speedy Conference on Campaign Reform Seen," 2233–38; "Congress Clears Campaign Financing Reform," 22–23; Adamany and Agree, "Election Campaign Financing," 212–14.

15. *New York Times,* October 14, 1974.

16. *Washington Post,* October 16, 1974.

17. *Buckley v. Valeo,* 424 U.S. 1 (1976).

18. "Court Decision Forces New Campaign Law," *Congressional Quarterly Almanac* 32 (1976), 461–62; "Campaign Financing: Growing Pressure to Go Public," *Congres-*

sional Quarterly Weekly Review (March 30, 1974), 797; Ronald Dworkin, "The Curse of American Politics," *New York Review of Books* (October 17, 1996), 19–24; Burt Neuborne, "One Dollar, One Vote?," *Nation* 263 (December 2, 1996), 21; "Democracy vs. Free Speech?," *Progressive* 61 (January 1997), 8. The legal historian Cass R. Sunstein has said that "the decision probably ranks among the strongest candidates for overruling of the post-World War II period." See: Sunstein, "Political Equality and Unintended Consequences," *Columbia Law Review* 94 (May 1994), 1400.

19. "Court Decision Forces New Campaign Law," 461–62; *New York Times,* May 12, 1976.

20. Congress, House, House Administration Committee, *An Analysis of the Impact of the Federal Election Campaign Act, 1972–78, from the Institute of Politics, John F. Kennedy School of Government, Harvard University* (Washington, D.C.: U.S. Government Printing Office, 1979), 9.

21. Ibid., 2, 4–6; Frank J. Sorauf, *Money in American Elections* (Glenview, Ill.: Scott, Foresman, 1988), 73–74; Robert J. Samuelson, "The Campaign Reform Failure," *New Republic* (September 5, 1983), 31.

22. There are many different kinds of political action committees. The only legal requirement is that a PAC must receive contributions from more than fifty people and contribute to at least five federal candidates. Most scholars break PACs into three groupings. First, there are connected PACs, which are affiliated with larger organizations—labor unions, corporations, and membership organizations such as the Sierra Club—and which solicit only from members, owners, or employees. The second category consists of nonconnected PACs, which are run by independent political entrepreneurs and are free to solicit from a national constituency. Finally, there are leadership PACs, or personal PACs, which serve the specific agenda of one person, usually a prominent political figure. Most scholars also distinguish between ideological PACs, which support candidates because of their positions on specific issues, and pragmatic PACs, which coordinate campaign giving with lobbying efforts by developing close ties with incumbents. Organized labor is the best example of an ideological PAC, while most corporations follow a pragmatic strategy. See Frank Sorauf, "Political Action Committees," in *Campaign Finance Reform: A Sourcebook,* ed. Anthony Corrado et al. (Washington, D.C.: Brookings Institution, 1997), 124–26.

23. Edwin M. Epstein, "Business and Labor under the Federal Election Campaign Act of 1971," in *Parties, Interest Groups, and Campaign Finance Laws,* ed. Michael Malbin (Washington, D.C.: American Enterprise Institute of Public Policy Research, 1979), 146–47.

24. Bernadette A. Budde, "Business Political Action Committees," in *Parties, Interest Groups, and Campaign Finance Laws,* ed. Malbin 9–25; David Adamany, "The New Faces of American Politics," *Annals* 486 (July 1986), 18–21; *New York Times,* August 19, 1979.

25. Adamany, "The New Faces of American Politics," 21; *New York Times,* August 19, 1979. Having realized the problem, labor worked with its allies in Congress to restrict corporate PACs when Congress adopted the new amendments in 1976. The

new law permitted company committees to seek contributions only from stockholders and executive and administrative personnel and their families, and it limited union soliciting to members and their families. Twice a year, however, union and corporate PACs were permitted to use "crossover" rights and seek donations from all employees.

26. Mark J. Green, "Take the Money and Reform: Breaking a $3,000 Habit," *New Republic* 202 (May 14, 1990), 27; *Washington Post,* October 30, 1989.

27. Cohn, *Congressional Campaign Finances,* 16–17; Karen Peart, "Government for Sale?," *Scholastic Update* (November 1, 1996); Congress, Senate, Committee on the Judiciary, Subcommittee on the Constitution, *Hearing on Campaign Finance Reform,* 101st Congress, 2d Session (February 28, 1990), 7.

28. Hugh Davis Graham, "Legacies of the 1960s: The American 'Rights Revolution' in an Era of Divided Governance," *Journal of Policy History* 10 (1998), 273–75.

29. Michael J. Malbin, "Looking Back at the Future of Campaign Finance Reform: Interest Groups and American Elections," in *Money and Politics in the United States,* ed. Michael Malbin (Washington, D.C.: American Enterprise Institute for Public Policy Research, 1984), 248–49; Ross K. Baker, *The New Fat Cats: Members of Congress as Political Benefactors* (New York: Priority Press, 1989), 1–4.

30. William H. Chafe, *The Unfinished Journey: America since World War II* (New York: Oxford University Press, 1991), 463; *Washington Post,* August 16, 1984; *An Analysis of the Impact of the Federal Election Campaign Act, 1972–78,* 11, 87; Maxwell Glen, "Independent Spenders Are Gearing Up, and Reagan and GOP Stand to Benefit," *National Journal* (December 17, 1983), 2627; *Los Angeles Times,* May 14, 1989.

31. Green, "Take the Money and Reform: Breaking a $3,000 Habit," 27; Carol Matlack, James A. Barnes, and Richard E. Cohen, "The Money Chase," *National Journal* (June 16, 1990), 1448; Ronald Kessler, *Inside Congress* (New York: Pocket Books, 1997), 101.

32. Green, "Take the Money and Reform: Breaking a $3,000 Habit," 27; Matlack, Barnes, and Cohen, "The Money Chase," 1448; *An Analysis of the Impact of the Federal Election Campaign Act, 1972–78,* 4.

33. Matlack, Barnes, and Cohen, "The Money Chase," 1448; Green, "Take the Money and Reform," 27; *New York Times,* December 26, 1996.

34. *An Analysis of the Impact of the Federal Election Campaign Act, 1972–78,* 16; *Washington Post,* February 12, 1997.

35. *An Analysis of the Impact of the Federal Election Campaign Act, 1972–78,* 23.

36. Dom Bonafede, "Some Things Don't Change—Cost of 1982 Congressional Races Higher than Ever," *National Journal* (October 30, 1982), 1832.

37. Anthony Corrado, "Party Soft Money," in *Campaign Finance Reform,* ed. Corrado, 167–71; *New York Times,* January 10, 1980.

38. Corrado, "Party Soft Money," in *Campaign Finance Reform,* ed. Corrado, 171–73.

39. *New York Times,* May 16, 1992; *Los Angeles Times,* October 3, 1988.

40. *Los Angeles Times,* October 3, 1988; *Washington Post,* May 10, 1992.

41. *Christian Science Monitor,* May 10, 1993; *Boston Globe,* February 4, 1993; Jane Mayer, "Inside the Money Machine," *New Yorker* (February 3, 1997), 33–34.

42. Richard Stengel and Eric Pooley, "Masters of the Message," *Time* (November 18, 1996), 76; George Stephanopoulos, "The View from the Inside," *Newsweek* (March 10, 1997), 27.

43. *Washington Post,* February 9, 1997; Stengel and Pooley, "Masters of the Message," 76; *Washington Post,* November 9, 1997.

44. *Washington Post,* February 9, 1997.

45. *Los Angeles Times,* December 22, 1997; Stengel and Pooley, "Masters of the Message," 76; *Washington Post,* February 9, 1997.

46. *Washington Post,* February 9, 1997.

47. Deborah Beck et al., "Issue Advocacy Advertising during the 1996 Campaign," Annenberg Public Policy Center, University of Pennsylvania, 1997, 3–6.

48. *Washington Post,* February 9, 1997.

49. Jonathan Alter and Michael Isikoff, "The Real Scandal Is What's Legal," *Newsweek* (October 28, 1996), 30; *Washington Post,* November 3, 1996; Peter Stone, "The Green Wave," *National Journal* (March 9, 1996), 2410.

50. Jonathan Rauch, "Blow It Up," *National Journal* (March 29, 1997), 604; Alter and Isikoff, "The Real Scandal Is What's Legal," 30–32; *New York Times,* November 2, 1997.

51. Stone, "The Green Wave," 2410.

52. *New York Times,* September 8, 1996.

53. *Washington Post,* April 21, 1997.

54. Kent Jenkins, Jr., et al., "Showdown over Reform," *U.S. News & World Report* (October 13, 1997), 30, 32; *New Orleans Times-Picayune,* October 14, 1997.

55. Bradley Smith, "Faulty Assumptions and Undemocratic Consequences of Campaign Finance Reform," *Yale Law Journal* 105 (January 1996), 1049–91; Curtis Gans, "Common Gridlock," *New Democrat* (May 1993), 16; Major Garrett and Timothy J. Penny, *The 15 Biggest Lies in Politics* (New York: St. Martin's Press, 1998), 92–112.

56. *Minneapolis Star Tribune,* February 24 and 27, 1998.

57. *New York Times,* April 6, 1997; Eliza Newlin Carney, "Defending PACs," *National Journal* (July 13, 1996), 1518; *USA Today,* June 13, 1997.

58. Thomas L. Gais and Michael J. Malbin, "Campaign Finance Reform," *Society* (May 15, 1997), 56; Eliza Newlin Carney, "Taking on the Fat Cats," *National Journal* (January 18, 1997), 110.

59. *Denver Post,* March 12, 1997; *New York Times,* December 26, 1996.

60. Rauch, "Blow It Up," 604.

Conclusion: A Few Final Observations

1. Robert K. Merton, "The Unanticipated Consequences of Purposive Social Action," *American Sociological Review* 1 (December 1936), 894–904.

2. Louis Hartz, *The Liberal Tradition in America* (New York: Harcourt, 1955); Daniel J. Boorstin, *The Genius of American Politics* (Chicago: University of Chicago Press, 1953); Robert G. McClosky, "The American Ideology," in *Continuing Crisis in American Politics,* ed. Marian D. Irish (Englewood Cliffs, N.J.: Prentice-Hall, 1963), 14; Michael Kammen, *People of Paradox: An Inquiry concerning the Origins of American Civilization* (New York: Oxford University Press, 1972); Daniel T. Rodgers, *Contested Truths: Keywords in American Politics since Independence* (New York: Basic Books, 1987); Gordon Wood, *The Creation of the American Republic* (Chapel Hill: University of North Carolina Press, 1969), 70.

Index